From the Dining Car

Also by James D. Porterfield

Dining by Rail

From the Dining Car

The Recipes and Stories Behind
Today's Greatest Rail Dining Experiences

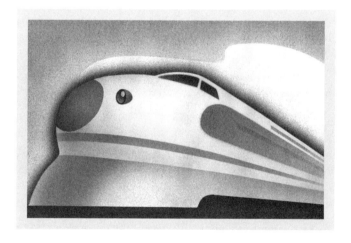

James D. Porterfield

St. Martin's Press　New York

www.stmartins.com

Library of Congress Cataloging-in-Publication Data

Porterfield, James D., 1942–

From the dining car: the recipes and stories behind today's greatest rail dining experiences

James D. Porterfield.—1st ed.

p.   cm.

Includes index (page 271).

ISBN 0-312-24201-8

EAN 978-0312-24201-5

1. Cookery, American. 2. Railroads—United States—Dining-car service.

I. Title.

TX715.P849 2004

641.5'75—dc22

2004046759

10 9 8 7 6 5 4 3 2

For Lori Stine,
who knows why

Contents

Dinner Trains   125

The Passenger Railroads   193

From the Business Car   238

Acknowledgments

This book, meant to capture and share the work of railroad chefs throughout North America and beyond, would not have been possible without the help of the chefs themselves, and of many others. For that, I am indebted, at the very least, to the following men and women. To any whose name I have overlooked, I offer my apology and accept full responsibility for the error.

From the working railroads: At Amtrak, executives Peter Welch, Jack Davis, Brian Rosenwald, Matt Cahoon, Peter Humphries, and Deborah Varnado, and Executive Chef Lamar Gilbert Sr. At Gate Gourmet, Executive Chef Tim Costello and Corporate Relations Director Sherry Cox. At VIA Rail Canada, Executive Chef and Senior Officer James Kleiner, Chef Ron Woods, and Malcolm Andrews. On behalf of the Louisville & Nashville Railroad, Charles Castner of the Louisville & Nashville Railroad Historical Society. From the Great Southern Railway, C.E.O. Stephen Bradford, Food Service Manager Trevor Cook, and Office Manager Sally Murray-Dillon.

From the privately operated luxury trains: On the *American Orient Express,* Executive Chef Warren McLeod, Patissiter William Poole, President Peter Boese; on Montana Rockies Rail Tours, Marcia Pilgeram, President, and Mike Phillips, General Manager; on the Princess Tours' *Midnight Sun Express,* Food and Beverage Manager Steve Heinle, and Vice President Thomas Dow; on the *Rocky Mountaineer,* Executive Chef Mark Jorundson, and Mairi Welman in Public Relations; on the *Royal Canadian Pacific,* Morgan Burgess, Manager of Hospitality Operations, and Chefs Pierre Meloche, Denis Sirios, and Alain Maheux; and on *The Royal Scotsman,* Head Chef Alan Mathieson.

Among those with the American Association of Private Railroad Car Owners, *Private Varnish* editor John Kuehl, Executive Director Diane Elliott, and Patrick Henry, as well as John Kirkwood, Chef Matt Gipson, and Terry Gainer from the *Belle Vista*; Nona Hill, Clark Johnson, and Chef Clay Hollifield from the *Caritas*; DeWitt Chapel, Mike Danneman, and Chef Robbie Williams from the *Chapel Hill*; Jack Heard, and Chefs Nat Jones, Ralph Graves, and Kevin Langton from the *Georgia*

300; Executive Chef John Mickey from the *J Pinckney Henderson*; Dave Hoffman and Chef Dave Kugler from the *Northern Sky*; Tom Whitted and Chef Nanette Casanova from the *Palmetto State*; Dean McCormick and Chef Shaun Murphy from the *Scottish Thistle*; Dante Stephenson and Chef Gay McClelland from *The Survivor*; Chef Connie Luna from the *Tamalpais*; and Wade and Julia Pellizzer and Chef Katherine Mitchell from the *Virginia City*.

From the dinner trains included here: Leslie Holloway, Lance Burack, and Chef Doug Trulson from the *Cafe Lafayette Dinner Train*; Ella Cooper and Chef Richard Kelp from the *Grand Traverse Dinner Train*; Chef Paul Swofford from the *Great Smokey Mountain Railroad*; General Manager Michael Beckham from the *Michigan Star Clipper*; General Manager Michelle Marquart and Chef Jacob DeLeon from the *Mt. Hood Dinner Train*; General Manager and Executive Chef Robert Perry from *My Old Kentucky Dinner Train*; General Manager Erica Ercolano and Chef S. Patrick Finney from the *Napa Valley Wine Train*; Bob Andrews and Chef Robert Cornett from the *Newport Dinner Train*; Jan Anderson, Valerie Fallert, and Executive Chef Michael M. Slay, from *Rail Cruise America*; Executive Chef Pat Morgan from *Scenic Rail Dining*; Jeff Forbis and Chef Ed Hines from the *Shasta Sunset Dinner Train*; and Eric Temple and Doug Bacon, and Chefs Rick Pinney and Brian Hedland, from the *The Spirit of Washington*.

Among those associated with business cars: from the Quad/Graphics business train, Jerry Blaski, Corporate Communications Manager Clair Ho, Quad/Cuisine Manager Gary Chitwood, and Quad/Cuisine Chef Bob Clairmont; from the Burlington Northern Santa Fe Railway, Manager of Business Car Operations Donna M. Marlin, Assistant Food Service Manager Danny Barth, and Chef Dave Nixon; and from Montana Rail Link, Linda Frost, Susan Twiford, and Executive Chef Norma Geng.

And elsewhere, for information and illustrations on Rufus Estes, Dianna Seay, and Steve Quinn; for adaptations from the Harbor Court Hotel, Chef Christian DeLutis; for artwork, Tex Wilson; for railroad china, Richard Luckin; and for other recipes found here, Chef Max Hansen, owner of Max & Me Catering, and Executive Chef Paul Goodmundson; for help assembling the illustrations, Jamie Baker, Digital Image Specialist, and the entire staff of The Film Center; for the special cartoon, Curt Katz; and for keeping me informed on brewpubs in railroad settings, Sandy Mitchell.

A special note of gratitude is reserved for Hal Carstens, owner of Carstens Publications and Publisher of *Railfan & Railroad*, as well as for my editors there—Jim Boyd, Steve Barry, Mike Del Vecchio, and Walt Lankenau. Without their encouragement and support, including the checks that arrived each month in payment for riding and then writing about so many wonderful trains over the past twelve years, this book would not have been possible.

From the Dining Car

Introduction

This book is a love song. Its composition began twelve years ago with the publication of my first cookbook, *Dining by Rail: The History and Recipes from America's Golden Age of Railroad Cuisine,* which is a social history with recipes. Working on that book rekindled in me two dormant passions: great trains and good food. Pursuing those passions to research that book, I discovered a number of vibrant contemporary spinoffs on the rail-dining theme. Train stations were being restored for use as restaurants. Dining cars had been converted into dinner trains. Old train cars had been modernized and put to use by private owners. Whole train sets were being converted into privately operated luxury trains. And connecting me to all of this, Amtrak, the National Railroad Passenger Corporation, whose long-distance trains—with dining cars—run all over the contiguous United States. It turns out, I was happily reminded, there are still hundreds of chefs hard at work conjuring fine meals for passengers in all kinds of railroad settings across North America—indeed, on trains running throughout the world.

Because of the uniqueness of their workplace, these chefs have special knowledge that is valuable for those of us who like cook at home, even for those who don't like to but have to cook. Consider this, for example. For a period in the 1990s, Amtrak sent its dining car chefs and food specialists to the Culinary Institute of America in Hyde Park, New York, to receive refresher training and to compete for recognition of their creations before a panel of judges. The CIA chef-in-charge, Anton Flory, cited the difficulties a railroad chef faces, noting that they not only work in a confined space, but in one that is moving; that they must work quickly because their "dining room" has to serve several hundred people at each meal in a series of seatings that occur over a short period of time; and that, because their patrons range from sophisticated gourmands to fussy children and fast-food mavens, their dishes have to compare favorably with those of chefs at fine hotels, resorts, and restaurants, and with those of hurried line cooks, even with those in a fast-food chain.

Further, a railroad chef needs to use fool-proof planning in order to have everything needed at hand, or be adept with last-minute substitutions in a pinch. As Joe Begia, director for the now defunct *Texan Dinner Train,* once quipped, "Unlike a chef at a restaurant, who can send someone to the store, or to a nearby establishment to borrow something missing, you can't just run out for another head of lettuce." If you forget it, or run out of it, you are going to have to get creative.

Does any of this sound familiar? Small kitchen, short on time, work with what's on hand, make something good. It reminds me of my own kitchen, and the kitchens of just about everyone I know, at dinnertime.

That my increasing knowledge of contemporary rail dining and the challenges of rail chefs would result in another cookbook, however, grew unintentionally out of the fickle nature of the writer's life. When I undertook writing *Dining by Rail,* I saw it as one book in a planned eclectic writing career. My next book was to have been a history of the oil fields of Pennsylvania. However, while promoting *Dining by Rail,* I was asked to do a feature on the winners of Amtrak's then-new "Chef of the Year" competition, and to give the subject an historical perspective (which in turn led to a long-term quarterly "Foodstyles" column for the in-room magazine of a major international chain of hotels). My next assignment was a rail dining column in *Railfan & Railroad,* which has so far yielded more than 150 columns and features about all aspects of rail dining. Work on these pieces, and on the "Annual Guide to Dinner Trains" that now appears in the magazine each June, has provided me entrée into the corporate offices, kitchens and commissaries, and trains and equipment of dozens of railroads, museums and historic sites, private cars, dinner trains, freight railroads, and luxury trains in North America and beyond.

Memories abound. Spending a crisp fall evening in New Hampshire's White Mountain National Forest on board the *Cafe Lafayette Dinner Train.* Conversing with a chef who is slicing fresh zucchini in the galley of Amtrak's *Coast Starlight,* the Pacific Ocean's beach flashing by outside the window. Watching the sun set on Narragansett Bay from the *Newport Dinner Train* in Rhode Island. Getting a guided tour of the private car *Belle Vista*'s new state-of-the-art kitchen by the chef who designed it, to include all the childproofing the owner insisted on. Gliding through Glacier National Park en route to Seattle in June—the month of the longest days— over dinner on Amtrak's *Empire Builder.* Taking in reminders of America's industrial might from the observation platform of the private car *Georgia 300* while departing Baltimore, Maryland. Enjoying an improvised curried chicken dinner named in honor of my presence that evening—"Chicken à la Jimmy"—on Amtrak's *Southwest Chief* to Los Angeles. Three days of spectacularly varied scenery and frequent conversations with a team of skilled chefs on VIA's *Canadian* on a run from Toronto to Vancouver. Speeding along the Mississippi River on a BNSF business car train—a route the railroad's predecessor line, the Chicago, Burlington & Quincy, once touted in its advertising as "300 miles where Mother Nature Smiles"—on a run rail fans call "rare mileage" because it no longer sees passenger trains, two of the railroad's CIA-trained chefs swapping stories about life and work.

Nice work if you can get it!

The work also revealed that while technique has changed (for example, today there is greater reliance on seasonings than on fats for flavor) and the technology has changed (today's dining car kitchens are powered by electricity, not fueled by coal) since the era covered in *Dining by Rail*—which ended in the early 1950s—the skills, attitudes, and work ethic required of the men and women who cook in dining cars today are pretty much the same as they were in that earlier era. Further, the similarity of the working conditions these men and women encounter to those you and I encounter remain: We want to make and serve delicious foods despite fast-paced and time-stressed circumstances, despite the decidedly unrestaurant-like constraints our kitchen equipment and layout imposes, and despite the fact that we shop in grocery stores—and then only on occasion—instead of having a variety of vendors deliver fresh or unique ingredients to our door several times a day.

It was to capture and share this relevant work of today's railroad chefs, to showcase their methods and wonderful foods, and to motivate or inspire others to try cooking by demonstrating what is truly possible, that I began to collect recipes everywhere I went. If in reading my book and trying the recipes, you are encouraged to try a dinner train for a special event, to take an excursion on a private car or train for one of your vacations, or to take the train when you travel, so much the better.

Or if you, like me, find yourself longing for a return to truly relaxing travel that offers great scenery, affable companionship, and good food as part of the trip. There is no better way to travel than by train.

To create fine dining on a train requires concentration on four factors. The first is FLAVOR. That is, on the selection of ingredients, often unique to a region or a history, and on the combining of textures. Second, FOCUS, by which I mean the selection of appropriate technique, most notably for a railroad chef the reduction of preparation steps, but also the ability to work in steps to finish items just prior to serving them. Third, ORGANIZATION, including good planning and careful shopping to keep supplies on hand. Finally, CREATIVITY, or as Max Sanoguet, Jr., an Amtrak chef who was using champagne to make stuffing one evening on Amtrak's Chicago–Los Angeles *Southwest Chief,* put it, "being a chemist." These are the culinary principles you'll find throughout the recipes in *From the Dining Car.*

All the recipes in this book are cooked and served on moving trains, which fall into five categories:

- Private luxury trains, a form of land cruise wherein passengers are transported in luxuriously appointed, restored or new, railcars to noteworthy scenic or historic sites or events. Some of these trains provide sleeping accommodations on board the train, which may change locations overnight, while others operate during daylight hours and put guests up in hotels overnight.

- Privately chartered rail cars, a wide variety of restored and upgraded passenger cars that meet Amtrak and VIA Rail Canada requirements—generally to be capable of traveling at speeds up to 110 miles per hour, to have self-contained waste disposal systems, and to be capable of passing electrical current from the locomotive through to the cars that follow—and that are attached to the rear of regularly scheduled trains to be transported to destinations of choice.

- Dinner trains, of which more than eighty such excursion trains operate locally throughout North America. They offer meal service that ranges from a train ride to a restaurant and back, known as a "ride-'n'-dine," to meals served while underway that are catered by a locally prominent restaurant and to meals cooked on board by the train's own chef (only the latter have been included here).

- Scheduled trains on working railroads, including numerous Amtrak and VIA Rail Canada trains that transport passengers great distances and generally offer both sleeping cars and a dining car in the train's set of equipment, known in railroad parlance as a consist.

- Business cars, the offices-on-wheels that transport railroad executives, shippers, and others over the respective railroad's right-of-ways to meetings or on inspection tours, or to and from special events.

From selected carriers in these categories, each chef was invited to submit recipes for a typical meal to be found on the menu of the car or train on which he or she works. I then adapted the recipes to the standardized format you'll find in the book. They were tested and revised as necessary—although no ingredients were changed—and when possible returned to the chef with questions and, finally, for approval.

The result is an astonishing array of delicious foods made of a wide range of ingredients which, thanks to the Internet, can be found and purchased by cooks everywhere. (Occasionally, a side dish is called for in more than one chef's menu; in those cases, a cross-reference is provided.)

Throughout the book, you'll find rail chefs' tips and tricks, all of which can be used by the home cook. Recipe notes suggest ingredient substitutions and cooking techniques that can work in a pinch. Chefs' tips relate to cooking in general and are applicable to a variety of circumstances on or off a train. Here, for example, you'll encounter the concept of the "planned-over" (never a "leftover"): preparing more of a sauce or other recipe element than you immediately need, so that the excess can be used later, often the same day, on another dish (e.g., the use of a luncheon salad dressing as a marinade for a dinner entrée).

My hope and expectation is that if you cook in a small kitchen, as I do—my eight-foot-by-six-foot "Pullman kitchen" holds a refrigerator, two ovens and a range, a microwave, two sinks, and a dishwasher, and very little counter space—and have a tight schedule, and several people with varying tastes to satisfy, but nonetheless want something that excites the food lover in you, you will find the inspiration, techniques, and recipes here that will work for you.

Meanwhile, the countless hours and miles of breathtaking train rides across North America and on into the continent's fascinating back country, with accompanying meals "taken in the cars," has inspired an affection for and appreciation of the men and women who prepare consistently delicious meals on the rails. This book is meant to capture their passion and experience, and to share it with you. The next time you want a good meal while you travel, I hope you'll consider taking the train. And by the way, if you're on Amtrak, I'll likely be in the sleeping cars forward.

NOTES: (1) All recipes included here have been prepared on board a working train. However, chefs and menus change regularly. As a result, the menu items you will find here may not be available on the respective trains at the time you choose to book a trip. My experience indicates that you can look forward to other equally good menu items being offered for your enjoyment. (2) While the focus in organizing the book's chapters and recipes has been on the trains and equipment, the chefs working in private car service pose a unique problem: they work under contract to various car owners at different times. For that reason, the names of the cars associated with the various private car chefs are to be considered "home cars," that is, the car identified is the one on which the chef most commonly works. Making the home car determination was the decision of the author, and any errors in that matter are, with apologies to an offended party, his alone. (3) When instructions prepare one serving, quantities can be increased arithmetically for each additional serving.

North America's Private Luxury Trains

Adjectives abound when one reads descriptions of private rail travel: "Luxurious," "evocative," "gracious," "romantic," "hospitable," "inviting," "charming," "unhurried," "enduring," "sumptuous," and "refined," to name a few. Throw in a couple of nouns like "civility," "luxury," and especially "fun," and you have a dead-on description of an array of such trains that operate around the world, from the *Eastern & Oriental Express* in the Far East to *The Blue Train* in South Africa, to the *Venice Simplon-Orient-Express* in Europe, and the many fine trains included here.

Perhaps the finest rail dining in history is to be found on these great privately operated luxury trains running today over once famous routes. They are described in their literature as rail cruises and offer sumptuous surroundings on board and stunning or exotic scenery and locales en route to touring destinations along their right-of-way. Meals are an important part of this experience, and each train's chefs work to prepare something you will remember for a lifetime. Then, perhaps, as was the hope of managements of the first-class railroads of yore, you will not only tell friends about your wonderful experience and urge them to take the trip as well, but you will think to ride the train again the next time you travel.

Sunday, August 19, 1995, marked the inaugural run of one such train in America. The *American Orient Express* (*AOE*) departed Washington, D.C., for Los Angeles, California, on a journey of 4,200 miles. It made history for the fact that it was the longest run a scheduled train had ever made in the United States. Today the *American Orient Express,* along with the *Rocky Mountaineer, Princess Tours, Montana Rockies Rail Tours,* and the *Royal Canadian Pacific,* also described in this chapter, offer dozens of varying routes through and across portions of North America each year. The *AOE* is typical of what one can expect to find on any of these premium trains. Come on board.

American Orient Express

www.americanorientexpress.com

Sunday mornings in the center of a great metropolis are always quiet. This day is no exception, as a group of tourists enter the grand and sparkling Union Station in Washington, D.C. The silence is broken momentarily while they pass through the otherwise deserted terminal en route to their train. Hushed murmurs convey that they are suitably impressed by the great structure. They descend to the platform along Track 25 to board an inviting line of passenger cars—gleaming cream and royal-blue smooth-sides resting atop a black under-frame, with gray roofs and gold stripes accentuating the length of the sixteen-car consist—and are greeted by formally attired attendants, today offering fresh strawberries dipped in chocolate. The congruity of the train set is broken only when one looks forward to see the two growling Amtrak locomotives coupled up to the head-end.

Once on board, the passengers see to their belongings, already placed in their compartments, then gather in small groups in one of the three inviting lounge cars. This voyage of the *American Orient Express* is scheduled to get under way shortly. For now, however, a conspicuously placed blue light glows atop a pole mounted on the rail off the rear of the train, a warning to other trainmen that workers are still in harm's way underneath the train, and to hold the train in place.

The informed watch and others wonder when, a few minutes later, the blue light

The American Orient Express, *which operates two complete train sets on various itineraries throughout North America. © Kerrick James*

flickers out and the train begins to glide forward, bound for Charlottesville, Virginia, and points west all the way to California. It rolls under the Capitol lawn, then affords its passengers a view of the city's landmarks fading to the rear. "For my part," Robert Lewis Stevenson wrote, "I travel not to go anywhere, but to go. I travel for travel's sake. The great affair is to move." That thought is echoed in an American Express advertisement of the day that quotes Geoffrey Kent, himself an authority on rail tours, saying, "To travel is to fulfill one's fantasies." It is also appropriate to consider what Lucius Beebe would have had to say about this train and its journey. Beebe, in books, magazines, and newspapers of the 1940s and '50s, glorified first-class rail travel. Where his beloved "steamcars" were concerned, Beebe did not tolerate slipshod conception or sloppy execution among railroad people (he very publicly quit patronizing one famous train when coaches found their way into the train's set of cars). So it is to his book *The Trains We Rode* (written with Charles Clegg) we can turn in search of comparisons to the *AOE* among the great trains of North American rail travel. Such comparisons are appropriate and favorable.

American railroads have historically concentrated on services to mark the exclusivity of the *Limited* train. Early riders, after all, were people who had a relatively high average income and appeared willing to pay a premium for comfort, speed, and luxury when traveling. Hence, the thinking of railroad managements went, the faster, more luxurious, and expensive the service, the more customers they would attract. As a result, the emphasis in the best trains was on luxury, high speed, and attention to every passenger comfort. The extra fare justified by these considerations took care of separating the high-and-mighty from the hoi polloi, and avoided the undemocratic concept of "classes" of accommodation such as were favored in Europe.

In the 1940s and '50s, rail standards were set by "the *Century* and the *Chief*"— that is, the New York Central's *20th Century Limited* from New York to Chicago, which Beebe described as "a name train whose legend and excellences have exhausted the superlative," and the Santa Fe's *Super Chief,* which rode on to Los Angeles. These prestigious trains, were regarded as the cream of limited train service, offering accommodations, personal services, amenities, and meals in a combination unequaled by other trains. On all these counts, today's *American Orient Express* can boast the same unparalleled status. But what about speed? The frequent squawk from detectors in the track coming over the conductor's radio will confirm that the train goes as fast as 79 miles per hour. While not as fast as some earlier trains, which could run at more than 100 miles per hour, it is a safe and comfortable rate, set by the railroads over whose tracks today's passenger trains run. But the *AOE* offers something more than the *Century* and the *Chief* did. It is also a work of historic preservation, a rail travel "experience," and entertainment for all senses, all of which separates it from anything Beebe rode.

Consider the *American Orient Express* train set. Its line of cars typically consists of four crew's cars followed by three sleeping cars, a lounge car, two dining "carriages," a dome lounge car, three more sleepers, and the Henry Dreyfuss–designed lounge/observation car *New York*. The *New York* was originally placed in service on the *Century* in 1948, while the others took to the rails sometime in the 1950s. Each of these cars enjoyed a previous life assigned to passenger trains running workaday schedules. All have since been adaptively restored to a new level of splendor. The interiors are a tasteful interpretation of what luxury rail cars would no doubt look like today if dozens of Class I railroads were competing for riders.

The cars are tied together as a unit with dark mahogany walls rubbed to a matte luster and adorned with delicate marquetry done up in varying shades of lighter wood, reminiscent of an early Pullman tradition. In the sleepers, compartment doors are marked with an inlaid pattern unique to each car. The rooms too are lined in mahogany, and vary in configuration but typically include a compartment-width sofa/berth, done in a muted rose-on-rose upholstery, that is both spacious and suitably firm. A soft paisley-print blind can be lowered over the window on those rare occasions—such as when modesty dictates—that one doesn't want to take in what is passing outside. Controls for lighting and climate are conveniently placed. A compact dressing area is done up with a rubbed stainless sink and counter with a bay-windowed mirror. A retractable table can serve for cosmetics or drinks served in the room. Each compartment includes a stand-alone bathroom equipped with commode and space to dress.

The lounge cars of the *AOE* recreate the zenith of luxury rail travel–parlor/lounge seating, well-stocked bars and congenial bartenders, and, in one car, a grand piano and live entertainment each evening. The cars are trimmed in mahogany to just above the windows and crowned with a car-length scenic mural that tapers into the ceiling. On a recent evening, as dusk engulfed the train while it hurried across Iowa, and as the library invited guests with newspapers, magazines, and books, as the pianist applies her skill to the keyboard, and as ice can be heard clinking in glasses over whispered small talk, one can't help wondering how a civilized people ever gave up this mode of transportation. Perhaps Beebe was right when he once scoffed at those who flew as people with an inflated sense of self-importance.

In the grand manner of railroads past, the managers of the *American Orient Express* recruit outstanding chefs for the train's kitchens. The culinary team includes a pearl diver (the cook who also washes dishes), a second cook, and the sous chef or the executive chef. Three waiters serve each dining car's forty-four eager diners. A chef for the crew dining room works forward. To help the kitchen staff communicate, and to minimize the likelihood of a staff member hustling through the dining room in search of an item in the other car's kitchen, the dining cars are set back to back, with kitchen ends connecting. Here is where you'll find Executive Chef Warren McLeod.

McLeod doesn't have to tell you he was a "Jarhead." His haircut, build, and manner announce that fact as soon as he enters the dining car *Chicago* to join his guests after dinner. What he reveals in conversation, what passengers say about him, is that he is a skilled and creative chef, a warm yet firm and demanding boss, and a natural-born leader. A talk with him is spiced with keen insight, disarming honesty, and hearty laughter.

For the record, Warren C. McLeod was in the United States Marine Corps from 1982 to 1987. "All over the Middle East," he summarizes after ticking off a list of duty stations in that region. A soldier's blunt descriptions thus pepper his answers to the questions and comments passengers and the occasional writer direct at him. "I'm not complicated," he says when asked about this.

Once discharged from the marines, he gravitated to the food service industry. His first job, as a server in San Antonio, Texas, got him excited about food. "We had to work one week in the kitchen as part of our training," he says. "That made me curious about what I was putting in front of people." At his next job his potential in the kitchen was recognized by Executive Chef Elmer Prambs, whom McLeod credits as his tutor and mentor. "When the Four Seasons Hotel opened in New York in 1995, Prambs encouraged me to go there to work."

Having found a career that satisfied him, McLeod realized that to rise to the top of the profession he'd have to be "certified," that is, to have formal culinary schooling. It is another insight into his character that he aimed high, attending the tough but prestigious Culinary Institute of America in Hyde Park, New York, for two years (1996 and 1997) to earn his degree. From there his career path is typical for a chef: He job-hopped to expand his skills. He worked under Mario Batali at the restaurant Po in Greenwich Village in New York, then at the Waldorf Astoria, and at the Peninsula Hotel. "Mario Batali encouraged me to go to Italy," he says. "So in 1999 I left for Castel Guelfo, near Bologna, where I worked at Lo Conda Solo Rola for eighteen months." Back in the United States he opened the restaurant Alain Ducasse at the Essex House in New York City.

That's where he was working when his friend Jay McCarthy, the Director of Operations with the *AOE,* called. "It was right after 9/11," says McLeod. "I'd worked for Jay twice before, starting at the Zuni Grill. He knew what I could do." Management of the *American Orient Express* wanted to elevate the train's cuisine. McCarthy thought McLeod was right for the job. "I told Jay I wanted to think about it and, if I was going to do it, to wrap up some things I was involved with in New York. I asked him to get back to me after the first of the year." The call came at 8:00 A.M. on January 1, 2002. " 'Well,' he said, 'what do you think?' I flew to Denver, we talked it over, and I started to work on January 6."

"Now you're lookin' at a guy who'd never been on a train," McLeod says, "except the subway. I had no idea about cooking with electric. I didn't know a thing about taking movement into account while cooking. I'd never had to concern myself with things like ballasting my pots. And our first trip was in just five weeks."

Being asked to "elevate the cuisine" is a polite way of saying "start over." That's what McLeod had to do. A daunting task under any circumstances, this had to be done to a menu already at the high end of the culinary ladder. Cuisine, after all, is one of the selling points of the train. "It started," says Chef Warren, "with a service concept to guide everything else I would have to do. Next I had to plan my menus. Then establish standards of service. Hire staff and train them in my vision, expectations, and techniques. Find purveyors for my ingredients. Set up procedures for provisioning the train."

The concept grew out of his experience: "I'm trained in American and Italian technique. I go for big, bold flavors. I serve creative comfort foods." McLeod will tell you he's a craftsman, not an artist. "What's the difference between an artist and a chef?" he asks. "An artist does it great once. If he tries to do it again it may not be as good. A chef does it once, and if it's great he has to do it great over and over and over again."

Concerning his menus and recipes, he says, "I knew what I wanted to do, but I didn't know my clientele. Will my food work for the people coming in to my dining room? I had to look at my first six months on the train as a test period. You know, try something, get a response, then tweak it and go out again." His Oven-Roasted Red Beet and Grand Marnier Soup (see page 17), for example, while tasty, needed texture. "So I diced a beet fine, sautéed it until it was crisp, and sprinkled it on as a garnish," he says. The result? Fragrance, flavor, texture, and color. He calls it "vibrant and sexy."

Concept and menus established, he set out to hire. "I had a stack of résumés and the telephone," McLeod says. "You can tell a lot about a chef just in conversation." Today, he oversees the offerings on two trains. McLeod works one train and handpicks the crew on the other. "But I give that crew creative freedom," he says. "The chef is allowed to do his thing as long as he maintains quality."

"I've had to learn how to be patient," he continues. "Executive chefs are teachers as well as chefs and managers. I was a dictator in the kitchen until I got here. But this place humbles you. And teaches you that you can't dictate. Too much teamwork is needed to get the job done." But if McLeod doesn't take credit for the output—he's always talking up his team to passengers—he does feel everything coming out of the kitchen reflects on him. And he is out talking to guests at every meal.

Dealing with purveyors to provision his train taught him some lessons, too. "When I got to Los Angeles for my first run," he says, "there were ten pallets of food delivered the first day. My heart sank. I didn't know where to put all of it." He dealt with it, and today routinely deals with a number of supply problems that would befuddle a traditional restaurant chef. "I don't just have to deal with seasonality," he says, "but with seasons that vary according to the train's schedule. Every change of schedule requires us to reprioritize our menu and our sources of ingredients. I have to find fennel in Savannah, Georgia, and fresh seafood in Montana." And, while his needs may be urgent to him, they are apt not to be to a supplier. "A purveyor will give priority to a regular year-round customer over someone like me. I may buy as much as any restaurant that serves one hundred dinners each evening, but I do it only once or twice a year at a given location."

The *AOE*'s Copper Canyon runs in Mexico create their own problems. The train is sometimes in very remote locations. When McLeod does find a grocery store open somewhere, there often isn't much selection. And if he needs one hundred pounds of potatoes, that might mean the grocer he wants to buy them from has no potatoes for townspeople for another week. "My creative skills are definitely called to the fore," he says.

Through it all, the last clue to McLeod's success with his people can be seen in his attitude. He's been heard to say, "I can smile till my face cracks." Or, "I'm still on the right side of the grass, aren't I?" When asked about leftovers, he says there is no such thing in his kitchen. "But," he added, "I do use planned-overs." He laughs heartily for the umpteenth time. And then he's off to be sure his kitchen is working okay without him.

Typically, a day's dining begins at 6:30 A.M. with fresh fruit, fresh pastries that are baked on board, and beverages being served in several of the lounge cars. From 7:00 A.M. to 9:00 A.M. the dining car is open for breakfast and offers a varied menu that changes daily. Entrées include an egg dish, a specialty item, unique pancakes or waffles, and a variety of cereals and fresh fruits.

Sides include several meats, breads, and juices, teas, and coffee. Here is one favorite specialty.

Roasted Lobster and Grilled Asparagus Frittata

6 lobster tails, bloomed
¼ cup extra-virgin olive oil, divided
salt and pepper to taste
2 tsp. paprika
1 bunch asparagus
2 tsp. garlic, minced

8 eggs, whole
¼ cup heavy cream
1 cup scallions, sliced on bias
1 cup crème fraîche
1 oz caviar, osetra (optional)

Before You Begin

You'll need: kitchen shears, roasting pan, large pot, sauté pan, small bowl

Preheat oven to 400°F.

Prep: 30 minutes

Cook: 5 minutes

Yield: 6 servings

Open up lobster tails by cutting down from the head end with a pair of sharp kitchen shears, stopping close to the last joint and without completely cutting the tail out. Carefully remove tail and place on top of shell, butterfly tail meat and remove vein. (**NOTE**: Tails may be purchased already prepared.) Coat tail meat with olive oil, salt, pepper, and paprika. Place in a roasting pan and roast in a 400°F oven, until pink, approximately 5 to 7 minutes. Meanwhile, in a large pot, blanch asparagus in lightly salted, rapidly boiling water for one minute, then remove and plunge into an ice-water bath to stop cooking. Quickly pat dry and toss in olive oil, then season with salt and pepper. Roll whole asparagus across grill top or in a hot sauté pan until marked. Remove lobster from oven, and from its shell. Dice lobster meat into bite-size pieces. Slice grilled asparagus into 1-inch pieces. In a small bowl, combine eggs, heavy cream, and salt and pepper to taste. For each portion, in a sauté pan over medium heat, heat 1 teaspoon olive oil and sauté garlic about 1 minute. Pour approximately ⅔ cup egg mixture into sauté pan. When eggs first begin to capture air bubbles, add a few pieces of lobster and an equal amount of asparagus. Flip open faced and cook until firm and heated through, 1 to 2 minutes. Remove to serving plate. Garnish with sliced scallions, crème fraîche, and a small dollop of caviar. Serve hot with Champagne or a chilled Riesling.

On those days when the train is moving to a new location instead of being "stabled" while passengers take in a local attraction, lunch consists of a soup, one cold and one hot entrée, and a choice between two desserts. Here is a typical warm luncheon main course:

Chicken Roulade with Maple-Chipotle BBQ Sauce

Before You Begin

You'll need: cleaver, small skillet, robot-coupe, large ovenproof sauté pan

Preheat oven to 400°F.

Prep: 30 minutes

Cook: 15 minutes

Yield: 4 servings

4 chicken breasts, boneless, skinless

3 Tbsp. olive oil, divided

3 shallots, diced fine

1 lb. pork fat, cubed

1 bunch sage

1 bunch rosemary

salt and pepper to taste

3 egg whites

½ cup heavy cream

1 lobe foie gras, B grade, sliced into 3" × ½" pieces

caul fat, as needed

3 cups mixed greens

Remove tenders from breasts and use the flat surface of a cleaver or heavy knife to pound breasts to ¼ inch thick. In a small skillet over medium heat, heat 1 tablespoon oil and fry diced shallots until crisp, about 5 minutes. Set aside. Lay out chicken breast, outer side down. Slice a small butterfly flap on both sides of each breast, and set aside. In a robot-coupe, combine the chicken tenders, pork fat, herbs, salt, pepper, egg whites, and heavy cream to form a mousse. While the mousse is emulsifying, season chicken breasts. When mousse is ready, keep it very cool and spoon it into the middle of the butterflied chicken breast. Top the mousse with a piece of foie gras, close flap, and tightly roll the breast. Spread caul fat out on a flat surface and place rolled chicken on top. Cut caul fat in a square slightly larger than necessary to tightly roll chicken within, roll, and trim off excess. In a large ovenproof sauté pan over medium-high heat, heat 2 tablespoons olive oil and sear the chicken on all sides until golden brown, about 3 minutes. Place pan in a 400°F oven to cook through, about 10 minutes (caul fat will cook off). To serve, spread ¾ cup bed of mixed greens on individual plates, then slice chicken breast into

5 or 6 slices to fan out around greens. Drizzle Maple-Chipotle BBQ Sauce over the slices. Top with fried shallots.

Maple-Chipotle BBQ Sauce

3 chipotle peppers in adobe
1+ Tbsp. olive oil, divided
1 cup chicken stock
1 medium onion, minced
6 cloves garlic, minced

⅛ tsp. ground allspice
½ cup ketchup
¼ cup maple syrup
1 cup coffee, cooled
lemon juice to taste

Before You Begin

You'll need: blender or food processor, 1-quart saucepan, 2-quart saucepan

Prep: 15 minutes

Cook: 30 minutes

Yield: 2 cups

In a blender or food processor, puree chipotle peppers with a little olive oil to form a paste, and set aside. In a 1-quart saucepan, bring chicken stock to a boil, reduce heat, and simmer until reduced by ¼. Meanwhile, in a 2-quart saucepan over medium heat, heat 1 tablespoon olive oil and sauté onion 2 minutes. Add garlic and allspice and sauté 1 additional minute. Add ketchup, maple syrup, chicken stock, coffee, and lemon juice, stir to mix, and return to simmer. Stir in chipotle paste and allow to simmer until reduced by ⅓.

At dinner, a five-course meal features an appetizer, soup, and salad, followed by a choice from among three entrees, and three dessert selections. For tonight . . .

Coriander-Crusted Scallops atop Tropical Fruit Salsa, Bathed in a Watermelon-Tomato Nage

2 cups coriander seeds
2 lbs. sea scallops, fresh, 20–30 count
1 cup extra-virgin olive oil, divided
1 cup white wine
¼ lb. lightly salted butter, divided
2 shallots, minced
12 plum tomatoes, peeled, seeded, chopped, juice reserved

3 jalapeño, seeded, minced
salt and pepper to taste
1 cup sherry
½ small watermelon, coarsely diced
1 cup cilantro, leaves only
2 Tbsp. shredded coconut

Before You Begin

You'll need: 2 large sauté pans, large plate, small bowl, whisk

Preheat oven to warm to hold sautéed scallops

Prep: 15 minutes

Cook: 45 minutes

Yield: 8 servings

Crack coriander seeds by rolling under a large sauté pan to just open, and spread them on a large plate. Season scallops with salt and pepper to taste, and press one side only into cracked coriander seeds to encrust. In a large sauté pan over medium-high heat, add 3 tablespoons olive oil and sauté scallops, coriander side down. When just turning golden brown, about 2 minutes, carefully turn and sauté other side about 1 minute longer. Remove to a plate and keep warm. Deglaze pan with white wine, bringing just a boil, and simmer to reduce until liquid sticks to a spoon, about 45 seconds. Pour into a small bowl and set pan and bowl aside.

Meanwhile, in a large sauté pan over medium heat, melt 2 tablespoons butter and sauté shallots until translucent, about 3 minutes. Add chopped tomatoes and all juice reserved. Add salt and pepper to taste, sherry, and 1 tablespoon olive oil. Let reduce by ⅔, stirring occasionally, and remove from heat. Heat pan in which scallops were sautéed, add half of reduced tomato mixture, watermelon and juice, and deglazed scallop pan liquid. When hot, whisk in three 2-tablespoon cubes of butter, blending one melted cube before adding another, until foamy. Reduce heat to keep warm. To serve, place a spoonful of Tropical Fruit Salsa (see below) in the center of a dinner plate. Lean 3 scallops on salsa, coriander crust side up. Ladle watermelon–tomato sauce over and around scallops. Garnish with fresh cilantro leaves, shredded coconut, and a few cracked coriander seeds.

Tropical Fruit Salsa

Before You Begin
You'll need: medium bowl
Prep: 20 minutes
Yield: 4 cups

1 papaya, peeled
1 pineapple, peeled, cored
1 mango, peeled
½ small watermelon
1 small red onion
¼ cup lime juice

1 cup cilantro, leaves only
sherry vinegar to taste
salt and pepper to taste
fruit juices to taste (orange, cranberry, pineapple, etc.) (optional)

Small-dice all fruit and red onion. Add lime juice and cilantro leaves. Stir in sherry vinegar. Add salt and pepper. Add fruit juices if using. Cover and refrigerate. **NOTE:** This step can be completed up to 24 hours ahead of time.

Oven-Roasted Red Beet and Grand Marnier Soup

1 cup red beets, small-diced (for garnish)

5 lbs. red beets, peeled, chopped

2 Tbsp. butter, divided

2 shallot bulbs, chopped

4 cloves garlic, chopped

2 cups Grand Marnier

2 cups heavy cream

2 cups orange juice

1 cup orange peel zested

1 cup extra-virgin olive oil

salt and pepper to taste

dash cayenne pepper

1 cup orange sections

Before You Begin

You'll need: large pot, 2 small skillets, electric beater, 2 large bowls, strainer, roasting pan

Preheat oven to 400°F.

Prep: 30 minutes

Cook: 45 minutes

Yield: 16 servings

In a small skillet over medium heat, melt 1 tablespoon butter, sauté diced beets until crispy, and set aside for garnish. In a large pot over high heat, place chopped beets in salted water to cover, bring to a boil, reduce heat, and cook until almost done, about 20 minutes. Meanwhile, in a small skillet over medium heat, melt 1 tablespoon butter and sauté shallots and garlic until soft, about 3 minutes. Deglaze skillet with a dash of Grand Marnier and set aside. In a large bowl, whip the cream with electric beater, adding a splash of orange juice and one-half of the orange zest. Remove and drain boiling beets in a strainer, reserving the liquid. In a large bowl, toss beets in olive oil with salt, pepper, and cayenne pepper. Place beets and reserved liquid in a roasting pan, then place in a 400°F oven until liquid is evaporated and beets begin to candy, allowing approximately 10 to 15 minutes. In a clean large pot, add shallots and garlic to beets. As pan begins to heat, add a small portion of the boiling liquid. Begin to puree, adjusting the consistency with Grand Marnier and orange juice to create a bold flavor and color. Serve hot, garnished with a small dollop of the whipped cream, diced beets, orange sections, and dash of zest.

Cucumber and Red Onion Salad with Mandarin Orange Sections and Toasted Caraway Seeds

Before You Begin

You'll need: small saucepan, baking sheet, spiral ribbon-slicing machine, large bowl

Preheat oven to 350°F.

Prep: 20 minutes

Cook: 10 minutes

Yield: 6 servings

½ cup dried currants
½ cup Madeira wine
½ cup caraway seeds
3 English/seedless cucumbers
1 small red onion
1 carrot, 3-inch julienne

½ cup rice wine
⅔ cup rice wine vinegar
⅓ cup sugar
salt and pepper to taste
1 11-oz. can Mandarin oranges
2 Tbsp. spiced mint oil

In a small saucepan over medium high heat, combine currants and Maderia wine, bring just to a boil, remove from heat and set aside to steep and cool, then drain. Spread caraway seeds on a baking sheet and place in a 350°F oven to toast, about 5 minutes, and set aside to cool. On a spiral ribbon-slicing machine, shave cucumbers, leaving skin on. Trim the ends of the onion, cut in half vertically, then slice thin and add to cucumbers. Add julienne carrot to cucumber and onion. In a large bowl, stir rice wine, rice wine vinegar, sugar, salt and pepper until sugar and salt are dissolved. Add cucumber, onion, and carrot mixture and stir. Add caraway seeds. To serve, quickly stir salad mixture and remove a medium handful to the center of a salad plate. Top with 3 mandarin sections and garnish with poached currants and a splash of spiced mint oil.

Cioppino

Before You Begin

You'll need: large stockpot

Prep: 30 minutes

Cook: 45 minutes

Yield: 16 servings

2 Tbsp. bacon rendering
1 red pepper, small-diced
1 onion, small-diced
2 carrots, small-diced
2 celery stalks, small-diced
1 fennel bulb, small-diced
1 cup white wine
2 qts. fish fumet or rich stock
¼ cup dried basil
1 stalk lemongrass, chopped coarse
salt and pepper to taste

10 Roma tomatoes, peeled, seeded, chopped coarse
1 cup Pernod
2 oz. tomato paste (optional)
½ lb. white fish, diced
½ lb. littleneck clams
½ lb. mussels
½ lb. jumbo lump crab meat
½ lb. 20- to 26-count shrimp
½ lb. 20- to 30-count sea scallops, quartered

In a large stockpot over medium heat, melt bacon rendering, add first five vegetables, cover, and sweat to soften, about 5 minutes. Uncover and continue to sauté until a slight caramelization builds on bottom of pan, about 5 more minutes. Deglaze with white wine, simmer to reduce liquid by ½, then add fish fumet. Stir in basil, lemongrass, salt, pepper, tomatoes, and Pernod. Add tomato paste to flavor and thicken, if desired. Heat to a simmer and cook until all vegetables are softened, about 5 minutes. Add seafood and continue to simmer to cook and heat through. Serve with a thick slice of grilled bread that has been rubbed with roasted garlic cloves.

For dessert, a choice of two favorites:

Bailey's Chocolate Custard

6 oz. semisweet chocolate, chopped
3 cups half & half
1 vanilla bean
1 egg

8 egg yolks
⅓ cup sugar
Bailey's Irish Cream to taste

Before You Begin

You'll need: double boiler, 2-quart heavy-bottomed saucepan, medium bowl, sieve, pitcher, 8 5-oz. molds, large baking dish or pan

Preheat oven to 325°F.

Prep: 30 minutes (plus 3 hours or more to chill)

Cook: 40 minutes

Yield: 8 servings

Melt chocolate in a double boiler over hot, but not boiling, water. In a 2-quart heavy bottom saucepan over medium-high heat, bring half & half, with vanilla bean added, to a boil. Remove from heat, and let sit for 10 to 15 minutes to allow vanilla flavor to infuse half & half. Remove vanilla bean. Meanwhile, in a medium bowl, beat egg and egg yolks together, add sugar, and beat until thick and of a lemon color. Add vanilla-flavored half & half, stirring to combine well. Add Bailey's and melted chocolate, and stir well to form a creamy mixture. Strain mixture through a sieve into a pitcher, skim any bubbles or foam off surface, and pour to equally fill individual molds. Set molds in a large baking dish or pan, fill baking dish with enough water to reach halfway up sides of molds, and place in a 325°F oven to bake until set, 35 to 40 minutes. Remove from oven and cool to room temperature. Cover and refrigerate at least 3 hours or overnight. Serve lightly chilled.

Or, from Patissier William Poole, another popular specialty:

Lemongrass Rice Impératrice

Before You Begin

You'll need: small saucepan, strainer, 2-quart heavy-bottomed saucepan, whisk, 2 small bowls

Prep: 15 minutes (plus 2–3 hours to chill)

Cook: 60 minutes

Yield: 8–12 servings

1 pint half & half

2 heaping Tbsp. dried lemongrass

3 oz. long-grain rice, rinsed and drained

2 egg yolks

3 oz. granulated sugar

1 pkg. unflavored gelatin

¼ cup water

6 oz. heavy cream

whipped cream (for garnish)

Rice Krispies (for garnish)

In a small saucepan, combine half & half with lemongrass and heat just to the boil. Remove from heat and let stand for 20 minutes to infuse. Meanwhile, rinse and drain rice. Strain half & half into a 2-quart heavy-bottomed saucepan. Add rice and bring to a simmer. Cover and simmer slowly until rice is tender, about 20 minutes. Reduce heat to lowest setting. Meanwhile, in a small bowl, whisk egg yolks, add sugar, and beat until thick and of a lemon color. In another small bowl, dissolve gelatin in water. Add a little of the hot rice mixture to the yolks, stir, then add the yolk mixture into the hot rice mixture and cook very slowly, stirring constantly. Add gelatin and continue stirring until mixture thickens, about 3 minutes. Refrigerate 2 to 3 hours to chill through. Whip heavy cream until it forms soft peaks, and fold into chilled rice mixture. To serve, pour into individual bowls, top with additional whipped cream, and sprinkle with Rice Krispies.

"The China Man"

www.chinaconcepts.net

There is one name known to the operators of all types of rail dining service today. Yet he's not a chef, he doesn't operate a dinner train, he doesn't own a private car, he isn't mentioned in any history of railroading or rail dining, he isn't even officially connected with a railroad. Who is this mystery man?

Meet Richard W. Luckin, known as The China Man, thanks to a private car owner who always hails him thus. Rich, his customary nickname, is the acknowledged leading authority on railroad china. He is the author of a half-dozen books, including *Dining on Rails: An Encyclopedia of Railroad China,* an exhaustive listing of the specialized china patterns and designs used in dining car service throughout railroad history. The book details nearly nine hundred patterns once used on trains, in railroad hotels and depot restaurants, and on ships owned or operated by railroads, and as a result has become the unofficial handbook of serious railroad china collectors everywhere.

Luckin is also the creative force behind the company China Concepts, playing a key role in designing new patterns, such as the business car china sold by the New York, Susquehanna & Western Technical & Historical Society, and in researching and replicating historic patterns for fund raising by rail preservation groups. The most extensive of these undertakings is his work reproducing the Atchison, Topeka & Santa Fe Railway's "California Poppy" pattern on a number of authentic pieces for the California State Railroad Museum.

His company created the demitasse sold as a memento on Amtrak's *Coast Starlight* (page 214). He designed the china used on board the *American Orient Express* (page 8) and other private luxury trains. His pieces grace a number of private cars, including the *Georgia 300* (page 60) and *Caritas* (page 68). He's also created china used on the CSX lounge/diner *Indiana,* on the D&RGW business cars *Utah* and *Kansas,* and on business cars of the Union Pacific, Kansas City Southern, and Morristown & Erie railroads.

Like many fans of rail travel and history, Luckin's interest in trains started with a gift. "It was Christmas 1952," he says. "I got a metal refrigerator car kit. Later, when my family moved to Rochester, New York, I found myself living near a New York Central System yard. Train watching became a pastime. When I began work in the advertising specialty industry in Chatham, New York, I rode the New York Central back and forth." In fact, he was known to kill an occasional day off just riding trains. "I was in Chicago once and rode the *Hiawatha*. On another trip I rode the *400*. Going to Chicago I'd ride the *Capitol Limited* or the *Twentieth Century Limited*. I rode every train I could. That's when I became taken by the dining car experience." So taken, in fact, that he began collecting pieces of dining car china. "My first piece was an Erie Starucca–pattern dinner plate I bought on an Erie-Lackawanna fan trip in the 1960s. They were selling it in the baggage car." Within ten years he would be an avid collector. In 1981 he launched China Concepts. His first reproduction order was for the D&RGW "Prospector" plate, an unusual and hard-to-find piece.

In addition to his work for private car owners, railroad business cars, and railroad historic societies, Luckin has designed china for executive aircraft, private yachts, and even the china found on board Cessna Aircraft's demonstrators. "I guess you could say that I specialize in mobile dining rooms,"

Richard Luckin's designs for china on the American Orient Express, *including a charger plate, a five-piece place setting, and various accompanying pieces, is typical of what a well-appointed dining car will offer. Like railroad china of yore, it features the bold colors, gold trim, and the train's logo. The unique soup bowl, standing in the center, is a popular item available for purchase in the* AOE *gift shop. China Concepts*

Luckin says. But not entirely. One of his clients was the family of a couple celebrating their fiftieth wedding anniversary, for whom he designed a set of twelve dinner plates featuring the family crest up front and a chronicle of the couple's life together in the backstamp. He has also designed china for the DeLorean Car Club, a neighborhood church, the president of Peru, and several private buyers.

It's a tribute to Rich Luckin's fastidiousness about his work that, when asked about things that went wrong—serious or silly—he couldn't think of anything. Pressed on the matter, and after several false starts, he finally confessed that, "Well, when the bouillon cups for the *Georgia 300* came in, the logo was mounted crooked." But even that had a happy ending. The car's owner gave them away to train crews.

Montana Rockies Rail Tours dining room. Mountain Rockies Rail Tours

Montana Rockies Rail Tours

www.montanarailtours.com

Want just a taste of luxury rail travel? Want to enjoy unique scenery in a manner similar to what earlier generations experienced on train trips to the Pacific Northwest? Want to take in some of America's oldest and most spectacular national parks in the manner they were accessed in days gone by? Want to traverse once popular rail routes that today are accessed by only one operator's passenger trains? A run of the *Montana Daylight*, operated by Montana Rockies Rail Tours, offers all of this, and delicious food to boot. At 478 miles, it is the longest multiple-day scenic rail journey in the United States.

Rail tours on board the *Montana Daylight*, designated a day train because guests are put up in hotels along the route of the train at night during the excursions, vary from three-day-and-two-night excursions between Spokane, Washington, and Livingston, Montana, to eleven-day-and-ten-night tours between Salt Lake City, Utah, through portions of the Canadian Rockies and Glacier National Park, and Spokane. The rail portion of all these trips has, since the company's inception in 1995, run between Livingston, Montana, and Sandpoint, Idaho. The route covers the original Northern Pacific Railroad right-of-way through southern and western Montana and northern Idaho. It includes climbing to Mullan Pass, Montana, where, in the summer of 1883, crews working for the Northern Pacific drove the final spike for what was the second transcontinental railroad in the United States, this one connecting Chicago to the Pacific Ocean in Washington.

The *Montana Daylight*'s 1950s-era streamlined rail cars, carefully collected and restored into an authentic representation of the classic American trains that once prowled the country, originally ran on such famous western trains as the Great Northern's *Empire Builder*, the Northern Pacific's *North Coast Limited*, the Santa Fe's *El Capitan*, and the Denver & Rio Grande's *Rio Grande Zephyr*. The recipes presented here are from the railroad's deluxe Montana Gold service.

Pasta Salad

½ Tbsp. minced garlic

1½ Tbsp. Dijon mustard

2 Tbsp. balsamic vinegar

6 Tbsp. olive oil

1½ lbs. rainbow rotini, cooked and
  drained

½ cup Kalamata olives, pitted, sliced

2 tomatoes, seeded and diced

2 cucumbers, diced

¼ cup chopped parsley

salt and pepper to taste

Before You Begin

You'll need: large bowl, whisk

Prep: 15 minutes (plus time to cook rotini and to chill before serving)

Yield: 8 servings

In a large bowl, combine garlic, mustard, and vinegar. Slowly whisk in olive oil until all is incorporated and emulsified. Add rotini, olives, tomatoes, cucumber, parsley, and seasoning. Carefully toss to combine and coat all ingredients. Chill to serve.

Prime Rib Sandwich with Roasted Red Peppers and Onions

Before You Begin

You'll need: roasting pan, griddle or large skillet, 2 medium sauté pans, small bowl

Preheat oven to 375°F.

Prep: 15 minutes (plus 1 hour to cook prime rib)

Cook: 10 minutes

Yield: 1 serving

Begin by mixing and refrigerating the sour cream/horseradish sauce, then put the prime rib to roast, and prepare the red peppers and onions while the meat roasts.

2 lb. prime rib (approx. 6 oz. per sandwich)
kosher salt
pepper
1 thick slice sourdough bread

1 tsp. butter
Roasted Red Peppers and Onions (approx. 3 oz. per sandwich)
¼ cup Sour Cream Horsey
¼ cup au jus

Season prime rib heavily with kosher salt and pepper. Place in a roasting pan and roast at 375°F until internal temperature reaches 125°F, about 1 hour. Let rest 15 minutes, then slice thin. Meanwhile, spread bread with butter and place buttered side on a griddle or large skillet to cook until golden brown, turn, and repeat, 1 to 2 minutes per side. Place bread on individual plate, top with 6 ounces of prime rib, and scatter sautéed peppers and onions on top. Serve accompanied by Sour Cream Horsey, au jus, and Pasta Salad (see page 23).

Roasted Red Peppers and Onions

¼ cup cooking oil, divided
1 large onion, sliced
1 12-oz. jar roasted red peppers, drained, ¼-inch julienne

salt and pepper to taste

In a medium sauté pan warm 2 tablespoons of oil over medium-high heat to smoking point, add onion, and stir to sauté and caramelize, about 3 to 4 minutes. In another sauté pan, warm 2 tablespoons of oil over medium-high heat to smoking point, add roasted peppers and sauté until they achieve the same color as the onions. Combine sautéed onions and peppers, season with salt and pepper, and hold hot.

Sour Cream Horsey

1 pint sour cream
3 tsp. horseradish

2 tsp. prepared mustard

In a small bowl, combine ingredients and refrigerate until ready to use.

Banana Cream Pie

1½ cups milk, divided
¼ cup sugar
¼ tsp. salt, or to taste
3 Tbsp. flour
1 egg yolk, well beaten
1 Tbsp. butter

½ tsp. vanilla
4 ripe bananas, sliced thin
8 4-inch tart shells (see NOTE)
1 cup Candied Walnuts
8 chocolate cigarettes (substitute:
    curled semisweet chocolate)

Before You Begin

You'll need: double boiler, small bowl, 8 4-inch tart pans, baking sheet, parchment

Preheat oven to 350°F.

Prep: 30 minutes (plus 1 hour to refrigerate)

Cook: 5 minutes (candied walnuts only)

Yield: 8 servings

NOTE: See pages 82–83 for pastry dough recipe to make tart shells, or purchase already made up.

In a double boiler over boiling water, scald 1 cup milk. Meanwhile, in a small bowl, combine sugar, salt, flour, and ½ cup milk and stir until blended and liquid. Stir flour/milk mixture into hot milk and continue to stir until thickened. Cover and cook 5 additional minutes. Stir in egg yolk and cook 1 additional minute. Add butter and vanilla and stir until melted and well mixed. Remove from heat and allow to cool. Fold in banana slices and pour mixture into tart shells. Refrigerate until ready to serve, at least 1 hour. To serve, remove tarts from pans, spread a portion of candied walnuts over each, and garnish with chocolate cigarettes.

Candied Walnuts

1 Tbsp. honey
2 tsp. granulated sugar

1 cup walnut halves
pinch salt

Preheat oven to 350°F. In a small bowl, combine honey and sugar. Add walnut halves and salt and stir until well coated. Using a slotted spoon, transfer glazed walnuts to a baking sheet lined with parchment and bake until golden brown, about 5 minutes. Remove and cool.

The International Experience: The Royal Scotsman

www.royalscotsman.com

The *Royal Scotsman,* described by its operators as "a country house on wheels," is a luxurious, evocative train. It serves as a traveling hotel for as many as thirty-six passengers who embark on one-, two-, and four-day excursions in the Scottish Highlands. The train is stationary overnight to allow those unaccustomed to sleeping while in motion a more restful accommodation. The term "stabled" is commonly used by luxury train operators to describe this phenomenon, which seems entirely appropriate for a mode of transportation once labeled "the iron horse." (**NOTE:** Some, who sleep even better while moving than they do at home in bed, find such a practice to be heresy.)

No matter what the sleeping accommodation, though, high cuisine is an integral part of the experience. Here, from *Royal Scotsman* Head Chef Alan Mathieson, is something to carry armchair travelers and gourmands to the mountains, glens, and moors of Scotland.

This inviting service on The Royal Scotsman *is typical of the scene waiting guests who enter the dining room of a private luxury train. Abercrombie & Kent International, Inc.*

Fillet of Sea Bass with Tomato Relish, Accompanied by Potato Salad and Beurre Blanc

Before You Begin

You'll need: medium bowl, large skillet, small skillet with lid

Prep: 20 minutes

Cook: 5 minutes

Yield: 4 servings

4 plum tomatoes, peeled, seeded, and chopped

1 small red onion, chopped fine

½ red chili, diced fine

4 Tbsp. olive oil, divided

juice of ½ lemon

1 Tbsp. fresh chives, finely chopped, divided

salt and fresh cracked black pepper to taste

4 6-oz. sea bass fillets

1 Tbsp. butter

4 oz. green beans or snow peas, julienned

In a medium bowl, combine tomatoes, red onion, chili, 2 tablespoons of olive oil, and lemon juice. Add chives, salt, and pepper, stir to mix and set aside. In a large skillet over medium heat, heat 2 tablespoons olive oil, and fry sea bass skin side down until crisp, about 3 minutes. Turn and cook for an additional 2 minutes. Meanwhile, in a small skillet over medium heat, melt butter, add cut green beans, cover, and sweat until tender, about 3 minutes. To serve, form a circle of Potato Salad in the center of individual serving plates. Place sea bass fillet on top, skin side up. Scatter green beans over, drizzle with Beurre Blanc, and sprinkle lightly with remaining chives.

Potato Salad

Before You Begin

You'll need: medium bowl, 3-quart saucepan

Prep: 10 minutes

Cook: 2–3 minutes

Yield: 4 servings

⅓ cup mayonnaise

2 tsp. minced garlic

2 large potatoes, peeled, ½-inch diced

½ Tbsp. chopped fresh chives

salt and fresh cracked black pepper to taste

In a medium bowl combine mayonnaise and garlic and set aside. Fill a 3-quart saucepan ⅔ full of water and bring to a boil. Add diced potatoes and blanch just until heated through, about 3 minutes. Drain potatoes and plunge into ice water to arrest cooking. Drain well and mix with garlic mayonnaise and chives. Season with salt and pepper to taste.

Beurre Blanc

Before You Begin

You'll need: 2-quart saucepan, whisk

Prep: 5 minutes

Cook: 30 minutes

Yield: approximately 7 cups

6 shallots, finely chopped

10 oz. white wine

2½ oz. tarragon vinegar

1 bay leaf

5 oz. vegetable or fish stock

5 oz. heavy cream

1½ lbs. lightly salted butter, well chilled, 1" cubes

salt to taste

In a 2-quart saucepan over medium heat, cook shallots in wine and vinegar until softened. Add bay leaf and simmer to reduce by ½. Add stock and simmer to again reduce by ½. Add cream and again simmer to reduce by ½. Carefully bring sauce just to the boil, reduce heat, and gradually whisk in butter cubes, one at a time, until sauce is of desired thickness and flavor. Do not boil. Season with salt if desired.

Princess Tours's *Midnight Sun Express*

www.Princess.com

A tour and cruise ship operator, Princess Tours offers fans of rail travel an array of seasonal runs on the *Midnight Sun Express,* a train that attracts 80 percent of its passengers from the company's various ship cruises.

Here, ten custom bilevel luxury rail cars come equipped with wraparound glass Ultra Dome ceilings on the upper level that offer unobstructed views. On the lower level, an open-air viewing platform provides additional opportunities to take in the sights. Also on the lower level, eight cars come equipped with a kitchen, and all cars have an elegant dining salon featuring five-foot picture windows and seating for thirty-two. At each of three seatings for each meal, up to ninety guests are greeted with crisp linen and fine china—both time-honored railroad traditions—and a menu of delectable entrées prepared to order by a staff of two in each kitchen.

On a run out of Anchorage, breakfast is served on the way to Talkeetna, lunch is served enroute to Denali, and dinner completes the run to Fairbanks. For such a trip, the pantry is stocked overnight, while a crew of between six and ten people prepares the cars for the trip. "The storage limitations imposed by a rail car necessitates multiple uses of our different food products," says Food and Beverage Manager Steve Heinle. The crew joins the train at 6:00 A.M. and readies everything for an 8:15 A.M. departure. That crew will lay over at the end of the run, and rejoin the train for its return trip the next day, to serve a different group of guests.

Following the route of the Alaska Railroad between Anchorage and Fairbanks, the *Midnight Sun Express* is a part of the various Princess Tours "Heart of Alaska" Cruisetours from mid-May through mid-September. The meals served are a team effort, and showcase the ingredients and cuisine of Alaska. Let's start at lunch.

Midnight Sun Express. *Princess Tours*

Alaskan Reindeer Chili

4 large sourdough boules
1½ lbs. reindeer sausage
1 large onion, chopped
1 celery stalk, chopped
3 large tomatoes, chopped
3 cups tomato juice
2 tsp. ground cumin
1½ tsp. powdered sage

1½ tsp. ground black pepper
1½ tsp. dry basil
1 tsp. oregano
2 Tbsp. chopped garlic
½ bottle Alaskan Amber beer
4 cups cooked red kidney beans
cheddar cheese, grated
green onions, diced

Before You Begin
You'll need: large skillet
Prep: 30 minutes
Cook: 40 minutes
Yield: 4 servings

Cut and save the upper 1½ inch off the sourdough boules, then, with a spoon, dig out and discard the insides of the boules. Set aside. In large skillet over medium heat, brown sausage and onion, about 5 minutes. Add celery during last 2 minutes, and, when celery is soft, add tomatoes, tomato juice, cumin, sage, black pepper, basil, oregano, garlic, and beer. Stirring occasionally, simmer for 20 minutes. Add kidney beans, continue stirring occasionally, and simmer 15 more minutes. To serve, set hollow boule on a plate, fill with hot chili, scatter cheddar cheese and green onions over, and place top alongside on the plate for dipping.

At dinner, begin with two appetizers:

Sweet and Spicy Alaska Spot Prawns

2 Tbsp. olive oil
16 oz. Margarita salsa
1½ Tbsp. cider vinegar
1 Tbsp. honey
½ tsp. salt

24 medium-to-large Alaska Spot prawns,
    peeled, deveined
red onion, sliced (for garnish)
fresh cilantro, chopped (for garnish)

Before You Begin
You'll need: large nonstick skillet
Prep: 10 minutes
Cook: 8 minutes
Yield: 6 servings

In a large nonstick skillet over medium heat, heat olive oil, add salsa, and stir and cook for 3 to 4 minutes. Stir in vinegar, honey, and salt. Add prawns and cook, stirring constantly, until done, about 3 minutes. (**NOTE:** Do not overcook or the shrimp will become soft.) To serve, place four prawns on individual plates, garnish with red onion slices and chopped fresh cilantro.

Hot Crab and Shrimp Spread

Before You Begin

You'll need: large ovenproof dish

Preheat oven to 350°F.

Prep: 10 minutes (plus 3 hours to chill)

Cook: 1 hour

Yield: 8 servings

½ cup mayonnaise

½ cup sour cream

½ cup grated Parmesan cheese

1 tsp. Old Bay seasoning

1 tsp. white pepper

14 oz. artichoke hearts, chopped coarse

1 cup chopped spinach leaves

1 cup Alaskan king crab meat, chopped coarse

6 Alaskan Spot shrimp, chopped coarse

loaf of sourdough bread, sliced thin

8 parsley sprigs (for garnish)

In a large ovenproof dish, combine mayonnaise, sour cream, Parmesan cheese, Old Bay seasoning, and white pepper. Stir in artichoke hearts, spinach, crab, and shrimp. Cover and chill for at least 3 hours, then bake at 350°F until internal temperature reaches at least 140°F, 50 to 60 minutes. Garnish with parsley sprig and serve accompanied by thin slices of sourdough bread.

Intended as an entrée, Alaskan Seafood Gumbo can also be served as a soup course.

Alaskan Seafood Gumbo

Before You Begin

You'll need: small bowl, 6-quart saucepan, 2-quart saucepan

Prep: 15 minutes

Cook: 1 hour

Yield: 4 or 8 servings

½ tsp. ground white pepper

½ tsp. cayenne

½ tsp. ground black pepper

½ tsp. ground cumin

½ tsp. dried basil

½ tsp. dried thyme

½ tsp. dried oregano

4 bay leaves

1 tsp. kosher salt

¾ cup vegetable oil

¾ cup flour

1 cup diced onion

½ cup diced celery

½ cup diced green bell pepper

1 lb. reindeer sausage (substitute: any spicy sausage)

5 cups fish stock

½ lb. Alaskan silver salmon, cut into 1" x 1" squares

½ lb. Alaskan Spot shrimp, peeled and deveined

4 cups cooked long-grain rice

4 green onions, sliced thin (for garnish)

In a small bowl, combine first nine ingredients well to form a seasoning mixture and set aside. In a 6-quart saucepan over medium-high heat, heat the oil until it shimmers, about 3 minutes. Slowly whisk in flour, stirring constantly to prevent clumping, until the mix is smooth and the roux begins to turn the color of an old penny, about 20 minutes. (**NOTE:** Be sure not to let the roux burn. If black specks form, this means it has burned and must be started again.) As the roux begins to darken, reduce heat to medium and add onion, celery, bell pepper, and sausage to cook until the vegetables are soft, about 5 minutes. Add 1½ teaspoons of seasoning mixture, stir to mix, and remove pan from heat. Meanwhile, in a 2-quart saucepan over medium heat, warm stock. Whisking continuously, carefully add stock to roux in a trickle. (**NOTE:** The roux is like lava and if cool, the stock will sizzle and spit.) Let stand for a couple of minutes, then continue whisking remaining stock into the roux. Return pot to the stove and bring to a simmer. Cook gently for 30 minutes. Adjust flavor with remaining seasoning mixture. Just prior to serving, add seafood to heat through, taking care not to overcook the seafood. To serve, divide rice into individual bowls, pour gumbo over, and sprinkle with green onions.

Ensalata Caprese

4 beefsteak tomatoes, sliced ½-inch thick

3 balls buffalo mozzarella, sliced ¼-inch thick

8 fresh basil leaves, cut chiffonade style

olive oil

balsamic vinegar

Before You Begin

Prep: 5 minutes

Yield: 4 servings

On individual plates, arrange three alternating slices of tomato and mozzarella. Sprinkle with fresh basil, olive oil, and balsamic vinegar.

Herb-Crusted French-Cut Pork Chops

1 sleeve saltine-style crackers

1 Tbsp. fresh chopped fresh rosemary

1 Tbsp. fresh chopped fresh parsley

1 Tbsp. chopped fresh garlic

1 tsp. salt

1 Tbsp. fresh cracked black pepper

1 French cut pork loin, approximately 8 bones

jar of spicy brown or Dijon mustard

Before You Begin

You'll need: food processor, large bowl, roasting pan

Preheat oven to 400°F.

Prep: 10 minutes

Cook: 2 hours

Yield: 4 servings

In a food processor, crush saltines until coarse. In a large bowl, mix cracker crumbs, rosemary, parsley, garlic, salt, and pepper. Rub pork loin with mustard and roll it in herb mix to coat. Arrange rack of pork crumb side up in roasting pan. Place in a 400°F oven to roast for 2 hours, or until thermometer inserted into center of meaty part registers 150°F. Remove pork from oven and let stand 10 minutes; temperature should rise to 160°F. Carve pork, cutting between ribs, and serve.

Yukon Gold Mashed Potatoes

Before You Begin

You'll need: 6-quart pot, colander, small saucepan, hand masher

Prep: 5 minutes

Cook: 30 minutes

Yield: 6 servings

3 lbs. Yukon Gold potatoes, peeled, cut in 1½-inch chunks

3 cloves fresh garlic, peeled

1 cup heavy cream

4 Tbsp. unsalted butter

1 tsp. salt

½ tsp. freshly ground white pepper

In a 6-quart pot over high heat, put potatoes and garlic in cold water, bring to a boil, and cook until a fork pierces the potato chunks easily, about 20 minutes. Drain in a colander 5 minutes to remove all excess moisture. Meanwhile, in a small saucepan over medium heat, put the cream, butter, salt, and white pepper, and heat until the butter melts. (**NOTE:** Do not allow to boil.) Stir to mix, reduce heat and keep mixture warm. Put potatoes back in their pot and pour half of warm cream mixture over. Using a hand masher, mash the potatoes well. Add remaining cream mixture and continue to mash, being sure to fully incorporate the cream mixture into the potatoes.

Green Beans and Carrots

Before You Begin

You'll need: vegetable steamer

Prep: 10 minutes

Cook: 3 minutes

Yield: 8 servings

1 lb. green beans, ends removed

1 lb. carrots, peeled, ⅛-inch julienne

salt and pepper to taste

In a vegetable steamer over boiling water, steam vegetables until hot, being sure not to overcook, about 3 minutes. You want these to be hot and crispy. Season with salt and pepper.

In a further nod to local specialties, dessert consists of Alaska Supreme Vanilla Ice Cream, made in Anchorage, topped with Alaska Wild Berry Syrup (see Appendix 2).

Throughout the history of railroading, special trains have served to promote ideas or products. Whether they were a succession of flat cars carrying tractors in a Depression-era "Prosperity Special" or tanks in a display of military might, or a string of twelve blue-and-white streamlined passenger cars and matching locomotive named "The Rexall Train" for the drugstore chain that sponsored its 29,000-mile journey, these trains have called the public's attention to a concept, to products, and to a point of view.

On September 7, 1995, Marlboro, the cigarette maker, unveiled its own special train, the *Marlboro Unlimited*. The company said it marked the return of "the golden age of rail travel" and "the opportunity to explore the American West," where Marlboro drew many of its advertising images. "The Marlboro Unlimited," it went on, "comprises state-of-the-art, custom-designed railcars manufactured by Denver-based Rader Rail Car, Inc. All passenger cars will be outfitted with large, maximum-view, domed rail cars called Ultradomes." As originally conceived, the $27 million train would include eight sleeping cars, eight lounge cars, two saloon cars, a dance club, and a spa car, complete with a 15,000-gallon hot tub, and would measure 17 feet tall and more than one-third of a mile long. The two 3,000-horsepower FP59PH1 locomotives, recognizable by their "swoopy" noses, were built by General Motors. "The ultimate adventure," the company said, "awaits 2,000 lucky sweepstake winners and their adult guests."

The media kit announcing the train included the following recipes as samples of what one could expect on board. They demonstrate how specialty cuisines, too, can be captured using the simple approach required when cooking in a dining car—just as it must have been required when rustled up by a cook working from a chuck wagon. And because the meal is expected to sustain cowhands out on the range, the menu is generous.

Buffalo Burgers

Before You Begin

You'll need: small bowl, waxed paper, or plastic wrap

Prep: 10 minutes (allow 4 hours for the butter to freeze)

Cook: 10 minutes

Yield: 6 servings

½ cup butter, room temperature
2 Tbsp. chopped cilantro or parsley
1 green onion, finely chopped
1 small hot red pepper, minced
2 lbs. lean ground beef or buffalo

6 thin slices Bermuda onion, rings separated
1 sweet green bell pepper
1 Tbsp. butter
salt and pepper to taste

In a small bowl, combine butter, chopped cilantro or parsley, onion, and red pepper. On waxed paper or plastic wrap, shape into a cylinder, 1-inch diameter and 8 inches long. Wrap and freeze. Shape meat into 6 large balls. Cut six ¾-inch lengths of the frozen butter. Keep remaining butter frozen for another day. Make a depression in the center of the meatballs, place a frozen butter pat into each and seal inside by wrapping the meat over. Using the palm of your hand, press meatballs into patties about 1 inch thick, being careful not to expose the butter. Broil or grill 4 inches from the heat to desired degree of doneness, about 4 to 5 minutes on each side. Meanwhile, in a small skillet over medium heat, melt butter and sauté pepper and onion until lightly browned, about 10 minutes, then season and use hot.

Buffalo Burger Buns

Before You Begin

You'll need: large mixing bowl, baking sheet

Do not preheat oven.

Prep: 3 hours

Cook: 25 minutes

Yield: 8 buns

1½ packages active dry yeast

2 cups lukewarm water

1 Tbsp. sugar

1½ tsp. salt

6 cups all-purpose flour

yellow cornmeal

1 egg white

1 tsp. water

In a large mixing bowl, soften yeast in warm water. Add sugar and salt and let stand until it is bubbly. Beat in flour 1 cup at a time until a smooth, soft dough is formed. Turn out onto a floured surface, cover, and let rest 5 minutes. Knead, adding more flour as needed, until dough is smooth and elastic, about 10 minutes. Put dough into a large buttered bowl, turning it to butter top. Cover and let rise in a warm place until doubled, about 1½ to 2 hours. Turn out and punch down, knead lightly, and cover and let rest 5 minutes. After dough has risen and been punched down, shape into 8 large buns. Place buns on a baking sheet that has been greased and sprinkled with cornmeal, and let rest 5 minutes. Lightly beat together the egg white and water; brush over buns. Sprinkle tops with cornmeal. With a sharp knife, slash tops, if desired. Place on the middle rack of a cold oven. Put a pan of boiling water in rack under loaves. Turn oven temperature to 400°F (do not preheat) and bake buns for 20 to 25 minutes or until done.

To serve, place bison burger on a bun and top with fried peppers and onion.

Crusty Corn Trout

1 egg

1 Tbsp. water

1 cup yellow cornmeal

¼ cup ground nuts (peanuts, pine nuts, walnuts, etc.)

1 tsp. salt

¼ tsp. cracked pepper

¼ tsp. paprika

¼ tsp. ground cumin

⅓ cup all-purpose flour

4 rainbow or brook trout, cleaned and boned

vegetable oil

In a broad, flat bowl, beat egg with water. In a second bowl, mix cornmeal, ground nuts, salt, pepper, paprika, and cumin. Place flour in third bowl. Roll trout in flour. Dip floured trout into egg/water mixture, and then into corn-meal. Meanwhile, heat about 1 inch vegetable oil in large skillet over medium heat. Cook trout, turning once, until both sides are brown and fish flakes, about 5 minutes per side.

Chef's Tip: Carry the cornmeal mixture and flour in paper bags. Toss in the trout, shake, and it is ready to fry.

Family Roundup Potato Salad

Before You Begin

You'll need: 4-quart saucepan, large mixing bowl, baking sheet, medium skillet

Preheat oven to 400°F

Prep: 45 minutes (plus at least 1 hour to chill)

Yield: 8–10 servings.

6 to 8 medium potatoes, peeled
½ cup clear Italian dressing
1 cup chopped celery
1 cup chopped cucumber
½ cup chopped parsley
½ cup chopped sweet red and/or green pepper

½ cup chopped green onion
½ cup sliced radishes
½ cup mayonaise
½ cup sour cream
½ lb. cooked bacon, crumbled
½ cup chopped walnuts, toasted

Place potatoes in a 4-quart saucepan and cover with water. Over medium-high heat, bring water to boil and cook potatoes until tender but not soft, about 15 minutes. Chop potatoes (about 6 cups) and put in a mixing bowl. While potatoes are still warm, pour Italian dressing over and allow to cool. Add chopped and sliced vegetables. Combine mayonnaise and sour cream, pour over potato/vegetable mixture and mix well. Chill 1 hour to blend flavors. Meanwhile, spread chopped walnuts on a baking sheet and place in 400°F oven to toast, about 5 minutes. Cook and crumble bacon. Before serving, toss potato salad and top with crumbled bacon and walnuts.

Pepper Slaw

Before You Begin

You'll need: large mixing bowl, small mixing bowl

Prep: 20 minutes (plus at least 3 hours to chill)

Yield: 10–12 servings.

6 cups chopped or shredded cabbage
2 cups sliced red and/or green bell peppers
1½ cups sliced celery
1 cup sliced onion
3¼ cup shredded carrots
½ cup vegetable oil

1½ tsp. celery salt
1 tsp. cracked pepper
½ tsp. celery seed
2 Tbsp. sugar
3 Tbsp. cider vinegar
1 Tbsp. dry mustard

Toss vegetables together in a large mixing bowl. In a small bowl, combine remaining ingredients and pour over vegetables. Toss to mix. Refrigerate for several hours or overnight to blend flavors.

Wild Berry Buckle with Vanilla Cream Sauce

Before You Begin

You'll need: food processor, rolling pin, 9" round or 8" × 11" baking dish

Preheat oven to 425°F.

Prep: 15 minutes (plus 1 hour to refrigerate dough)

Cook: 45 minutes

Yield: 6–8 servings

1½ cups all-purpose flour

1½ Tbsp. sugar

¼ lb. chilled butter or margarine, cubed

5 Tbsp. cold soda water

5 to 6 cups berries (blueberries, raspberries, gooseberries, etc.)

½ to ¾ cup sugar

4 Tbsp. butter

2 Tbsp. bourbon

Vanilla Cream Sauce

Put flour and 1½ tablespoons sugar in food processor. Add chilled butter and process until mixture becomes crumbly. With processor running, slowly pour in soda water, mixing until a ball forms. (**NOTE:** if mixing by hand, cut butter into flour and sugar; slowly add soda water, mixing with a fork.) Press dough mixture into a 4-inch circle, wrap in plastic wrap, and refrigerate at least 1 hour. Then, on a floured surface, pastry cloth, waxed paper, or plastic wrap, roll dough out to fit a 9" round or 8" × 11" baking dish, allowing a 2-inch overhang. Pour berries into crust; sprinkle ½ to ¾ cup sugar over fruit, dot with butter, and drizzle with bourbon. Fold edges of crust over fruit, leaving center open. Sprinkle with additional sugar, if desired. Place in 425°F oven and bake for 45 minutes. Cool to room temperature and serve with Vanilla Cream Sauce.

Vanilla Cream Sauce

Before You Begin

You'll need: small saucepan, medium mixing bowl

Prep: 5 minutes (allow 1 hour to cool)

Cook: 15 minutes

Yield: 2 cups

3 Tbsp. sugar

1 Tbsp. cornstarch

1 cup milk

1 egg yolk, beaten

1 tsp. vanilla extract

½ cup heavy cream

In a small saucepan over medium heat, combine sugar and cornstarch. Add milk. Cook and stir until mixture thickens. Beat a small amount of the mixture into the egg yolk, then stir egg yolk into hot mixture. Cook and stir 1 more minute. Add vanilla, and chill to use. Whip cream and fold into cooled pudding.

NOTE: Plans to operate the *Marlboro Unlimited* were canceled in February 1997, a fact attributed to mechanical difficulty encountered in building the complex rail cars, and to concerns about the weight of the cars when finished.

Rocky Mountaineer

www.rockymountaineer.com

Talk to veterans of rail touring and there's a better than even chance they are members of the chorus that sings the praises of food service on the *Rocky Mountaineer*. The *Rocky Mountaineer* was born of a Canadian federal government decision in 1990 to privatize VIA Rail Canada's two-year-old daylight operations in the Rockies. In a competitive negotiation, a newly formed venture, the Great Canadian Railtour Company, won the route and, according to company literature, "brought in (people with) 120 years of combined railroad expertise" to create a new "daylight tour service along the Canadian Pacific and the Canadian National lines through Canada's west and the Rocky Mountains." Such expertise did not overlook great food.

On board this day train there are two levels of service. RedLeaf Service is similar to traditional rail travel: Picture windows and oversized reclining seats, but with at-the-seat food service that is typically prepared on the ground and placed on board. The "Ahh"-inspiring GoldLeaf Service takes place in ten bilevel dome coaches, built between 1994 and 2001 by Colorado Railcar Manufacturing, LLC. Each car offers second-story dome windows stretching to the roof centerline, a private downstairs dining room, a state-of-the-art stainless-steel galley, and a spacious observation platform on the lower level. These cars seat seventy in the dome and thirty-five in the dining room, so meals are taken by turns. Each GoldLeaf Service dome coach has two attendants upstairs and two down. In the kitchen there is one sous-chef and two cooks. Meal service focuses on breakfast and lunch, with a light dinner served to passengers traveling from Banff to Calgary.

The man responsible for the wonderful dishes coming out of the GoldLeaf galley is Executive Chef Mark Jorundson, a native of Canada. Planning for the mid-April launch of a season's schedule, which concludes in mid-October, Chef Mark first perfects the dishes he expects to serve, then brings the on-board staff in two to three weeks before operations begin to train them in preparing and presenting the

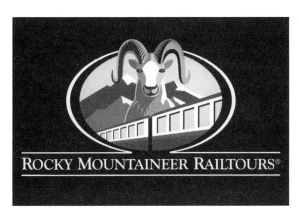

Rocky Mountaineer Railtours logo.
Rocky Mountain Railroads

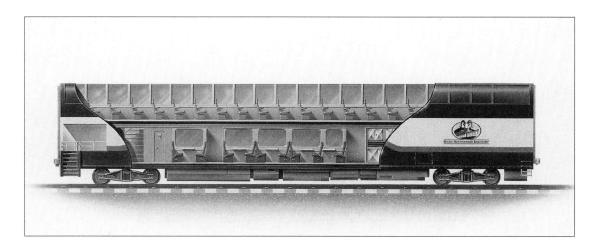

A cross section of the Rocky Mountaineer dining car. Rocky Mountain Railroads

dishes. Vegetables change to take advantage of local and seasonal specialties. Local Okanagan Valley wines complement the menu.

Asked what he found most challenging about working in the confines of a kitchen on a moving train, Chef Mark provided an unusual answer: "The best part of my job is working on the train. I get to cook. That is my passion. There is no telephone, no interference, no distractions, none of the interruptions you encounter in a restaurant kitchen. There is a rhythm, a team spirit, to working in a dining car kitchen. I find being isolated there is a benefit." When he first saw the size of the dining car galley, he wasn't fazed. "I was on Team Alberta and the Canadian National Culinary Team," he says. "We'd travel all over the world to compete and do demonstrations of our ingredients and cuisine. The kitchens we worked in then were quite small, as well. So this held few surprises."

Sugar Pumpkin Soup

3 Tbsp. butter
1 cup chopped onion
1 clove garlic, minced
1 bay leaf
¼ tsp. ground black pepper
½ tsp. ground cinnamon
½ tsp. ground allspice
¼ tsp. salt

4 cups vegetable broth
4 cups ½-inch cubed sugar pumpkin
  (see NOTE)
cranberry coulis or cranberry sauce (for
  garnish)
cilantro sprigs (for garnish) (optional)
roasted pumpkin seeds (for garnish)
  (optional)

Before You Begin

You'll need: 4-quart covered saucepan, slotted spoon, stick blender

Prep: 15 minutes

Cook: 30 minutes

Yield: 4 servings

NOTE: Any type of winter squash (hubbard, acorn, etc.) or pumpkin may be substituted.

In a 4-quart covered saucepan over medium-high heat, melt butter and sauté onion and garlic until tender, about 3 minutes. Add bay leaf, pepper, cinnamon, allspice, salt, and vegetable broth, and stir to mix. Bring to a boil, reduce heat, and simmer, covered, 10 to 15 minutes. Add squash, cover, and simmer an additional 10 minutes, or until squash is tender but retains shape. Remove bay leaf. With slotted spoon, remove 1 cup squash cubes. With a stick blender, puree remaining mixture. Return reserved squash and cook until heated thorough. To serve, ladle soup into serving bowls, top with cranberry coulis, and garnish with roasted pumpkin seeds and a sprig of cilantro.

Salmon with Blueberry-Lime Sauce

1 4-oz. skinless salmon fillet
salt and pepper to taste
3 oz. Wild Rice, prepared (see page 97)
2 oz. Blueberry-Lime Sauce

3 oz. vegetables of the season (see pages
  74, 82, and 217)
1 sprig dill (for garnish)

Before You Begin

You'll need: nonstick baking sheet, 1-quart saucepan

Preheat oven to 350°F.

Prep: 5 minutes

Cook: 30 minutes

Yield: 1 serving

Season salmon fillet with salt and pepper, place on a nonstick baking sheet, and put into a 350°F oven to bake until done, about 7 to 9 minutes. To serve, place wild rice mixture in the center of the plate. Place salmon fillet on top of rice and ladle Blueberry-Lime Sauce over. Place vegetables along side and in front of the salmon. Garnish with dill sprig.

Blueberry-Lime Sauce

1 lb. fresh blueberries (substitute: frozen
    blueberries)
1 cup granulated sugar

juice of 3 limes
zest of 2 limes
¼ cup red wine vinegar

In a 1-quart saucepan over medium-high heat, combine all ingredients and bring just to a boil. Reduce heat and simmer to reduce until mixture is shiny and adheres to a spoon, about 20 minutes.

Honey Lemon Ginseng Cheesecake

British Columbia, thanks to the dry climate in the Fraser and Thompson River valleys and Okanagan Valley, is a major grower of ginseng. While ninety percent of the province's output is exported to Asia, Chef Mark Jorundson promotes its virtues for locals with this specialty dessert:

Before You Begin

You'll need: electric beater, large mixing bowl

Preheat oven to 250°F.

Prep: 15 minutes (plus 3 hours to cool, then refrigerate overnight)

Cook: 4 hours

Yield: 1 cheesecake

18 oz. cream cheese, room temperature
¼ cup granulated sugar
3 Tbsp. honey
2 eggs
⅓ cup sour cream
⅓ cup heavy cream
juice of ½ lemon
1 oz. ginseng liquid (see note)

1 tsp. ginger powder
¼ tsp. cinnamon powder
2 Tbsp. sweet ginger puree (substitute
    crystallized ginger, minced)
1 graham cracker pie crust
½ cup lemon curd (decoration)

NOTE: Substitute 2 packs ginseng tea reconstituted in 2 cups water, then simmered until reduced to 1 ounce of concentrated tea.

With electric mixer set to Beat, use paddle attachment to cream the cream cheese. Add sugar and honey and continue to cream until smooth. Add eggs one at a time, mixing one thoroughly before adding the second. Add sour cream and heavy cream. Add lemon juice, ginseng liquid, ginseng powder, cinnamon, and ginger puree, and continue to beat until well blended. Pour mixture into graham cracker crust. (**NOTE:** Being rich in flavor, pour only 1 inch deep.) Bake in 250°F oven 1 hour and 15 minutes. Remove to cool thoroughly on a wire rack. Marble the top with lemon curd before serving.

Dining has played an important part in rail travel from the beginning. Cartoonists have not over-looked the experience. They, like the writers quoted on pages 89–92, have given their own unique interpretation to what they've experienced.

"*They're got rolls.*"

ABOVE, LEFT: © 1978 *The New Yorker* Collection. Warren Miller from cartoonbank.com. All rights reserved. ABOVE: © 1953 *The New Yorker* Collection. Mischa Richter from cartoonbank.com. All rights reserved. LEFT: © 1947 *The New Yorker* Collection. Mischa Richter from cartoonbank.com. All rights reserved. BELOW: *Cartoonist Curt Katz, an attendant on board Amtrak's* California Zephyr, *offers visual commentary on the state of railroading each month in* Railfan & Railroad, *one of America's oldest magazines covering the railroad community. This is his take on dinner trains. Courtesy of Curtis L. Katz and Carstens Publications*

"*I wonder if I might have a—er—glass of water.*"

RAILFUN   by CURT KATZ

Royal Canadian Pacific

www.cprtours.com

The very essence of private luxury rail travel, then and now, is superior service delivered in vintage rail cars, following an historic rail route through timeless natural splendor. Such is the goal of the Canadian Pacific Railway's *Royal Canadian Pacific* train tours. Employing a fleet of the railroad's business and parlor cars, built between 1916 and 1930 and restored to recreate comfortable and elegant travel accommodations, the railroad allows passengers to travel back nearly one hundred years.

Guests travel in cars once occupied by Sir Winston Churchill, Princess Elizabeth and the Duke of Edinburgh, and their Royal Highnesses King George VI, Queen Elizabeth II, and other luminaries. Surrounded by wood paneling with inlays that were once the trademark of makers of first-class rail cars, stately furniture, tables set with linen, silver, and china, and a discreet but busy staff attending to the passengers' every need, this rail experience achieves the craftsmanship, style, and grace of an earlier era.

In the company's signature trip, a 650-mile loop out of Calgary, Alberta, the *Royal Canadian Pacific* retraces the historic CPR right-of-way, completed in 1885 to form Canada's first transcontinental railway. Passengers catching their first glimpse of the majestic expanse of the Canadian Rockies are often stunned to silence. After touring the Rockies, the train heads north through the Columbia River

Royal Canadian Pacific *dining room. Canadian Pacific Railway— Rick Robinson/ CPR*

Valley to Golden, then east for another view of the Rockies, passing through Yoho and Banff National Parks, and the famous Mount Ogden spiral tunnel, en route back to Calgary.

In the kitchens, three accomplished Canadian Pacific chefs apply their art and chemistry to satisfying your culinary desires. Pierre Meloche, trained in Toronto and for more than fifteen years honed his California, French, and International specialties, before joining the Royal Canadian Pacific six years ago. Denis Sirois, inspired and taught by well-known Radio Canada host and culinary arts book publisher Chef Daniel Vezina, worked in Quebec City to master French technique, then moved to Vancouver, where he added the cuisine of the Pacific Northwest to his credentials. He, too, is a six-year veteran of "the cars." The newest member of the team, Alain Maheux, grew up in Montreal and graduated from the Institut du Tourisme at d'Hôtellerie du Québec, then spent seven years in an eclectic mix of hotel and restaurant kitchens before joining the *RCP* crew in 2001. Together or individually, their creations illustrate the limitless possibilities of a dining car kitchen.

Poached Pears with Stilton Blue Cheese, Cranberry Compote, and Toasted Poppy Seed Dressing

4½ oz. granulated sugar

⅔ cup cold water (approx.)

1¼ cups late-harvest (sweet) white wine, chilled (approx.)

6 pears

3 oz. Stilton cheese, room temperature

2 oz. Philadelphia cream cheese, room temperature

pinch of black pepper

Cranberry Compote

Toasted Poppy Seed Dressing

red grapes (for garnish)

walnut halves (for garnish)

Before You Begin

You'll need:
3-quart saucepan, slotted spoon, small bowl, 1-quart heavy-bottomed saucepan, fine strainer, small bowl, sheet pan

Preheat oven to 350°F.

Prep: 30 minutes (plus 1 hour to poach pears)

Cook: 45 minutes

Yield: 6 servings

In a 3-quart saucepan, combine sugar, and sufficient water and wine to cover pears. Peel and clean the pears and place them in the cold wine mixture. Over medium-high heat, bring to a boil, reduce heat to simmer, and poach pears until soft, allowing 45 to 60 minutes. Using a slotted spoon, remove pears from the liquid (retain 4 teaspoons poaching liquid for dressing mixture), allow to cool, cut in half lengthwise, and clean out the center pit. Meanwhile, in a small bowl, mix the cheeses and pepper together until smooth. Divide cheese mixture evenly among the cavities of the pears, and set aside.

Cranberry Compote

2½ oz. fresh cranberries
2 Tbsp. late-harvest (sweet) white wine
1 oz. granulated sugar
4 tsp. red currant jelly

2 Tbsp. water
zest and juice of one lemon
zest and juice of one orange

In a 1-quart heavy-bottomed saucepan over high heat, combine all ingredients and bring to a boil. Reduce heat and simmer 20 to 30 minutes. Using a slotted spoon or ladle, remove solids from liquid and set residue aside. Continue to simmer liquid in saucepan until reduced by ⅔. Return cranberries to the liquid when reduced, heat through, and set aside.

Toasted Poppy Seed Dressing

1 tsp. poppy seeds
¼ cup olive oil
4 tsp. lemon juice

4 tsp. poaching liquid
salt and pepper to taste

Scatter poppy seeds on a sheet pan and toast in a 350°F oven 3 to 4 minutes. Place all ingredients in a bowl and whisk until emulsified.

To serve, place two pear halves on individual plates, top with a dollop of cranberry compote, and drizzle with dressing. Garnish with red grapes and walnuts

Spinach Anaglotti with Scallop Mousse, Salmon Medallions with Champagne Saffron Cream Beurre Blanc

Begin by making the Pasta Dough, then prepare the Scallop Mousse. Next tackle the Anaglotti and make the garnish. Finally, cook the salmon, make the Champagne Saffron Beurre Blanc, and assemble.

Before You Begin

You'll need: small mixing bowl, food processor, pasta machine, 2½-inch round cutter, 4-quart saucepan, colander, large bowl, slotted spoon, small bowl, small saucepan, whisk, baking sheet

Preheat oven to 350°F.

Prep: 60 minutes

Cook: 30 minutes (total, all components)

Yield: 6 servings

Pasta Dough

Scallop Mousse

Anaglotti

Champagne Saffron Cream Beurre Blanc

¾ lb. salmon fillet, skinned, deboned

vegetable oil

¼ cup white wine

juice of 1 lemon

1 Tbsp. chopped dill

salt and pepper to taste

1 small leek (for garnish)

6 strawberries (for garnish)

Cut salmon fillet into twelve 1-ounce pieces and place on oiled baking sheet. Drizzle salmon with white wine, and lemon juice, then season with dill, salt, and pepper. Cover with foil and set aside or refrigerate until ready to cook. Just prior to serving, place salmon covered in foil in a 350°F oven for 7 minutes. Remove, discard foil, and position onto plate.

Pasta Dough

1 cup flour

dash of salt

1 egg, well beaten

4 tsp. water

1½ oz. cooked spinach, minced, squeezed dry

In a small mixing bowl, combine flour and salt and make a well in the center. Mix beaten egg, water, and spinach and pour in the well in the flour. Knead together to form a smooth dough. Cover and allow to rest for 30 minutes.

Scallop Mousse

½ lb. fresh scallops

salt and white pepper to taste

½ small beaten egg

1 tsp. whipping cream

In a food processor, season scallops with salt and white pepper, then puree. Scrape down sides and continue to puree until very fine. Add egg, set to Mix, and while the motor is running, add the whipping cream slowly. Do not over-puree; the mixture should be the consistency of whipped cream. Remove with a rubber spatula into a clean bowl, wrap and set aside in refrigerator until ready to use.

Anaglotti

Pasta Dough   1 egg, well beaten
Scallop Mousse   2 Tbsp. vegetable oil

Using the pasta machine, roll out the Pasta Dough to ⅛-inch thick. Stamp out with 2½-inch round cutter, place ½ teaspoon Scallop Mousse in the center of each round. Moisten the edges of the round with beaten egg, fold in half and crimp the ends. Fill a 4-quart saucepan ⅔ full of salted water and bring to a boil. Add anaglotti, return to the boil, and stir gently to cook for 5 minutes. Remove to drain in a colander and rinse under cold water to cool. Place in a large bowl, toss with oil, cover, and set aside. When ready to serve, in a fresh pan of boiling water, add anaglotti to cook just until hot. Remove with slotted spoon and position on plate.

Champagne Saffron Cream Beurre Blanc

2½ Tbsp. champagne   2 Tbsp. unsalted butter, cut in small
2½ Tbsp. whipping cream   cubes
pinch of saffron   salt and white pepper to taste

In a small saucepan over medium-high heat, combine champagne and whipping cream, bring to a boil, reduce heat, add saffron, and simmer until reduced by half. Remove from heat and whisk in cubed butter a couple pieces at a time. Season with salt and white pepper. Set aside.

For garnish, cut green part of leeks into thin strips, approximately 6 inches long, making 18 pieces. Poach in boiling water for 15 seconds, drain, and set aside to cool. Clean and quarter 6 strawberries to use as a flower garnish.

To serve, ladle 1 teaspoon of Beurre Blanc at the bottom of the plate. Place two salmon medallions over the sauce pointing toward the top of the plate. Lay two leek strips on either side of the medallions and one in the middle. Place an Anaglotti on the top of each strip to give the impression of a flower. To finish, place the quartered strawberry on the bottom of the plate to form a star making sure the bottoms of the leeks are under the strawberry.

Lemon Sorbet with Coconut Rum and Pineapple "Carpaccio"

1 small fresh pineapple
6 rounded scoops lemon sorbet

1 oz. coconut rum
12 pineapple leaves

Before You Begin

You'll need: chilled/frosted individual serving plates

Prep: 10 minutes

Yield: 6 servings

Trim, core, and cut the pineapple lengthwise into quarters, then slice the quarters very thin. Place a scoop of lemon sorbet in the middle of medium-sized frosted plates. Array pineapple slices around the sorbet. Sprinkle 1 teaspoon rum over the sorbet and pineapple. Slide two small pineapple leaves under the sorbet to finish.

Alberta Beef Tenderloin with Portobello Duxelle and Blueberry Ice Wine Demi-Glace

2¾ lbs. beef tenderloin
cracked black pepper to taste

vegetable oil
salt to taste

Before You Begin

You'll need: large skillet, baking sheet, meat thermometer, heavy-bottomed fry pan, 1-quart saucepan

Preheat oven to 400°F, then 450°F.

Prep: 30 minutes

Cook: 45 minutes

Yield: 6 servings

Clean and trim the tenderloin to remove any fat or silver skin and slice into 6 fillets (approximately 7 ounces each). Make an incision in the middle of the fillet for stuffing. Season both sides of each fillet with pepper and stuff with Portobello Duxelle. In a large skillet over medium-high heat, heat oil to just smoking, season fillets with salt, and sear, about 1 to 2 minutes per side. Place on a baking sheet and in to a 450°F oven to finish (measure an internal temperature of 135°F for rare, 160°F for medium), about 10 minutes.

Portobello Duxelle

2 Tbsp. butter
10 oz. fresh portobello mushrooms, medium diced
3 cloves garlic, peeled, fine diced

⅓ cup onion, peeled, fine diced
¼ cup white wine
salt and pepper

In a heavy-bottomed fry pan over medium heat, melt butter and add the mushrooms, garlic, and onion to sauté until tender, about 5 minutes. Add white wine and continue to cook, stirring occasionally, until mixture is almost dry, about 5 minutes. Season with salt and pepper, remove from heat and allow to cool slightly.

Blueberry-Ice Wine Demi-Glace

2 small garlic cloves, roasted, pureed
½ tsp. butter
1½ oz. shallots, fine-diced
4 tsp. Canadian ice wine

⅔ cup demi-glace
3 oz. fresh blueberries
salt and pepper

Peel and roast garlic in a 400°F oven until soft, about 5 minutes. In a 1-quart saucepan over medium heat, melt butter and sauté shallots. Puree roasted garlic and add to shallots. Add the ice wine, stir, and cook 1 minute. Add demi-glace and continue to simmer for 10 to 15 minutes. During last 5 minutes, add blueberries, bring sauce to a boil, season to taste, and remove from heat. Serve immediately.

To assemble, arrange beef tenderloin using Blueberry-Ice Wine Demi-Glace as noted below, and accompany with Steamed Asparagus with Sautéed Garlic Cherry Tomatoes and Roasted Cracked Pepper Red Baby Potatoes.

NOTE: Recommended consistency of Blueberry-Ice Wine Demi-Glace is that of au jus, in which case it is to be ladled over the tenderloin. If simmered to a consistency of gravy, serve under the tenderloin.

Steamed Asparagus with Sautéed Garlic Cherry Tomatoes

Before You Begin

You'll need: asparagus cooker, medium skillet

Preheat oven to 400°F.

Prep: 15 minutes

Cook: 15 minutes

Yield: 6 servings

1 lb. fresh green asparagus, medium size, trimmed
1½ oz. granulated sugar
salt and pepper to taste

2 Tbsp. unsalted butter
1 large shallot, peeled, fine-diced
3 cloves garlic, roasted, pureed
9 oz. cherry tomatoes

Peel and roast garlic in a 400°F oven until soft, about 5 minutes, then puree and set aside. Meanwhile, in an asparagus cooker's pot, combine sufficient water to cover thick part of asparagus stems with sugar, salt, and pepper. Bring to a boil over high heat. Peel lower areas of asparagus up to the stems and wash clean. Stand asparagus in cooker basket and place in boiling water mixture to cook until soft, about 10 minutes. Add hot water to cover tips and cook 5 minutes longer. Remove the asparagus and cool under cold water. Set the cooking liquid and asparagus aside. Just before serving bring the water to a boil once again and add the asparagus just long enough to heat them through. Meanwhile, in a medium skillet over medium heat, melt butter and sauté shallots and pureed garlic 1 minute. Add cherry tomatoes, stir to coat, and cook just until skins begin to break, stirring occasionally, about 5 minutes. Arrange asparagus spears on plate and spoon sautéed tomato mixture over. Season with salt and pepper and serve immediately.

Roasted Cracked Pepper Red Baby Potatoes

2 lbs. baby red potatoes (see NOTE)
2 Tbsp. vegetable oil

½ Tbsp. fresh cracked black pepper
salt to taste

NOTE: Substitute any size of most common variety if baby reds are not available.

Clean the potatoes and pat them dry. With a paring knife, carve away the bottom half of the potato, leaving enough to form a "mushroom stem." On the top area, cut away small circles of the skin to give the impression of the top of a mushroom. In a 4-quart saucepan over high heat, bring sufficient salted water to cover the potatoes to a boil. Add potatoes and cook until done, about 10 minutes. Drain well and toss gently in a large bowl with vegetable oil, pepper, and salt. Roast in a 450°F oven until lightly browned and crispy, about 5 to 10 minutes.

Before You Begin

You'll need: paring knife, 4-quart saucepan, large bowl

Preheat oven to 450°F.

Prep: 10 minutes

Cook: 20 minutes

Yield: 6 servings

❄ ❄ ❄

Orange Soup with Chantilly and Chocolate Zests

zest of two oranges, blanched
1 Tbsp. cornstarch
16 oz. orange juice
16 oz. frozen orange juice concentrate
8 oz. white wine
8 oz. water
9 oz. strawberries

½ cup orange liqueur (e.g., Bauchant, Grand Marnier, or similar)
¼ cup granulated sugar
20 orange sections
½ cup whipping cream
1 tsp. vanilla extract
2 Tbsp. granulated sugar

Before You Begin

You'll need: 1-quart saucepan, small bowl, 3-quart saucepan, strainer, large mixing bowl, electric beater, 2 medium mixing bowls, double boiler, waxed paper, pastry bag with nozzle

Prep: 30 minutes (total, both components) (plus 1 hour for soup to chill)

Cook: 5 minutes

Yield: 6 servings

Fill a 1-quart saucepan ⅔ full of water and bring to a boil. Drop orange zests in for 1 minute, drain, running cold water over to arrest cooking. In a small bowl, dissolve cornstarch in 2 tablespoons orange juice and set aside. In a 3-quart saucepan over medium-high heat, mix first ten ingredients (including cornstarch/orange juice mixture) together, bring just to a boil, reduce heat, and simmer lightly for 5 minutes. Strain into a large bowl, cover, and refrigerate to cool, at least 1 hour. Just before serving, in a medium mixing bowl, whip the cream until stiff. Continue to whip and add the vanilla and sugar. Whisk whipped cream into soup.

GARNISH:

3½ oz. white chocolate

3½ oz. dark chocolate

zest of orange, lemon, and lime, in equal amounts, blanched (see instructions, page 49)

½ cup whipping cream

1 tsp. vanilla extract

2 Tbsp. granulated sugar

fresh mint

fresh strawberries, sliced very thin

In a double boiler over simmering water, melt white and dark chocolates. Dip the zests into the chocolates and set onto waxed paper to cool. (**NOTE:** You can prepare these separately in white and dark chocolate if desired.) In a medium mixing bowl, whip the cream until stiff. Continue to whip, adding the vanilla and sugar, until stiff peaks form. Using a pastry bag with nozzle, pipe the cream on the upper area of the soup in the form of a bird's nest. Add the chocolate zests in the nest, garnish with fresh mint and strawberry slices.

Libation 1

Fine wine selections and wine tastings are a part of rail dining from Amtrak's *Coast Starlight* to the *Napa Valley Wine Train* and *Spirit of Washington Dinner Train* and the tours off of the *American Orient Express*. Often, local vineyards are spotlighted. The wines suggested by the chef to accompany the *Royal Canadian Pacific* meal here are:

Whites

Bouchard Aine & Fils Pouilly Fuisse 1999

Hugel Gentile Alsace, France 1998

Chapoutier Les Meysonniers Crozes Hermitage 1998

Reds

Château Cheval Brun St. Emilion Grand Cru 1998

Bolla Amarone Della Valpolicella, Italy 1996

Joseph Drouhin La foret Bourgogne Pinot Noir 1999

Château Belgrave Grand Cru Haut—Médoc 1997

And for dessert, or to accompany the main course

Mission Hill Vidal Ice Wine 1999

Private Varnish— Private Chefs

I t's early evening on a mild Sunday in October. At New Orleans's Union Terminal, Amtrak train Number 2, the Miami-bound *Sunset Limited,* is backing slowly to the head end of Track 6. Number 2 customarily takes the track to the bumper. Tonight, however, a special move has been called. Awaiting Number 2 on Track 6 are three private cars—the *Ohio River 364,* the *Missouri-Kansas-Texas 403,* and the *Georgia 300*—positioned there earlier in the day by a switching crew. The cars are returning home from the annual meeting of AAPRCO (pronounce that "aah-PER-co"; it's the accepted moniker for the American Association of Private Railroad Car Owners). On the station platform, a small group made up of the cars' owners and crews falls quiet to watch.

After the mandatory brake-check stop and three short signal blasts from the locomotive's air horn, the silver line of Superliners begins to back slowly toward the waiting cars. Fittingly, the sleeping car swaying toward the group is Amtrak's Number 32009, the *George M. Pullman.* Two Amtrak car men approach from the opposite direction on the platform, exchange greetings with the owners, and watch the action. Under the tutelage of Number 2's conductor, standing in 32009's upper rear door, the cars couple up. Head End Power (HEP) on Number 2 is cut. A blue metal flag is hung on the locomotive's cab, signaling that men were working under the train. The car men satisfy themselves that the brakes are on and venture between the cars.

Their first order of business is to hook up the main air hose and main reservoir line. An electrician unplugs the 480-volt loops at the end of 32009 and connects them to matching receptacles on each side of the lead private car. The HEP loop is complete. One of the car men turns the angle cock open. Air charges through the train and reservoir air lines into the added cars. The entire train is "stretched" several inches forward to check the connections. The electrician signals the head end to send power back. New Orleans–originating passengers can now wander down

The inviting charm and romance of rail travel is apparent on this cold winter's night that finds the private car Chapel Hill *attached to Amtrak's Chicago-Seattle* Empire Builder *as the train awaits departure from Havre, Montana. Mike Danneman*

the platform to their accommodations. They gawk at the brightly colored string of Private Varnish now bringing up the rear of their train. The car men begin the ritual of the brake test, first calling for brakes to be set. Then, walking forward, they flash their lights over each set of trucks in the entire consist, verifying the brake shoes are seated against the wheels.

"Now they'll walk 'em off," says Jack Heard, owner of the *Georgia 300,* for the first time taking his eyes off the activity between his car and the *George M. Pullman.* He's referring to a visual check that the brakes are disengaged. There is a hiss from under the cars. In a barely perceptible motion, the brake shoes are released from the wheels. From the front of the train, swinging lanterns trace the progress of the car men as they again search under each car, this time checking to be sure the brake shoes have lifted. In a matter of minutes the procedure is complete. The blue flag is pulled. The conductor calls "All aboard." Amtrak's car attendants pick up their stair steps and hop into their cars. The private car owners climb to the platform of the *Georgia 300,* each owner heading to his own car to await departure. The destination: Jacksonville, Florida. Entering the *300*'s observation-end sitting room, the platform door eases shut behind the group with an authoritative and reassuring thud.

Two long blasts from the air horns forward and the train is moving. Several hundred yards out, a slight tug on the train indicates the running brake test—a third and final check of the brakes, this one to assure that they work while under way—

has been carried out. Clear signals and a clear evening welcomes Number 2 as she accelerates out of the yard heading east.

Inside, the *Georgia 300* is a cozy, comfortable car tastefully decorated in what might be called "the club look," featuring a corridor off which the stately bedrooms are located, a formal dining room (see page 61), a bar-lounge, wet bar, and wine cellar. At the end of the train, an observation room overlooks the rear platform and the track receding behind.

Among the highlights is the car's fully equipped stainless-steel kitchen. A model of efficiency typical of railroad car kitchens, this one has a sink and counter along the bulkhead to the left and a refrigerator, counter, and stove along the outer wall. Here, Chef Nat Jones does his magic, while Steward Ralph Graves remains poised on a stool in the corner opposite to help or kibitz as the situation demands. All the while, Graves keeps an eye down the car and listens for the buzzer to signal that someone has entered off the platform.

Private cars have always been the province of the well-to-do. *Georgia 300*'s owner Jack Heard, a successful Florida businessman, fell in love with private business cars at an early age. "When I was growing up in Moultrie, Georgia, I was in the school band. We were playing an event in 1965 that included a Southern Railway steam-powered train arriving at Moultrie's station. On that occasion, the Georgia Northern Railway moved its office car *Moltrie* out of storage and spotted it in front of the station. I got one look at that car, and at all the dignitaries going in and out, and was bitten. Of course, as a youngster I couldn't go in the car. So I just stood there and watched. I said to myself, 'One day I am going to own one of these things.' " Twenty-one years later, he got his chance.

The *Georgia 300* was built in 1930 by the Pullman Company originally as a ten-section mid-train sleeper with lounge, and named the *General Polk*. It was assigned to the Southern Railway's *Queen* and *Crescent Limited*. Retired from revenue service in 1953, it was converted into an office car by the Georgia Railroad in 1954 and sent out as the *300*. Declared surplus by the time the Seaboard Coast Line acquired the Georgia Railroad in 1982, it was sold to a buyer in Cincinnati. There it sat, idle, when it was called to Jack's Heard's attention, in 1986. "I learned it was set to be scrapped or sold into Maintenance of Way service," Heard recalls. "When I got a look at it, the rust streaks coming down from the windows looked for all the world to me like the car was crying. I just had to save it. I bought it that same day."

Since then, the car has undergone several upgrades. The first was carried out right away. Heard restored grandeur to the interior with new paint, carpeting, upholstery, and drapes. Outside, the observation platform deck was replaced and the car was painted. Abandoning the Georgia Railroad's flat Pullman green scheme—working railroads have historically shied away from exterior ostentation on their business cars for fear of appearing to their stockholders to be the robber barons of old—the car emerged painted bright blue and trimmed in aluminum to recall the Georgia Railroad's passenger diesels.

In 1989, the *Georgia 300* was shopped for a major mechanical upgrade: 1955 General Steel Industries high-speed six-wheel outside swing-hanger trucks, taken from another car and rebuilt, were placed underneath. The brake system was upgraded. The electric system was converted from 32-volt to 110-volt throughout. The propane generator was replaced by a diesel generator. The car was made fully Amtrak-compatible by the addition of full–Head End Power, a 27-pin communications train line, and main reservoir air line. Installing environmentally friendly stainless-steel Microphor treatment tanks for waste, an electric hot water heating system, and a new all-stainless-steel kitchen, completed the overhaul.

Each of the major projects—acquiring, inspecting, and rebuilding trucks, installing HEP and the Microphor system, becoming fully Amtrak compatible—represented an investment of tens of thousands of dollars, which explains why the number of cars that attain the *Georgia 300*'s level of luxury, comfort, and sophistication is small.

The exact number of privately owned cars is hard to pin down. AAPRCO Executive Director Diane Elliott estimates there are between 150 and 160 privately owned, working, Amtrak-certified cars. (Several hundred more cars are in operation but are not Amtrak compatible, running in excursion or dinner train service.) An inestimably greater number of passenger cars sit inoperable, belonging to rail fan groups, private individuals, or other organizations who may have restored them, or are working at getting them restored—may even hope someday to see them running again—but are sitting track-bound.

To help offset the expense of keeping a private car—a bad wheel, for example, will cost $2,000 plus shop expense and labor to replace—many owners charter their car to individuals and groups for personal celebrations or business functions (see Appendix 1 for information on how to contact AAPRCO). Jack Heard does this on a modest scale, taking referrals from Amtrak, the AAPRCO Directory, and word-of-mouth. Among those taking up residence in his car have been Presidents George Bush (1992) and Bill Clinton (1996). Amtrak reports that typically the company executes more than five hundred private car moves each year.

For each trip, Heard lines up his crew, which consists of a steward and a chef. Also accompanying the *Georgia 300* on each trip is a mechanic. "A car that fails an Amtrak inspection anywhere on the system will be cut out and left to sit until the owner can deadhead it home for repair," Heard says. To help assure that never happens, the mechanic oversees, inspects, and repairs anything that goes wrong, from adjusting a door that ever-so-slightly scrapes the jamb when it closes, to muscling a misbehaving generator back to order. "His job," says Heard, "is to be sure the car is operated properly throughout its run, to oversee coupling up, answer questions ground crew may have, top off water or generator fuel, and the like, and to oversee repairs if any are needed."

Two weeks before the move, the car is inspected and any repairs made. The batteries are watered. Fuel and lubrication are applied where needed. Inside, the linen closet is inventoried and replenished. The car is cleaned and the silver polished and set out. All systems are checked to be sure everything is fully operational. The menu is planned and a shopping list drawn up. "I don't buy anything from a chain store," Heard says. "I use institutional distributors—the ones that provision the best restaurants—to get meat and poultry. We shop farmers' markets for fruit and vegetables. Seafood comes from the docks. A local bakery does my bread and rolls." Jack has been known to shop station stops, too: "I pick up collard greens at Palatka, Florida, if I can, and citrus fruits at other stops in Florida." All of this, plus anything needed for the bar, are picked up and loaded the day before the trip.

On the day of the trip, the car receives a detailed final inspection just before the switching locomotive picks it up. The air conditioner is turned on. The beds are made up, and linen placed throughout. Fresh flowers and fruit are arranged at appropriate locations. The day's newspaper is placed on board, a practice carried out each day the car is on the road. Music is selected for the stereo system.

Guests are greeted on board and given a book of safety rules to observe. Cocktail hour and meal times are established. This run, uneventful but for the special surroundings of a private car, comes to an end in Jacksonville. The three private cars are uncoupled from the *Sunset Limited* and left where they sit, at the north end of Track 1 at Amtrak's station. The *Sunset Limited* departs. CSX locomotive #6159, backs down to the cars and couples up to the *300*. The main brake line is hooked up and the angle cock opened. The air horn sounds, and the short but stately consist, just begging for a steam locomotive, is pulled unceremoniously away. North of town, at Jacksonville's intermodal ramp, the three cars are wyed. Coming back through the station, the Ohio River 364 is repositioned to be picked up by Amtrak's northbound number 98, the *Silver Meteor*.

The *Missouri-Kansas-Texas 403* and the *Georgia 300* are taken to a storage track at Jack Heard's car park in Orange Park, adjacent the CSX/Amtrak main line. There, among other private cars, the *Georgia 300* will await orders from Heard as to where he and his guests want it to go next.

Chartering space on a private car, or chartering the entire car, may be railfanning at its best. Anyone, even those with modest means, can share an experience once enjoyed by Jay Gould, J. P. Morgan, Lucius Beebe, and a long list of other luminaries. And after taking in the sights and sounds of the Gulf Coast countryside after midnight, at 79 miles per hour, sitting in a folding director's chair on the platform of a heavyweight private car, it can be said this is an experience not to be missed.

Georgia 300

www.aaprco.com

Chef Kevin Langton's emergence as a leading private car chef was an evolution. After graduating from Loyola College in Maryland and going on to earn a two-year certificate in the culinary arts, he began working from time to time on the business cars of CSX, a major freight railroad. He subsequently went to work on the private

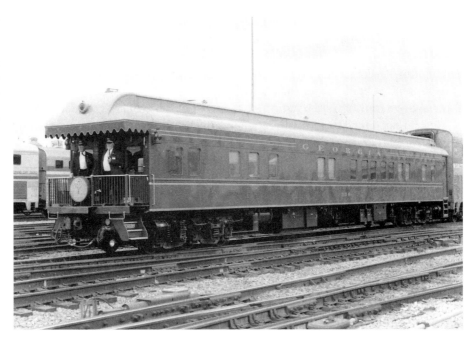

The private car Georgia 300, coupled up to an Amtrak Intercity train, departs Chicago under careful supervision. John H. Kuehl

car *Caritas* (see page 68), and filled in occasionally on the *Chapel Hill* (see pages 71–74). Around these assignments, he's worked in country clubs, restaurants owned by the Colgate family in Jacksonville, Florida, and at the Epping Forest Yacht Club. "It became my ambition, though, once I'd mastered cooking in a rail car, to work primarily on a first class private business car. When the opportunity arose to chef for Jack Heard on the *Georgia 300,* I found my home car." His meals, such as this one, are the culmination of more than twenty years on trains.

Chef Kevin's Butternut Squash Soup

Before You Begin

You'll need: large roasting pan, 3-quart sauté pan, blender

Preheat oven to 375 °F.

Prep: 20 minutes

Cook: 90 minutes

Yield: 6–8 servings

½ cup unsalted butter, divided

2 2-lb. butternut squash, peeled, cut into 2-inch cubes

salt and pepper to taste

1 diced medium onion

1 cup celery cut into 1-inch cubes

1 medium leek, chopped fine

1 large carrot, cut into 1-inch pieces

¼ cup of shallots, diced

1 Tbsp. finely chopped ginger

1 Tbsp. fresh thyme, chopped fine

2 qts. chicken stock

½ cup heavy cream, chilled

crème fraîche or sour cream (for garnish)

2 medium scallions, chopped (for garnish)

In a large roasting pan, melt ¼ cup butter, add squash pieces, toss to coat, season with salt and pepper, and place uncovered in 375°F oven to roast until squash is tender, about 35 to 40 minutes. In a 3-quart sauté pan melt ¼ cup butter, add onion, celery, leek, carrot, and shallot to cook over medium heat until vegetables are barely soft, about 3 minutes. Add ginger, thyme, roasted squash, and chicken stock, bring to a boil, then cover and lower heat to simmer until vegetables are tender, about 20 minutes. Allow soup to cool sufficiently to handle, then place in a blender in batches and puree until smooth, repeating as necessary, about 5 minutes per batch. Reheat the soup, season with salt and pepper to taste, whisk in cream, and cook until smooth and heated through, about 5 minutes. Ladle soup into bowls and garnish with a dab of crème fraîche or sour cream and a scatter of chopped scallions.

Smoked Cheddar and Andouille Sausage Bruschetta

1 Tbsp. cooking oil
1 cup diced Andouille sausage
1½ cups shredded smoked cheddar cheese
¼ cup sour cream
¼ cup chopped green onion
3 Tbsp. Worcestershire sauce
Creole seasoning to taste
24 cocktail rye toasts

Before You Begin

You'll need: medium skillet, medium bowl, baking sheet

Preheat oven to 350°F.

Prep: 10 minutes

Cook: 12 minutes

Yield: 6–8 servings

In a medium skillet over medium-high heat, warm oil and sauté Andouille sausage for about 2 minutes, and set aside. In a medium bowl, mix cheddar cheese, sour cream, green onion, Worcestershire sauce, and Creole seasoning well. Smooth the cheese mixture atop the rye toasts and top with Andouille sausage. Place on a baking sheet and bake in 350°F oven until cheese is melted, about 12 minutes. Serve warm.

Stuffed Olives with Blue Cheese and Shrimp

¼ lb. wedge blue cheese, crumbled
2 Tbsp. olive oil
2 Tbsp. minced garlic
cracked black pepper to taste
24 large queen olives, pitted
24 36–40 count shrimp, cooked, peeled, deveined, tail off

Before You Begin

You'll need: small bowl, frill toothpicks

Prep: 15 minutes

Yield: 6–8 servings

In a small bowl, mix blue cheese, olive oil, garlic, and pepper together to form a soft paste. Stuff cheese mixture into olives, wrap each olive with a shrimp, and secure together with a frill toothpick.

Stone Mountain Asparagus Salad

Before You Begin

You'll need:
asparagus steamer, blender

Prep: 15 minutes

Yield: 6–8 servings

1 lb. asparagus, allow 5 spears per
   serving

1 head radicchio lettuce

3 vine-ripened tomatoes, seeded, diced

1 red onion, diced

¾ cup extra-virgin olive oil

¼ cup balsamic vinegar

1 Tbsp. minced oregano

1 tsp. minced garlic

salt and Creole seasoning to taste

¼ cup minced, cooked bacon

¼ cup crumbled blue cheese

Steam asparagus for about 1 minute, until slightly firm, then remove from heat and transfer into a bowl of ice water to cover. Strain and set aside. Cut radicchio at the bottom to get individual lettuce cups. On a chilled salad plate, place radicchio and arrange asparagus, then tomatoes and onions separately. Vegetables should appear to be falling out of the radicchio "basket." In a blender, place olive oil and set on Low/Mix. Gradually add vinegar, oregano, garlic, and seasoning. Drizzle dressing over salad and garnish with bacon and blue cheese.

Savannah Pecan Grouper

Before You Begin

You'll need:
blender or food processor, small bowl, large bowl, sheet pan, large sauté pan, ovenproof platter

Preheat oven to 250°F.

Prep: 15 minutes

Cook: 15 minutes

Yield: 6 servings

1 cup pecan pieces

1 cup all-purpose flour

salt and pepper to taste

2 eggs, whipped

3 Tbsp. milk

6 7-oz. grouper fillets

6 Tbsp. butter, divided

¼ cup white wine

½ cup chutney

¼ cup key lime juice

1¼ cups heavy cream

zest of 1 orange

zest of 1 lemon

Place pecan pieces in a blender or food processor and chop until pecans are very fine. In a small bowl, combine flour, salt, pepper, and pecan pieces with a fork. Whisk the eggs and milk in a large mixing bowl. Season both sides of fillets with salt and pepper. Place fillets, one at a time, in the egg/milk mixture, remove from wash, dredge in pecan flour, and transfer to dry sheet pan. In a large sauté pan over medium-high heat, melt 3 tablespoons of butter, then place three fillets in pan to sauté for about 2½ minutes per side. Remove fillets to a clean sheet pan and repeat same using remaining fillets. Place sheet pan with 6 fillets in a 250°F oven to keep warm. Meanwhile, deglaze sauté pan with white wine, then stir in chutney, key lime juice, and heavy cream. Continue to cook until sauce thickens. To serve, remove grouper fillets from oven and place on serving plate. Top with chutney sauce and garnish with lemon-orange zest. Serve with potato or rice of choice, and any fresh, indigenous vegetables of the season, such as:

Wilted Fresh Spinach with Garlic

2 Tbsp. butter
4 cloves garlic, chopped
½ cup portobello mushrooms, sliced

juice of ½ lemon
salt and pepper to taste
1 lb. fresh spinach, thoroughly washed

Before You Begin

You'll need: large skillet

Prep: 5 minutes

Cook: 10 minutes

Yield: 6 servings

In a large sauté skillet over medium heat, melt butter and sauté garlic until golden, about 2 minutes. Add mushrooms and continue to sauté until soft. Sprinkle lemon juice over and season to taste. Add spinach and toss lightly until heated through and slightly wilted, about 3 minutes.

Georgia 300 Peach and Pecan Sundae

½ cup chopped pecans, roasted
4 large fresh Georgia peaches (substitute 2 8-oz. canned, drained, if not available)
juice of 1 lemon (optional, if holding fresh peach cubes)

6 Tbsp. unsalted butter
½ cup light brown sugar
3 Tbsp. heavy cream
3 Tbsp. bourbon
1 qt. vanilla bean ice cream
mint leaves

Before You Begin

You'll need: baking sheet, medium bowl, 2-quart saucepan

Preheat oven to 350°F.

Prep: 10 minutes

Cook: 20 minutes

Yield: 8 servings

Spread pecans on a baking sheet and place in a 350°F oven until lightly browned, about 10 minutes. Meanwhile, peel and pit peaches, then cut into 1-inch cubes and place in a bowl of water to cover to which the juice of one lemon has been added to prevent discoloring. Set aside. In a 2-quart saucepan over medium heat, melt the butter and brown sugar, stirring occasionally, until thick enough to adhere to the spoon, about 2 to 3 minutes. Slowly add heavy cream and stir until thick and smooth. Add bourbon and mix well. Drain peach cubes and add them and toasted pecans, reduce heat and simmer 15 minutes. Serve in champagne glasses over vanilla bean ice cream and garnish with a fresh mint leaf.

One pleasantry afforded by sleeping in the drawing room of a well-constructed railroad car is the near-total darkness created by tight-clearance doors and snug-fitting window pulls. Add the smooth yet gently swaying ride produced by a Pullman heavyweight, and insomnia research becomes irrelevant. On one trip, a guest's slumber in such luxury is interrupted only when Steward Ralph Graves of the private car *Georgia 300* presses the discreet room buzzer and announces, just above a whisper, "Breakfast is about to be served in the dining room." For one who is usually up at 5:30 A.M., the "8:30" looking back from a wristwatch is its own alarm. A quick shower, a hurried application of dress, and a few brisk steps down the corridor to the dining room, and one joins host and car owner Jack Heard for breakfast.

The scene is a timeless one from the railroad life, at least as lived by a line's executives, or the well-to-do, and their guests. Pale blue walls, underlined by dark wainscoting and accented with vivid, floral-print, pulled-back window curtains, set the mood. Classic black-and-white photographs of Georgia Railroad motive power, matted and framed, flank the door to the bar/lounge and beyond. On the opposite wall a huge mirror crowns a credenza adorned with bouquets of fresh flowers that surround silver hollow-ware on a tray and a silver bowl filled with fresh fruit. Muted sunlight streams in through thin-slatted blinds.

At table, a formal setting worthy of the presidents, both national and corporate, who have dined here. Crisply pressed white linen tablecloth and napkins. Heavy, well-balanced Atlantic Coast Line flatware. Customized *Georgia 300* china, white, trimmed in the car's exterior colors—a broad blue band edged in silver along the outer rim and a thin blue stripe around the edge of the well—with a red Georgia Railroad logo accenting the top rim of each piece. An array of heavy silver hollow-ware within easy reach. Awaiting, too, at each place setting, is a six-piece silver Combination Server, designed originally for dining cars on the Union Pacific, centered on a plate, hinting of something good to come.

This scene is the work of railroad veterans Ralph Graves and his kitchen colleague, Nat Jones. Their uniforms echo the private/business car theme as well: dark gray dress slacks and white jackets. Steward Graves wears a formal jacket with blue piping accenting the sleeves, epaulets, and upright collar. Brass buttons, a red Georgia Railroad logo on the right shoulder, and the words *Georgia 300* in black on the shirt cuffs. Chef Jones wears an all-white military-style shirt, his name in script over the right breast pocket, the car's name printed over the left pocket, and the Georgia Railroad logo on his right shoulder, all in red.

Graves, a native of Jacksonville, Florida, entered the work force in 1943 in the kitchen of that city's Roosevelt Hotel. He began his railroad career with Seaboard Air Line on December 7, 1945. "The day I applied I was made second cook and put on a train, the *Silver Meteor* going north. Because I'd worked in a kitchen and been trained, I was promoted to Chef six months later." His work eventually got him into kitchens on the *Comet,* the *Star,* the *Orange Blossom Special,* the *Palmland,* and the *Gulf Wind.* "I worked as Chef until 1964. In that year I was asked by G. R. Thorne, our Vice President of Operations, to work in his office car." Graves remained on the office car staff until he retired in 1987 from by-then CSX, rising to the top: Chef to Thomas Rice and other of the railroad's CEO's. He started to work on the *Georgia 300* in January 1988. Among those he's encountered in his work are President Eisenhower's wife Mamie, movie mogul Cecille B. DeMille, entertainer Jackie Gleason, and President Jimmy Carter.

"Working an office car has its advantages and disadvantages," Graves points out. "Men'd often take the job for the prestige associated with working on business cars. It was the top of our profession. Plus, you also got to stay home more. You only traveled when the executive was out on the system. But," he adds, "the work is confining. You are on the same car for the duration of your trip. And you have to be on call."

Among Graves's culinary contributions to railroading legend is the Seaboard Air Line's specialty Cream of Peanut Soup. He says of that creation: "Often the cooks in dining cars had no culinary training. They were merely shown how to prepare the recipes on our menus by the traveling chef. So they often just poured a little stock, or even water, into peanut butter and served that. I knew to add a little cream and to always use stock to assure a smooth and flavorful soup."

Nat Jones, too, comes from a restaurant background, including training as a pastry chef, and didn't start work for the railroad until 1965. Why did he switch? "The railroad paid better and had benefits," he says. Like Graves, he went through the Seaboard Air Line-Seaboard Coast Line-CSX metamorphosis, and likewise retired in 1987. His career, however, was more of a checkerboard. "I began as a number 2 cook, then rose to be a Chef on the *Silver Meteor* and the *Star*. When the SCL was formed, I went into the Commissary. That's were I learned how to cut meat for the trains. After another brief stint on the trains, I transferred to the CSX mailroom, then into the law department. It was in the early 1970s that I hired out to the business cars. I worked them until I retired."

Georgia 300
dining room.
John H. Kuehl

This Sunday, breakfast begins with grapefruit sections marinated in maraschino cherry juice and topped with a cherry, served set in ice in the Combination Server. Next, a Nat Jones specialty: light, fluffy-and-flavorful Georgia Peach Hotcakes, accompanied by sides of scrambled egg whites, pork sausage, and bacon. Buttered rolls and plenty of hot coffee complete the meal.

"Timing your cooking can be crucial," offers Jones. "My biggest disaster was once trying to cook an egg custard pie. I'd just gotten it poured into the shell and placed in the oven when the train departed. I spent most of the rest of the trip cleaning burnt custard from my oven."

Jack Heard usually notifies Nat and Ralph two or three weeks before a move. He tells Nat how many guests to expect and how many meals will be served. "I've learned," Nat interjected, "that if Mr. Heard says there will be four guests, I plan for six. If he says six, I just know there'll be eight." Jones then plans the menu and, the day before the move, goes shopping at local grocery stores. The day of the move, he picks up any last-minute items and loads the car.

Both Jones and Graves agree that it was important to learn the preferences of the executives whose cars they worked. Ralph Graves once even had to go to the wife of one of his executives for help. "He wouldn't eat. I'd ask him, 'Is everything all right?' He'd say, 'Yes, everything tastes great.' But he wouldn't eat. So I met his wife and asked her what he ate at home. Once I knew his preferences, I cooked things he enjoyed." This lesson serves them when working for Jack Heard, too. He is partial to ingredients from his home state of Georgia.

Later that day, at lunch, Nat serves up the perfect club sandwich, railroad style: Layers of toasted white bread separated by thin slices of smoked turkey breast, bacon, lettuce, tomato, and mayonnaise, cut into four crisp, absolutely straight and level wedges, accompanied by a chilled dill pickle wedge. Coffee and an array of chocolate wafers complete the meal.

Sitting in the elegant dining room, enjoying this unique culinary moment, one is reminded of how the everyday work of these dedicated, hardworking, even inspired men, and many other men and women like them throughout railroad history, made (and make) rail travel the special experience it has always been.

Nat Jones's Georgia Peach Hotcakes

Before You Begin

You'll need: griddle, large mixing bowl, medium mixing bowl.

Prep: 30 minutes

Cook: 5 minutes

Yield: 4 servings

4 cups flour

1 cup packed light brown sugar

2 Tbsp. granulated sugar

1 Tbsp. baking soda

1 Tbsp. baking powder

2 tsp. salt

4 cups buttermilk

1 cup unsalted butter, melted

2 tsp. vanilla extract

1 cup finely diced peaches

Peach slices (for garnish)

Cane syrup

Heat griddle to medium hot, about 375°F, and grease just before using. In a large bowl, mix dry ingredients well. In a separate bowl, combine buttermilk, butter, and vanilla and mix well. Slowly stir liquid into dry ingredients to just moisten (do not overbeat). Let stand for 20 minutes. Pour batter onto hot greased griddle using a ¼-cup measure. Sprinkle with diced peaches.

When bubbles form over the hotcake, approximately 1 to 2 minutes, turn to finish, allowing another 1 to 2 minutes. Serve with cane syrup. Garnish with peach slices (optional).

CHEF'S TIPS, COURTESY OF NAT JONES: (1) Fry sausage until browned on both sides, then set on paper towels and pat dry. Place fried sausage (or bacon) in boiling water for 2 to 3 minutes to draw out grease, and again set on clean paper towels and pat dry. Return to a clean skillet to which chicken stock or water and chicken bouillon has been added. Simmer until heated through. (2) When deep frying: Peel a small onion and a small potato (or halves if large), and place both in hot oil to absorb grease and reduce odor produced by deep-frying. When onion and potato turn black, remove and replace if needed.

Belle Vista

www.railventures.com

Matthew Gipson, Chef de Cuisine for a number of private car owners, is currently the manager of a fleet of private railcars owned and chartered out by a company called Rail Ventures. Some of these cars see service in the summer as the first-class Montana Gold service on *Montana Rockies Rail Tours* (see pages 23–25).

The Rail Ventures car Chef Matthew is most often affiliated with is the *Belle Vista,* a former Union Pacific dome car that recently underwent a thorough restoration. Gipson oversaw the design of the newly outfitted car. He was given great liberties with the design, especially when it came to the kitchen, a walk-through stainless-steel beauty that would be the pride of chefs everywhere. Throughout, the *Belle Vista* is a spacious and modern setting that includes dome and rear-platform seating from which to view the passing countryside or enjoy dinner under the stars, two master bedrooms with queen beds, two staterooms, and a state-of-the-art audio-visual installation.

Chef Matthew began his career onboard privately owned railcars when he had a catering business in Sonoma County, California. His specialty was pairing food with wine for events sponsored by the wineries there. The then-president of the Chateau St. Jean winery, Allan Hemphill, who later became president of Gauer Estate Vineyards, came up with the concept of using a private railcar as a marketing tool. He proposed traveling the United States in the private wine cars *Sonoma Valley* and *Golden Mission,* and showcasing Chateau St. Jean wines and the cuisine of

Belle Vista *dining room. Rail Ventures, Inc.*

California's wine country along the way. To that end, fresh Sonoma produce, meats, and fish were flown in every day to meet the train in cities throughout the United States, thus bringing a "taste" of the California wine country to people all over the country. When the wine industry struggled in the mid-1990s, cutbacks in entertainment expenses persuaded Chef Matthew it was time to expand his catering operation to include providing professional services on other private rail cars.

Chef Matthew created the recipes here with elegance and ease of preparation in mind. They are extremely easy to prepare, and yet very impressive when presented at the dining table.

Sun-Dried Tomato and Basil Toasts

Before You Begin

You'll need: large baking sheet

Preheat oven to 350°F.

Prep: 15 minutes

Cook: 8 minutes

Yield: 24 toasts

1 thin baguette, cut into ⅛-inch slices
¼ cup olive oil
1 cup cured sun-dried tomatoes

salt to taste
4 oz. Muenster or Fontina cheese, cubed
12 fresh basil leaves, julienned

Brush both sides of the baguette slices with olive oil and bake at 350°F until golden brown and crisp, about 5 minutes. Drain tomatoes and blot excessive oil with paper towel. Finely mince tomatoes. Top each toast round with ½ teaspoon minced tomato, lightly season with salt, and add a cube of cheese. Return to the 350°F oven and bake until cheese is slightly melted, about 3 minutes. Remove from oven and top with fresh basil. Serve hot.

Roasted Butternut Squash Soup

1 large butternut squash
olive oil
1 cup minced onion
1 Tbsp. butter
6 cups chicken stock, divided
1 tsp. curry powder

⅛ tsp. nutmeg
1 cup heavy cream
salt and pepper to taste
6 tsp. sour cream (for garnish)
2 Tbsp. chopped chives (for garnish)

Slice squash lengthwise and remove seeds. Lightly brush cut side with olive oil and place on a cookie sheet cut side up. Bake at 425°F until golden brown and flesh is soft, about 45 minutes. Set aside to cool, then scoop flesh out with a spoon, taking care to avoid the skin. In a medium skillet over medium heat, melt butter and sauté onions until soft, about 3 minutes. In a food processor, add onions and squash, and puree with 1 cup chicken stock until smooth, adding more stock if needed. Transfer pureed squash to a 3-quart saucepan, add remaining chicken stock, curry powder, and nutmeg, and bring just to the boil. Reduce heat to low, add cream, and simmer until hot, being careful not to bring soup to a boil. Season with salt and pepper. To serve, top each portion with 1 teaspoon sour cream and sprinkle with chopped chives.

Autumn Pear Salad with Gorgonzola and Spiced Pecans

Dressing

½ cup balsamic vinegar
1 cup vegetable oil

2 Tbsp. maple syrup
pinch of salt and pepper

In a small mixing bowl, whisk all ingredients together well to infuse. Set aside.

Salad

1 cup pecan halves	salt
½ cup granulated sugar	6 servings mixed salad greens
½ tsp. nutmeg	1 pear, cored, sliced
½ tsp. cinnamon	½ cup crumbled Gorgonzola cheese

In a medium skillet over medium heat, lightly toast pecans, tossing occasionally and taking care not to let burn, about 5 minutes. Evenly spread sugar over pecans and continue to heat until sugar caramelizes, now constantly moving pecans so they do not burn. Evenly sprinkle nutmeg and cinnamon over caramelized pecans, remove from heat, and spread out on lightly greased cookie sheet. Lightly salt and set aside to cool. Then, in a large bowl, combine greens and pear. Drizzle dressing around the inside edge of bowl and toss greens until lightly coated. Top with spiced pecans and crumbled Gorgonzola.

Spiced Pork Medallions with Wild Mushroom Sauce

Before You Begin

You'll need: medium bowl, large skillet, aluminum foil, cookie sheet, meat thermometer, medium skillet

Preheat oven to 500°F.

Prep: 20 minutes (plus 1 hour to marinate tenderloins)

Cook: 35 minutes

Yield: 6 servings

1 Tbsp. fresh rosemary, minced	½ cup olive oil
4 cloves garlic, minced	2 pork tenderloins, sinew removed
2 Tbsp. fresh ginger, minced	1 tsp. seasoned salt
1 Tbsp. cumin powder	sprig of rosemary (for garnish)
1 tsp. cracked pepper	

In a medium bowl, combine well the rosemary, garlic, ginger, cumin, pepper, and olive oil. Toss pork tenderloins to coat, then set aside to marinate for 1 hour. Remove tenderloins from marinade, reserving the marinade, season with seasoned salt, and place in a large skillet over medium-high heat to lightly brown on all sides. Transfer to a foil-lined cookie sheet and place in hot oven. Immediately turn oven down to 350°F and cook until medium rare, reaching an internal temperature of 140°F, approximately 15 to 20 minutes. Remove and let stand for 5 minutes. To serve, slice tenderloin crosswise into medallions. Spoon Wild Mushroom Sauce onto plate and fan medallions over. Garnish with sprig of fresh rosemary.

Wild Mushroom Sauce

pork marinade
3 cups sliced wild mushrooms
    (substitute: domestic)
½ cup shallots, chopped

2 cups Madeira wine
½ cup orange juice
1 Tbsp. light or dark brown sugar
½ tsp. cumin powder

While pork tenderloin is cooking, in a medium skillet over medium heat, add reserved marinade, shallots, and mushrooms, and sauté until mushrooms are tender, about 3 to 5 minutes. Add Madeira wine and simmer to burn off alcohol, about 5 minutes. Stir in orange juice, brown sugar, and cumin, and simmer until reduced by ⅓. Adjust taste accordingly.

Garlic Mashed Potatoes

8 russet potatoes, peeled, halved
2 cups chicken stock
12 cloves garlic, peeled
2 cups milk (approximately, see
    instructions)

8 Tbsp. butter
salt and pepper

Before You Begin

You'll need: large pot, 2 small saucepans, colander, electric beater

Prep: 15 minutes

Cook: 30 minutes

Yield: 6 servings

In a large pot, add potatoes, cover with cold water, and place over high heat. Bring to a boil and cook until fork tender, about 20 minutes. Meanwhile, in a small saucepan over medium-high heat, add chicken stock and garlic, bring to a boil, then reduce heat and simmer until garlic cloves are very soft, about 15 minutes. In another small saucepan over low heat, heat milk until just before boil. Once potatoes are done, drain off water with colander. Return potatoes to the pot. Add garlic and stock and whip potatoes with an electric beater until smooth. Add butter and, depending on the size of the potatoes used, gradually whisk in milk until desired consistency is reached. Season to taste.

Autumn Apple and Black Currant Crowns

Before You Begin

You'll need: brush, large muffin tin, large skillet

Preheat oven to 375°F.

Prep: 15 minutes

Cook: 15 minutes

Yield: 6 servings

6 sheets phyllo

6 Tbsp. butter, melted

3 Tbsp. butter, unmelted

6 Granny Smith apples, peeled, cored, sliced

1 cup dried black currants

1 tsp. cinnamon

1 cup sugar

1 Tbsp. fresh orange zest

vanilla bean ice cream

fresh mint (for garnish)

Brush 1 phyllo sheet with 1 tablespoon of melted butter. Top and repeat with remainder of phyllo sheets and butter. Divide and cut into 6 squares, then trim each square to 5-inch diameter rounds. Using a large muffin tin, press one square of layered phyllo into each muffin cup. Place in a 375°F oven until golden brown, about 5 to 10 minutes. Meanwhile, in a large skillet over medium heat, melt 3 tablespoons of butter. Stir in apples, black currants, cinnamon, sugar, and orange zest, and sauté, stirring frequently, until soft, about 10 minutes. To serve, place a scoop of vanilla ice cream into each phyllo crown and top with warm apple mixture. Garnish with a sprig of fresh mint.

Caritas

www.highirontravel.com

The Pullman Company sleeping car *Pierre LaClede* was built in 1948 for the St. Louis–San Francisco Railroad, known as the "Frisco." The car served in a number of trains, including the St. Louis–Dallas–Fort worth–San Antonio–Houston *Texas Special,* operated jointly by the Frisco and the Missouri-Kansas-Texas, the "Katy." It was sold to the Canadian National Railroad in 1964, where it was renamed the *Churchill Falls*. In 1983 it was acquired by High Iron Travel Corporation and completely rebuilt to be the home-away-from-home that private cars are for their owners and passengers. Renamed *Caritas*, High Iron Travel describes it as a "cruise ship on wheels"

Caritas dining room. John H. Kuehl

that can sleep ten guests in four double bedrooms that maintain the original configuration and style.

The fully equipped galley, staffed by chef and attendant, caters to the tastes of the passengers. This dinner from one of those chefs, Clay Hollifield of Jacksonville, Florida, captures perfectly the simple elegance that can be achieved following the high-speed cuisine principles of high-quality and readily available ingredients, and just a few preparation steps.

Butter Bibb Lettuce with Strawberry Vinaigrette

½ cup raspberry vinegar
¼ cup frozen strawberries, thawed
   (substitute: raspberries)
1½ cups vegetable oil
salt and pepper to taste

2 to 3 heads Bibb lettuce
1 red onion, thinly sliced
4 fresh strawberries, sliced (substitute: raspberries)

Before You Begin

You'll need: small mixing bowl

Prep: 20 minutes

Yield: 4 servings

In a small mixing bowl, whisk together vigorously the raspberry vinegar and thawed frozen strawberries. Continue to whisk and slowly add vegetable oil until infused. Finish with salt and pepper to taste. Meanwhile, wash and dry Bibb lettuce, and arrange on four chilled plates. To serve, drizzle with strawberry vinaigrette, garnish with slices of red onion and sliced strawberries.

Broiled Salmon with Lobster Cream Sauce

2 Tbsp. cornstarch
½ cup cooking sherry, divided
1 pint heavy cream
2 Tbsp. lobster base (substitute: chicken base)

white pepper to taste
2 lbs. salmon fillet, boneless, skinless
2 Tbsp. butter
1 cup white wine, or as needed

Before You Begin

You'll need: small bowl, 1-quart saucepan, whisk, baking pan with ½-inch sides

Preheat oven to Broil.

Prep: 15 minutes

Cook: 30 minutes

Yield: 8 servings

In a small bowl, dissolve cornstarch in ¼ cup cooking sherry and set aside. For lobster cream sauce (or velouté if chicken base is used), in a 1-quart saucepan, bring ¼ cup cooking sherry to a boil. Slowly stir in heavy cream and reduce heat to simmer. Whisk in lobster base. Bring sauce to a boil, stir in cornstarch mixture, and continue stirring until sauce reaches sufficient thickness to coat the back of a spoon, 10 to 20 seconds. Add white pepper to taste, and set aside. Spray the baking pan with cooking spray. Place salmon in pan and dot with butter. Pour in white wine to ¼-inch depth and place 5 inches under the broiler and watch carefully until salmon flakes easily with a fork, about 10 to 12 minutes. To serve, on 8 individual plates, place pool of lobster cream sauce, set portion of salmon over, and drizzle remaining cream sauce on top. Accompany with asparagus spears (see page 240) and Rice Pilaf.

Rice Pilaf

Before You Begin

You'll need: small saucepan, heavy 1-quart saucepan, 9" × 9" baking pan, aluminum foil

Preheat oven to 350°F.

Prep: 10 minutes

Cook: 30 minutes

Yield: 8 servings

2 cups chicken stock or broth

1 small white onion, peeled and diced

2 Tbsp. clarified butter

1 cup long-grain white rice

1 bay leaf

In a small saucepan over medium-high heat, bring chicken stock to a boil. Meanwhile, in a heavy 1-quart saucepan over medium heat, sauté onion in clarified butter until translucent, about 3 minutes. Stir in rice until well coated. Stir in chicken stock. Add bay leaf. Pour mixture into a 9" × 9" baking pan, cover with aluminum foil, and bake at 350°F until moisture is absorbed, about 25 to 30 minutes.

Apple Brown Betty

Before You Begin

You'll need: 2-quart casserole or 9" × 13" pan, mixing bowl

Preheat oven to 425°F.

Prep: 20 minutes

Cook: 55–65 minutes

Yield: 8 servings

1 cup flour

²/₃ cup granulated sugar

1 cup brown sugar

1 to 2 Tbsp. cinnamon

½ cup butter

6 to 8 apples, peeled, cored, and sliced

Grease a 2-quart casserole or 9" × 13" pan with butter and set aside. In a mixing bowl, mix together flour, sugar and brown sugar. Add cinnamon and cut in butter until crumbs form. Layer apples in casserole or pan until ½ full. Sprinkle on ½ of crumb mixture. Repeat. Bake at 425°F for 15 minutes and then reduce heat to 350°F for an additional 40–50 minutes, or until apples are tender when pierced with a fork. Serve warm with ice cream or whipped cream.

NOTES: (1) You may also add a layer of pecan halves between the apples and the crumbs. (2) 3 or 4 cans of sliced, unsweetened apples may be substituted for fresh apples.

CHEF'S TIP: Reduce the flour slightly and add some quick-cooking oats for variety in the crumb texture. This recipe can handle a lot of variation, and it has over the years.

Chapel Hill

www.chapelhillrail.com

The business car *Chapel Hill* was built in 1922 by American Car & Foundry to be the private car *Hussar* for the personal use of investment banker and businessman E. F. Hutton and his wife Marjorie Merriweather Post. It is what is known as a heavy-weight passenger car, built before smooth- or silver-sided streamlined equipment was introduced in the 1930s. Acquired by the Chesapeake & Ohio Railroad in 1937 for use as an office car, it was bought in 1971 by present owner DeWitt Chapple, Jr.

After its most recent remodeling into what the owner describes as "the atmosphere of a private club on rails," one enters the *Chapel Hill* to find a mahogany-paneled observation lounge from which to "look out and absorb the breathtaking beauty of America." A similar experience can be had from the open platform off the rear of the car, once the very symbol of gracious travel. At meals there is seating for eight in a formal dining room. At night, retire to either a master bedroom, one of two double bedrooms, or a single room, and let the train's motion, and the soothing sound of steel wheels on steel rail, induce restful sleep.

Robert ("Robbie") Williams is the master of the tiny kitchen found forward on the *Chapel Hill*. A veteran of the New York Central System, and before that of the Erie Railroad, Chef Williams can spin any number of recipes off the top of his head

Chapel Hill
dining room.
John H. Kuehl

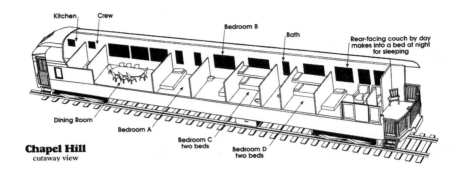

A cutaway view of the Chapel Hill *shows the typical private car floor plan, with a seating area at the rear or observation end of the car, followed by a series of private bedrooms, a dining room, and the kitchen and crew's quarters forward.*
John H. Kuehl and DeWitt Chapple

Kitchen | Crew | Bedroom B | Bath | Rear-facing couch by day makes into a bed at night for sleeping

Dining Room

Bedroom A

Chapel Hill
cutaway view

Bedroom C
two beds

Bedroom D
two beds

without consulting a single note. One suspects that, as with all railroad chefs of note, he can comfortably adjust ingredients on the spot to satisfy a passenger's special request, or to meet the demands of the "what do I have on board" manner of planning. Following a "traditional approach" at mealtime, dinner begins with a cocktail hour, featuring drinks and hors d'oeuvres.

Brie with Chutney and Bacon

Before You Begin

You'll need: large skillet, ovenproof serving plate

Preheat oven to 250°F.

Prep: 15 minutes

Cook: 5 minutes

Yield: 8 servings

3 strips bacon

1 lb. disk of Brie cheese

¼ cup mango chutney

loaf Italian bread, sliced thin

In a large skillet over medium heat, cook bacon crisp, drain, and crumble. Cut Brie in half horizontally, spread bottom half with chutney and top with crumbled bacon. Close Brie and place on an ovenproof serving plate. Place in 250°F oven to just warm and soften, watching carefully, about 5 minutes. Serve with thin sliced bread.

Waldorf Salad

Before You Begin

You'll need: medium bowl

Prep: 10 minutes (plus time to chill)

Yield: 6 servings

1 cup diced celery

1 cup diced red apple, skin on

½ cup chopped walnuts

½ cup mayonnaise

2 cups lettuce, broken

1 Tbsp. fresh chopped parsley

In a bowl, mix first four ingredients and refrigerate to chill. To serve, arrange a bed of lettuce or romaine on individual plates, mound salad mixture on lettuce, and sprinkle with chopped parsley.

Roast Leg of Lamb with Gravy

1 tsp. paprika

1 tsp. salt

½ tsp. pepper

4-lb. leg of lamb, bone removed

4 springs rosemary

4 cloves garlic, slivered

1 cup flour to coat, divided

1 medium onion, diced fine

1 large carrot, diced fine

2 stalks celery, diced fine

¾ cup water

Before You Begin

You'll need: small bowl, string, roasting pan, whisk, meat thermometer, sieve or strainer

Preheat oven to 350°F.

Prep: 20 minutes

Cook: 1 hour to 1 hour 15 minutes

Yield: 8 servings

In a small bowl, combine paprika, salt, and pepper, and set aside. In the cavity left from removing the bone from the lamb, spread rosemary and garlic evenly, then roll and tie for roasting. Rub lamb roast all over with seasoning and coat generously with flour. Place onion, carrot, and celery in the roasting pan, sift ½ cup flour over, and stir to coat. Add water and mix until smooth. Place lamb on rack and in roasting pan over vegetables. Roast in 350°F oven to desired degree of doneness. (**NOTE:** An internal temperature of 140°F for rare, 160°F for medium, about 1 hour to 1 hour 15 minutes.) Stir vegetables occasionally to blend with lamb juices, adding water as need to keep well moistened. Remove lamb and allow to rest 10 minutes before serving. Meanwhile, whisk vegetable mixture and press through a sieve to make gravy.

Pan-Fried Potatoes

4 russet potatoes, peeled, ¼-inch slice

½ cup cooking oil, divided

salt and pepper to taste

Before You Begin

You'll need: medium bowl, large skillet, paper towels

Prep: 20 minutes

Cook: 15 minutes

Yield: 8 servings

Peel and slice potatoes, then immerse in a bowl filled with ice water to chill. In a large skillet over medium-high heat, warm ¼ cup oil to hot. Meanwhile, drain sliced potatoes, pat them dry, and carefully place into hot oil. Toss to coat with oil, then stir occasionally to cook until tender, about 10 minutes. (**NOTE:** Do not overcook potatoes until soft.) Remove potatoes and set aside to drain on paper towels. About 10 minutes before serving, again in the large skillet over medium-high heat, bring ¼ cup oil to hot. Carefully place partially cooked potatoes into skillet, toss to coat, and continue to cook, tossing frequently, until well browned and crispy. Season to taste and serve hot.

✳ ✳ ✳

Buttered Green Beans

Before You Begin

You'll need: baking sheet, large saucepan, colander, large bowl, large skillet

Preheat oven to 400°F.

Prep: 10 minutes

Cook: 5 minutes

Yield: 8 servings

½ cup slivered almonds, toasted

2 lbs. fresh green beans, tips removed

1 tsp. salt

1 tsp. baking soda

4 Tbsp. butter

Spread slivered almonds on a baking sheet and place in a 400°F oven until lightly browned, about 5 minutes. Set aside. In a large saucepan over high heat, bring lightly salted water sufficient to cover beans to a boil. Meanwhile, fill a large bowl with enough ice and water to cover beans, and stir in baking soda to dissolve. (**NOTE:** This will enrich the green color of the cooked beans.) Plunge beans into boiling water. Allow water to return to boil, then remove beans immediately, drain, and plunge into ice water to cool for 5 minutes. Drain and dry beans and set aside. Meanwhile, in a large skillet over medium heat, melt butter. Add blanched beans and stir constantly until heated through, about 5 minutes. Stir in slivered almonds and serve hot.

✳ ✳ ✳

Buttermilk Coconut Pie

Before You Begin

You'll need: electric mixer, mixing bowl 9-inch pie pan

Preheat oven to 350°F.

Prep: 20 minutes

Cook: 40 minutes

Yield: 1 pie

½ cup butter, room temperature

2 cups sugar

5 eggs

¾ cup buttermilk

1½ cups shredded coconut

1 9-inch pie crust shell (see page 82)

Using an electric mixer at a low speed, cream butter and sugar until smooth. Continue beating and add eggs one at a time, making sure each egg is well blended into the mixture before adding another. Continue beating and add buttermilk, then coconut. When mixture is beaten fine, pour into pie crust shell and place in a 350°F oven to cook until set and a knife inserted in the center comes out clean, about 40 minutes.

Rufus Estes entered dining car service when he was twenty-six years old. Born a slave in Tennessee, he worked in a restaurant in Nashville, between 1873 and 1878. In 1883, he, like hundreds of other African-American men, hired on with The Pullman Company in Chicago, a leading manufacturer of railroad passenger cars in the United States. Assigned to private car service, he writes of his experience: "I was selected to handle all special parties. Among the distinguished people who traveled in my car were . . . President Cleveland, President Harrison (and) Princess Eulalie of Spain." In 1897, Arthur Stillwell, president of the Kansas City, Pittsburg & Gould Railroad, hired him away from Pullman for work in his private car. When that railroad went into receivership seventeen months later, the car was bought by John W. "Bet-A-Million" Gates. Rufus Estes worked for Gates until 1907. He finished out his career as a chef with United States Steel in Chicago.

All of this is known because Rufus Estes wrote a cookbook, *Good Things to Eat as Suggested by Rufus,* published in 1911. When it was reprinted in 1999 by Howling at the Moon Press, the publisher, Dianna Seay, did research that suggested it was the first published cookbook to have been written by an African-American chef. The 591 recipes Chef Rufus shares offer insights into the techniques employed by early dining car chefs, working as he did in a small moving kitchen (in his case, sans air conditioning), using wood and coal for heat and ice for refrigeration. Despite these challenging conditions, Chef Rufus turned out dishes and service suitable for the

LEFT: *Rufus Estes. Howling at the Moon Press* RIGHT: *In a setting recreated by the illustrator Steve Quinn, Rufus Estes is seen with guests traveling on board a private car owned by the celebrity pianist Ignace Ian Paderewski, who often employed Estes when the car was out on the line. Steve Quinn*

celebrities who found themselves on his cars. Join him this evening, perhaps en route to the World's Columbian Exposition in Chicago in 1893, to enjoy the timeless quality of his dishes as described in his own words.

Bird's Nest Salad

Have ready as many crisp leaves of lettuce as may be required to make a dainty little nest for each person. Curl them into shape and in each one place tiny speckled eggs made by rolling cream cheese into shape, then sprinkle with fine chopped parsley. Serve with French dressing hidden under the leaves of the nest.

Salmon Soup

Take the skin and bones from canned salmon and drain off the oil. Chop fine enough of the fish to measure two-thirds of a cup. Cook a thick slice of onion in a quart of milk 20 minutes in a double-boiler. Thicken with one-quarter cup of flour rubbed smooth with one rounding tablespoonful of butter. Cook ten minutes, take out the onion, add a saltspoon of pepper, one level teaspoon of salt, and the salmon. Rub all through a fine strainer, and serve hot. The amount of salmon may be varied according to taste.

Browned Beef Hash Cakes on Buttered Toast Points

Chop cold corned beef fine and add a little more than the same measure of cold boiled potatoes, chopped less fine than the beef. Season with onion juice, make into small cakes, and brown in butter or beef drippings; serve each cake on a slice of buttered toast moistened slightly.

Broiled Mackerel with Black Butter

Take some mackerel, open and remove bones. Season with butter, pepper, and salt. Place the fish on a gridiron and broil over a clear fire. Put a part of the butter in a saucepan and stir it over the fire until it is richly browned, squeezing into it a little lemon juice. Place the fish on a hot dish, arrange some sprigs of parsley around it, and pour over it the butter sauce, and serve hot.

Deviled Chicken with Mustard Sauce

Split the chickens down the back and broil until done, lay on a hot dripping pan and spread on a sauce, scatter fine crumbs over and set in a quick oven to brown. For the sauce heat a rounding tablespoon of butter light with one-half teaspoon of mixed mustard, one teaspoon of vinegar and a pinch of cayenne.

Potato Croquettes

Take four boiled potatoes and add to them half their weight in butter, the same quantity of powdered sugar, salt, grated peel of half a lemon and two well beaten eggs. Mix thoroughly and roll into cork-shaped pieces and dip into the beaten yolks of eggs, rolling in sifted breadcrumbs. Let stand one hour and again dip in egg and roll in crumbs. Fry in boiling lard or butter. Serve with a garnish of parsley.

Cauliflower Cone in Mayonnaise

Select some large, cold boiled cauliflowers and break into small branches, adding a little salt, pepper and vinegar to properly season. Heap them on a dish to form a point. Surround with a garnish of cooked carrots, turnips and green vegetables, pour some white mayonnaise sauce over all, and serve.

Add for dessert, a delicacy of the day: Fresh Vanilla Ice Cream with Raspberry Sauce.

Vanilla Ice Cream

Put two cups of milk in a double boiler, add a pinch of soda and scald, beat four eggs light with two cups of sugar, pour the hot milk on slowly, stirring all the time; turn back into double boiler and cook until a smooth custard is formed. Cool and flavor strongly with vanilla because freezing destroys some of the strength of flavoring. Stir in a pint of sweet cream and freeze.

Raspberry Sauce

"If you think that a good ice cream is yet not quite fine enough," Chef Rufus suggested, "pour a raspberry sauce over each portion as served." Here adapted from his two recipes, are instructions for making same:

1 pint fresh raspberries	1 Tbsp. water
¼ cup granulated sugar	1 Tbsp. fresh lemon juice,
1 heaping tsp. arrowroot	strained

Put raspberries in a preserving kettle with water to cover. When boiled soft, strain through a flannel bag to acquire juice. In a small saucepan, combine sugar with 1 cup of raspberry juice, bring to a boil, and simmer 5 minutes. Meanwhile, in a small bowl, combine arrowroot and water to make a paste. Add to simmering raspberry sauce and cook 5 minutes more. Add lemon juice and let boil up once. Cool and serve.

J. Pinckney Henderson

www.jphenderson.com

The distinctions of the *J. Pinckney Henderson* began with its construction. It was the first all-stainless-steel car built by the Pullman-Standard Car Manufacturing Company. A 72-seat coach named after the first governor of the American state of Texas, it was delivered to the Missouri-Kansas-Texas Railroad in 1954 for service on the MKT's "Texas Special." Acquired by Amtrak, it continued in service as a coach on long-distance trains in the west through the 1970s until placed in storage in the Amtrak yard at Sunnyside, New York. Stripped and heavily vandalized, the car was acquired a private owner in 1983, moved to Hartsville, South Carolina, and completely rebuilt into its current configuration as a Lounge-Dining Car-Sleeper.

The reconfigured *J. Pinckney Henderson* returned to mainline service as a private car for charter in 1989, and in 1991 was chosen by Amtrak for an experimental high-end service to run between New York and Pittsburgh, Pennsylvania. Named "Keystone Classic Club," as many as ten passengers could enjoy privacy, specially prepared meals, and the attentive service of a chef and steward, all while enjoying a run across New Jersey to Philadelphia, then through Amish country and over the Allegheny mountains by way of historic Horseshoe Curve just west of Altoona. That service ended in 1993. The *J. Pinckney Henderson* was acquired by its current owner, the Lancaster & Chester Railway Company, in 1997.

J. Pinckney Henderson's executive chef, John Mickey, has, since 1975, earned his stripes in the kitchen. Along the way he has won a number of honors, including being a three-time winner of the Chef of the Year award granted by the American Culinary Federation chapter in Charlotte. Of his work on the car, Chef John says, "I prefer to offer our guests an array of regional cuisine to enhance their rail journey. These are some of my favorite recipes."

J. Pinckney
Henderson *dining
room.* Pressly Hall

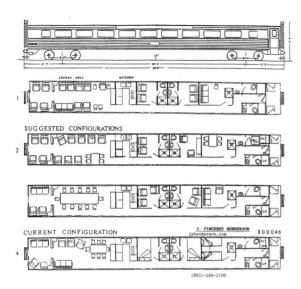

This J. Pinckney Henderson *floor plan is representative of what one might find in a private rail car. However, part of the charm of this means of transportation is to be found in the wide variety of cozy alternatives. The Lancaster & Chester Railway Company*

Crab Cakes Henderson

1 lb. jumbo lump crab meat
1 egg, slightly beaten
juice of 1 lemon
1 tsp. horseradish
1 Tbsp. mayonnaise
½ cup bread crumbs
dash Worcestershire sauce

dash hot sauce
½ tsp. kosher salt
½ tsp. restaurant-grind black pepper
2 Tbsp. olive oil
2 Tbsp. butter
Our Own Remoulade Sauce

Before You Begin

You'll need: large bowl, large skillet, small mixing bowl

Preheat oven to 350°F.

Prep: 10 minutes (plus 1 hour to chill Remoulade sauce)

Cook: 15 minutes

Yield: 16–20 mini-cakes (see NOTE)

Combine first ten ingredients in a large bowl and toss carefully so as not to break up crab lumps too much. Shape mixture into the desired number of patties and set aside. In a large skillet over medium-high heat, blend and warm olive oil and butter until of a light brown color, about 2 minutes. Cook patties until browned on both sides, about 2 minutes per side. (**NOTE:** Cakes can be removed and chilled at this point to finish later, or finished now). To finish, place cakes in a 350°F oven for about 7 to 10 minutes. Serve accompanied by Our Own Remoulade Sauce on the side.) **NOTES:** (1) Recipe can also make six 3-ounce cakes for dinner portions. (2) "I prefer to finish off the cakes in the oven because I may need to make burner space available to prepare other items."

Our Own Remoulade Sauce

1 cup mayonnaise
¼ cup horseradish, drained
juice of 1 lemon
few dashes Worcestershire sauce
few dashes hot sauce

1 Tbsp. Creole mustard
2 Tbsp. finely chopped green onion
3 Tbsp. capers, drained
½ tsp. kosher salt
½ tsp. restaurant-grind black pepper

In a small bowl, combine all ingredients, stir well, and refrigerate for 1 hour to chill and allow flavors to blend.

Mixed Greens Salad with House Vinaigrette

Before You Begin

You'll need:
medium mixing bowl, large bowl

Prep: 20 minutes

Yield: 4 cups

1 bag spring or mesclun mix of baby greens
1 cup balsamic vinegar (substitute: white balsamic vinegar)
1 tsp. Dijon mustard
1 shallot, finely chopped
2 cloves garlic, finely chopped

few sprigs fresh parsley, stems removed, finely chopped
juice of 1 lemon
1 tsp. kosher salt
1 tsp. restaurant-grind black pepper
3 cups extra virgin olive oil

In a large medium mixing bowl, combine vinegar, mustard, shallot, garlic, parsley, lemon juice, salt and pepper. Slowly whisk in the olive oil until infused. Toss greens in ⅓ cup of dressing.

CHEF'S TIPS: (1) I like to supplement this blend of greens with chopped hearts of romaine. (2) Because this mix of greens is already rather colorful, I suggest using golden teardrop tomatoes and julienne of jicama to garnish.

Beartooth Bison

Before You Begin

You'll need: 1-gallon freezer bag, large skillet, meat thermometer

Prep: 10 minutes (plus 1–2 hours to marinate fillets)

Cook: 15 minutes

Yield: 6 servings

1 cup olive oil
1 cup red wine
6 bay leaves
½ cup onion, diced

3 cloves garlic, diced
2 Tbsp. black peppercorns
6 8-oz. bison fillets

In a 1-gallon freezer bag, mix olive oil, wine, bay leaves, onion, garlic, and peppercorns well, and add bison fillets. Seal and toss to coat fillets well with marinade. Place in refrigerator for 1 to 2 hours to marinate. Then, in a large skillet over medium-high heat, sear fillets, turning once, until they are no more than medium rare, or an internal temperature of 145°F, about 6 minutes per side. (**NOTE:** Can be cooked in a similar fashion on a grill.) Serve with Roasted Tomato and Pepper Medley Chipotle Salsa, accompanied by Roasted Garlic Asiago Mashed Potatoes and Grilled Vegetables.

Roasted Tomato and Pepper Medley Chipotle Salsa

1 small can chipotle peppers
2 large tomatoes, halved
1 yellow bell pepper, halved, seeded
1 red bell pepper, halved, seeded
1 green bell pepper, halved, seeded
olive oil

salt and pepper
1 small purple onion, diced
juice of 2 limes
1 chipotle pepper, seeded, diced (NOTE: Add extra peppers for extra heat.)
1 tsp. cumin

Before You Begin

You'll need: strainer, roasting pan

Preheat oven to 400°F.

Prep: 20 minutes (includes roasting tomatoes and peppers) (plus 1 hour to chill)

Yield: 6 cups

Drain and reserve broth from can of chipotle peppers. Toss tomato and pepper pieces with oil to coat, sprinkle lightly with salt and pepper, place in a roasting pan, and roast at 400°F for 10 to 15 minutes. Cool, then peel skin from pieces and dice small. In a bowl, combine tomatoes, peppers, onion, lime juice, chipotle broth, chipotle pepper, cumin and salt and pepper to taste, and refrigerate for 1 hour to chill and allow flavors to blend.

Roasted Garlic Asiago Mashed Potatoes

4 lbs. russet potatoes, peeled and quartered
1 bulb garlic
1 Tbsp. extra-virgin olive oil
¼ cup butter

¼ cup sour cream
1 cup Asiago cheese, grated
salt and fresh cracked black pepper to taste

Before You Begin

You'll need: large pot, roasting pan, small bowl

Preheat oven to 300°F.

Prep: 15 minutes

Cook: 20 minutes

Yield: 8 servings

In a large pot over high heat, bring potatoes in water to cover to a boil and cook until tender, 15 to 20 minutes, then drain and return to pot. Meanwhile, separate and peel garlic cloves, toss with olive oil to coat, and place in a roasting pan. Place garlic in a 300°F oven to roast until tender, about 10 minutes. Remove garlic from oven, chop fine, then toss with a dash of the olive oil in which the cloves roasted. In the pot, combine cooked potatoes, garlic, butter, sour cream, Asiago cheese, salt and pepper, and mash well.

Grilled Vegetables

Before You Begin

You'll need: 1-gallon freezer bag, grill or large skillet

Preheat grill to hot.

Prep: 5 minutes

Cook: 5 minutes

Yield: 8 servings

2 lbs. zucchini, yellow squash, or asparagus (or some of each)

¼ cup olive oil

2 Tbsp. chopped fresh parsley

pinch dried thyme

salt and fresh cracked black pepper to taste

Trim and quarter the zucchini and/or squash if using. In a 1-gallon freezer bag, combine olive oil and seasonings. Add vegetables lightly toss to coat.

Place vegetables on a hot grill and turn to mark, or sear in a large skillet, about 1 minute per side.

Chocolate Pecan Tart

Before You Begin

You'll need: tart pan, large mixing bowl, medium mixing bowl, pastry blender, rolling pin

Preheat oven to 350°F.

Prep: 20 minutes

Cook: 45 minutes

Yield: 8 servings

Pastry Crust

3 eggs lightly beaten

1 cup dark Karo syrup

½ cup light brown sugar

3 tbs. butter, melted

1 tsp. pure vanilla extract

dash salt

¼ cup Kentucky bourbon

1 cup semisweet chocolate chips

1½ cups pecan halves

whipped cream (for garnish)

fresh berries (for garnish)

Prepare one Pastry Crust recipe, place dough in tart pan, and gently press to a snug fit. Weight pie shell with rice to keep crown from forming, and blanch by placing it in a 350°F oven for 5 minutes. Discard rice. Meanwhile, in a large bowl, combine all filling ingredients in order listed. Pour mixture into tart pan and place in a 350°F oven to bake until firm (toothpick inserted will come out clean), about 35 to 45 minutes. Let stand 2 hours or refrigerate 1 hour before serving. Serve with whipped cream and garnish with fresh berries.

Pastry Crust

1½ cups all-purpose flour

½ tsp. salt

½+ cup butter, room temperature

4+ Tbsp. ice cold water

In a medium mixing bowl, combine flour and salt. Cut butter into flour with pastry blender or beater attachment of KitchenAid or similar mixer. Slowly add water until moistened enough for dough to form into a ball. Let dough sit for 10 minutes, then use a rolling pin to roll it out to desired diameter.

NOTES: (1) This recipe can be doubled to make sufficient dough for pie recipes elsewhere here that call for a top crust. (2) For a sweet crust, add 1 tablespoon of confectioners' sugar to dry ingredients.

Northern Sky

www.northernsky.com

The dome car *Northern Sky* came into existence in 1955 at the American Car & Foundry Company's plant in St. Charles, Missouri, near St. Louis. It was purchased by the Union Pacific Railroad for use in the Los Angeles–Chicago *City of Los Angeles,* a train it operated in cooperation with the Milwaukee Road. Built as a blunt-end observation-dome-lounge car, it was one of the comparatively few cars built specifically for this train. As one of the last dome cars built for revenue service by a Class I railroad, Number 9003, as it was shown on the Union Pacific's roster, was also the highest expression of this post–World War II innovation in rail travel. In the dome, twenty-four low-backed divans were offset at a 10-degree angle to the outside to improve on the already sweeping view a dome provided. On the main level there was a card room at the head end (front) of the car that seated five, a cocktail lounge with bar and room for nine revelers beneath the dome, and seating for nineteen in the observation lounge at the end that carried the markers and drumhead bearing the train's name.

Current *Northern Sky* owner David Hoffman, a successful Wisconsin highway contractor, acquired the car in 1992 and had it rebuilt in its current configuration by Northern Rail Car Cooperation, a Wisconsin company with extensive experience at restoring and rebuilding domed passenger cars. Today it is a completely

Northern Sky
dining room.
John H. Kuehl

self-contained luxury moving hotel that sleeps eight in four double bedrooms, accommodates fourteen for meals or seats twenty for sightseeing in the dome, and typically houses a crew of two. The owner's experience suggests the ideal way to travel on board: "Sleep downstairs, use the lounge with its entertainment center primarily as a movie theater, and dine, converse, and take in the view in the dome."

The dining experience is the domain of Chef David Kugler. Educated in the "school of hard knocks," Chef David's first rail-dining experience was his role in the start-up of Quad/Cuisine in 1986 (see pages 254–255). In 1989 he started his own firm, Gold Award Foods, to make and market specialty sauces for the trade. In 1992, Delta Publishing, a publisher of magazines for the culinary professional, named his Mushroom Sauce "Best in Nation—New Condiment." He joined *Northern Sky* in 1994 at the request of a friend from his days at Quad/Cuisine who then managed the car. Meanwhile, he became an American Culinary Federation–Certified Executive Chef in 1996, and today, when he's not on the rails, he creates and markets two specialty desserts for restaurants.

Mandarin Orange Salad

Dressing

Before You Begin

You'll need: small saucepan, whisk, baking sheet, large skillet, large bowl

Preheat oven to 350°F.

Prep: 20 minutes

Cook: 5 minutes

Yield: 8 servings

1 cup sugar

1 Tbsp. fresh lemon juice

1 tsp. grated red onion

1 tsp. paprika

5 Tbsp. red wine vinegar

5 Tbsp. honey

1 tsp. dry mustard

1 tsp. celery salt

2 11-oz. cans Mandarin oranges, drained, divided (reserve liquid for future products)

Place first eight ingredients in a saucepan and stir to mix. Add ⅓ of the drained oranges to the sauce. Over medium-high heat, bring to a boil and remove from heat. Whisk to break up the oranges in the dressing. Keep warm, but not hot.

Salad

⅓ cup slivered almonds, toasted

¼ lb. double hickory-smoked bacon, sliced thin

2 to 3 heads red-leaf lettuce

remaining oranges (see above)

½ cup julienned red onion

On a baking sheet, scatter slivered almonds and place in a 350°F oven to toast until golden, about 8 minutes, then set aside to cool. In a large skillet over medium heat, sauté bacon slices until crisp, drain, crumble, and set aside. Wash and tear lettuce, then dry with paper towels. Place lettuce in a large bowl, add ⅔ of the warm dressing, and toss. Salad will be slightly wilted. (**NOTE**: Dressing should not be too hot or the salad will become over wilted.) Add more dressing as needed. Place on 8 salad plates. Top with remaining oranges, crumbled bacon, toasted almonds, and red onions.

CHEF'S TIP: All parts of this salad can be prepared ahead of time. Store lettuce in a plastic bag in the refrigerator. Reheat, but do not boil, the dressing. Finish at the last possible moment and serve immediately. For a lunch, this makes a terrific entrée served with something like Cajun grilled shrimp.

Cream of Asparagus Soup with Shrimp Quenelles

Shrimp Quenelles

⅓ cup coarse-chopped carrot
⅓ cup coarse-chopped celery
⅓ cup coarse-chopped onion
3½ tsp. kosher salt, divided
½ Tbsp. black peppercorns

8 oz. raw shrimp, shelled, deveined
⅛ tsp. white pepper
1 Tbsp. chopped fresh dill
½ cup whipping cream

Before You Begin
You'll need:
3-quart saucepan (used twice), fine-mesh strainer, blender or food processor, bowl, vegetable steamer, small skillet, whisk

Prep: 1 hour (plus 3 hours for mousse to chill)

Cook: 30 minutes

Yield: 12 serving

In a 3-quart saucepan, place carrots, celery, onion, 1 tablespoon kosher salt, and black peppercorns in 6 cups of cold water, bring to a boil, reduce heat and simmer 50 minutes to make a court bouillon. Strain cooked vegetables from broth and set broth aside. Meanwhile, place shrimp, ½ teaspoon kosher salt, and white pepper in a food processor and work until smooth, about 1 minute, stirring once or twice to ensure all pieces are incorporated. Add dill and pulse to blend. Add cream and blend just until it is well blended, about 30 seconds. (**NOTE**: Do not overblend or this mixture will break up during poaching.) Place mixture in refrigerator to chill until firm, about 3 hours. To finish, heat court bouillon to just barely simmering. (**NOTE**: For proper poaching, liquid is to be just moving in the kettle.) Scoop mousse mixture with a teaspoon to form an egg shape. Drop into court bouillon and continue until ⅓ of the mousse is used. Poach about 7 to 8 minutes, stirring gently two or three times to ensure even cooking. Scoop out, place into a bowl filled with ice water to stop cooking, and drain. Continue until all mousse is prepared.

CHEF'S TIP: Quenelles can be made up to two days in advance and refrigerated until ready to use.

Soup

1 lb. asparagus	⅓ cup flour
8 cups chicken stock, cold	2 cups whipping cream
¼ lb. butter, clarified	salt and pepper to taste

Cut tips from asparagus spears just large enough to fit on soup spoon, about 1½ inches long. (NOTE: If the spears are fat, split tips lengthwise.) In a vegetable steamer, bring water to a boil and steam tips until tender, about 3 minutes. Refrigerate to chill, about 1 hour. Chop remainder of asparagus. Place cold chicken stock in a 3-quart saucepan and add asparagus pieces. Over high heat, bring stock to a boil, reduce heat to simmer, and cook until stock is reduced to 6 cups, about 20 minutes. Meanwhile, in a small skillet, warm clarified butter and whisk in flour, stirring constantly, until of a pourable consistency, about 3 minutes. Stirring constantly, slowly add butter/flour mixture to broth, making sure broth remains boiling at all times. After incorporating, reduce to a simmer and stir in cream a little at a time. Cook for 5 to 10 minutes to thicken, skimming the surface of any residue that rises to the top. Strain, using your finest mesh strainer, into another kettle, and, over low heat, keep warm. Meanwhile, heat quenelles and asparagus tips in a microwave set on Low for 1 minute, or simply toss in the soup to heat through. Arrange quenelles and asparagus tips into warmed soup bowls and add boiling soup. Serve immediately.

Beef Tenderloin Fillet on Wild Mushroom Ragout with Demi-Glace

Before You Begin

You'll need:
1-gallon freezer bag, large skillet or electric griddle

Preheat griddle to 400°F if using.

Prep: 15 minutes (plus 3 to 4 hours to marinate)

Cook: 15 minutes

Yield: 8 servings

8 5 to 6 oz. beef tenderloins, preferably certified Angus	2 Tbsp. coarse cracked black pepper
¼ cup chopped fresh garlic	⅓ cup canola oil
	1 cup demi-glace

Rub steaks with garlic and pepper, then with oil, then place in 1-gallon freezer bag and refrigerate 3 to 4 hours ahead. Preheat a large skillet over medium-high heat, or a griddle to 400°F, then pan-fry tenderloins until of desired temperature, approximately 7 to 8 minutes per side.

Wild Mushroom Ragout

2 Tbsp. olive oil

1 cup shallots, fine diced

½ tsp fresh thyme, chopped fine

2 lbs. portobello mushrooms, diced

1 lb. shitake mushroom caps, diced

1 lb. white mushrooms, diced

¼ cup demi-glace or heavy cream

salt and pepper to taste

Before You Begin

You'll need:large skillet

Prep: 30 minutes

Cook: 10 minutes

Yield: 8 servings

In a large skillet over medium heat, warm olive oil and sauté shallots and thyme until clear, about 3 minutes. Add mushrooms, stir to mix, and cook until moisture gone, about 5 more minutes. Stir in sufficient demi-glace or cream to moisten and bind. Season with salt and pepper to taste, and set aside.

CHEF'S TIPS: (1) Mushroom Ragout can be made 1 or 2 days ahead and held in refrigerator. (2) Use any excess as a "planned-over" in omelets.

Dauphenoise Potatoes

granular garlic to taste (substitute: garlic powder, but use less)

2½ lbs. russet potatoes, peeled, thinly sliced

1 lb. Vidalia onions, peeled, thinly sliced (see CHEF'S TIPS)

butter, room temperature

kosher salt and pepper to taste

nutmeg

1 cup whipping cream

Before You Begin

You'll need: 9" × 5" bread loaf pan, aluminum foil

Preheat oven to 350°F.

Prep: 15 minutes

Cook: 1 hour

Yield: 8 servings

Butter a 9" × 5" loaf pan, then sprinkle lightly with granular garlic. Place a layer of potatoes in the bottom of the loaf pan, followed by a layer of onions. Sprinkle lightly with kosher salt and pepper. Repeat until all potatoes and onions are in place. Top with a light sprinkle of nutmeg. Pour cream over potatoes, cover with foil, and cuts slits in foil. Bake in a 350°F oven until tender, about 1 hour. Let stand 5 minutes before slicing or spooning onto plate to serve.

CHEF'S TIPS: (1) This recipe can be prepared 1 or 2 days ahead and then refrigerated. To reheat at service time, chilled potatoes can be cut into slices and placed in a 375°F oven for 10 minutes. (2) If Vidalia onions are not available, blanch cooking onions in boiling salted and sugared water 20 seconds, then plunge in ice water. This will not only sweeten the onions but will reduce their overpowering flavor.

Steamed Zucchini and Yellow Squash

Before You Begin

You'll need: large covered frying pan

Prep: 10 minutes

Cook: 5 minutes

Yield: 8 servings

1 lb. zucchini

1 lb. yellow squash

juice of two lemons

salt and pepper to taste

Cut vegetables into petal shapes (3 to 5 per plate) and place in a large frying pan skin side up. Add ⅓ cup water, drizzle with lemon juice, and season with salt and pepper. Bring to a boil, cover, and steam until tender, approximately 2 minutes.

To serve the meal, on individual serving plates which have been warmed, place potatoes and meat side by side on the center of the plate, meat on the left. Place the mushrooms in front of the meat, vegetables pointing out surrounding the potatoes, and demi-glace surrounding all.

Raspberry Bavarian with Chocolate Sauce and Fresh Raspberries

Before You Begin

You'll need: 2-quart saucepan, small bowl, 2 small saucepans, squirt bottle, spray bottle, or brush, metal rack with small grill, 8 molds

Prep: 20 minutes (plus 3 hours or more to chill Bavarian)

Cook: 20 minutes

Yield: 8 servings

Bavarian

1¼ cup raspberry puree, strained

1¼ cup light Karo syrup

1½ lemons, juiced

2 Tbsp. unflavored gelatin

1 cup whipping cream, whipped

small cookies or pirouettes (for garnish)

In a 2-quart saucepan over medium heat, mix raspberry puree and syrup and warm. In a small bowl, dissolve gelatin in lemon juice. Add gelatin mixture to puree and continue to heat until it dissolves. Remove from heat and allow to cool to under 120°F. Meanwhile, whip cream until stiff peaks form. Fold whipped cream into cooled puree. Pour into molds and refrigerate 3 hours to set.

CHEF'S TIP: Use 1½-inch PVC pipe cut into 2-inch lengths, bottoms covered with plastic wrap that is secured in place with rubber bands to keep mixture from running out, and lined with a strip of waxed paper.

Chocolate Sauce

3 oz. dark chocolate

2 Tbsp. unsalted butter

1 tsp. vanilla

½ cup whole milk

1 Tbsp. light Karo syrup

In a small saucepan over medium heat, combine all ingredients and heat to just boiling. Pour into a squirt bottle and set aside.

Raspberry Garnish

1 pint raspberries

½ cup water

1 cup sugar

1 Tbsp. Grand Marnier

In a small saucepan over medium-high heat, combine water, sugar, and Grand Marnier, stir to mix, bring to a boil, and remove from heat to cool. Put mixture into a spray bottle. Arrange raspberries on a rack and apply a light coating of syrup to berries. (**NOTE:** If you do not have a spray bottle, syrup can be brushed on.)

To serve, squirt a pattern of chocolate sauce onto individual plates. Remove plastic wrap from bottom of mold and place Bavarian onto plate. Surround with raspberries. Accompany with a small cookie or pirouette, or place the cookie under the Bavarian as a base.

Famous Writers On Rail Dining

With trains having roamed North America for more than 175 years, it is little wonder that they populate the work of writers past and present. Here is some of what writers, from Stephen Crane to David Balducci, have to say about rail dining:

Stephen Crane

Crane, perhaps most famous for his Civil War novel *The Red Badge of Courage,* has the characters in his 1897 story "The Bride Comes to Yellow Sky" riding an all-Pullman *Limited.* In this brief scene he captures the apprehension felt by many travelers during the Golden Age of passenger service about entering the fine dining atmosphere of a limited train's dining car; and the memorable experience it ultimately was for them:

> *The great Pullman was whirling onward with such dignity of motion that a glance from the window seemed simply to prove that the plains of Texas were pouring eastward. . . .*
> *"Ever been in a parlor-car before?" (Jack) asked, smiling with delight.*
> *"No," she answered. "I never was. It's fine, ain't it?"*

"Great! And then after a while we'll go forward to the diner and get a big layout. Finest meal in the world. Charge a dollar."

"Oh, do they?" cried the bride. "Charge a dollar? Why, that's too much—for us—ain't it Jack?"

"Not this trip, anyhow," he answered bravely. "We're going to go the whole thing." . . .

At last they went to the dining car. Two rows of negro waiters in glowing white suits surveyed their entrance with the interest and also the equanimity of men who had been forewarned. The pair fell to the lot of a waiter who happened to feel pleasure in steering them through their meal. He viewed them with the manner of a fatherly pilot, his countenance radiant with benevolence. The patronage entwined with the ordinary deference was not plain to them. And yet as they returned to their coach they showed in their faces a sense of escape.

Theodore Dreiser

In his autobiography, *Newspaper Days* (1922), Theodore Dreiser, an American novelist of the early twentieth century, offers this account of a time when he was traveling on a train with his life's savings in his pocket, and decided to treat himself to an elegant breakfast:

I have often smiled since over the awe in which I then held the Pullman car, its porter, conductor, and all that went with it. To my inexperienced soul it seemed to be the acme of elegance and grandeur. Could life offer anything more than the privilege of riding about the world in these mobile palaces? And here was I this sunny winter morning with enough money to indulge in a breakfast in one of these ambling chambers, though if I kept up this reckless pace there is no telling where I should end. I selected a table adjoining one at which sat two drummers who talked of journeys far and wide, of large sales of binders and reapers and the condition of trade. They seemed to me to be the most fortunate of men, high up in the world as positions go, able to steer straight and profitable courses for themselves. Because they had half a broiled spring chicken, I had one, and coffee and rolls and French fried potatoes, as they did, feeling all the while that I was indulging in limitless grandeur. At one station at which the train stopped some poor-looking farmer boys in jeans and "galluses" and wrinkled hats looking up at me with interest as I ate, I stared down at them, hoping that I should be taken for a millionaire to whom this was little more than a wearisome commonplace. I felt fully capable of playing the part and so gave the boys a cold and repressive glance, as much as to say, Behold!

Graham Greene

From the novel *Stamboul Train,* first published in 1932, a meal taken in the midst of the intrigue that accompanies a mysterious group traveling across Europe on a Limited train:

Coral Musker stared with bewilderment at the menu. "Choose for me," she said, and was glad that he ordered wine. . . . The lights of Vienna fled by them into the dark, and the waiter leant across the table and pulled down the blind . . . (Myatt) was back in familiar territory. . . . The wine list before him, the napkin folded on his plate, the shuffle of waiters passing his chair, all gave him confidence . . . she had to focus her eyes more clearly on reality, the swaying train, men and women as far as she could see eating and drinking between the drawn blinds . . .

All down the restaurant cars fell the sudden concerted silence which is said to mean an angel passes overhead. But through the human silence the tumblers tingled on the table, the wheels thudded along the iron track, the windows shook and sparks flickered like match heads through the darkness . . . "Braised chicken! Roast veal! . . ." The waiters called their way along the carriage and broke the minute's silence. Everyone began talking at once. . . . The angel had gone, and noisily and cheerfully with the thud of wheels, the clatter of plates, voices talking and the tingle of mirrors, the express passed a long line of fir-trees and the flickering of the Danube . . . the driver turned the regulator open, and the speed of the train was increased by five miles an hour.

James Beard

Writing about dining on the French railroad in 1956 James Beard observed:

What they do on trains here is amazing—in a kitchen about as big as mine in New York, with a coal stove, and sometimes four sittings. Wisely enough they have only one menu. Going to Bordeaux, the four of us had a Pullman compartment, and they served our lunch there—hors d'oeuvre, with five different vegetables in sauce Grecque, stuffed eggs, sardines and sausage. Then trout amandine, an excellent tournedos Rossini with chip potatoes and haricots verts, a salad of endives, cheese, and a fruit ice cream with wafers and coffee. And a large choice of wines. Coming back, they served Henry McNulty and me at the fourth sitting at quarter to ten at night—soup, quiche Lorraine—fresh and hot as it could be—rare roast filet with Lyonnaise potatoes and braised endive, salad, cheese, and fruits. I think they do a fantastic job. Imagine that meal on the 20th Century served the way it is . . . And we had hot plates for hot things, cold for cold, and silver for each course.

Ridley Pearson

Although this opening to the 1999 crime novel, *The Pied Piper,* is clearly set on the (unnamed) *Spirit of Washington Dinner Train,* it could describe any of the more than 80 dinner trains that operate in North America today:

The train left the station headed for nowhere, its destination also its point of embarkation, its purpose not to transport its passengers, but to feed them.

David Baldacci

In his 2002 book *The Christmas Train,* this author of bestselling thrillers, in a lighthearted moment, has several of his characters meet for dinner in the dining car of Amtrak's Washington–Chicago *Capitol Limited*:

As Tom surveyed the dining room, his mind drifted to his rail-travel touchstone, North by Northwest. *In the film Cary Grant, on the run from the police and the train conductor—as a poor fugitive from justice, Cary had no ticket—comes into the elegant dining car. The splendidly attired maitre d' escorts him past fashionably dressed diners, to the table of the ravishingly sexy Eva Marie. Turns out she'd tipped the waiter to seat Cary with her. Beautiful women were always doing that to poor Cary Grant. They order, they drink, they laugh; they conduct a sort of sophisticated verbal foreplay right there at the table, one of the more subtly erotic movie scenes ever Tom felt. . . .*

On Amtrak, diners were seated to encourage conversation and the forming of friendships, however fleeting. In this tradition, Tom was seated across from two people, a middle-aged man and a woman who, unfortunately, looked nothing like . . . Eva Marie. . . . Across the aisle from them at another table were Steve and Julie. They were drinking glasses of red wine, holding hands, talking in low voices, and still looked nervous. Young love. . . .

They placed their orders. The menu was very good, and Tom could actually smell the meals being cooked in the downstairs kitchen, which would then be sent up to the dining car via dumbwaiters. He ordered the prime rib and, instead of the salad, asked for a screwdriver as his appetizer. He was just putting it to his lips when he felt himself propelled to the side of the dining car. He turned and there was Agnes Joe wedging next to him, leaving him about six inches in which to eat his dinner.

Palmetto State

www.members.aol.com/tomgville/

The *Palmetto State* had humble origins. Built by Pullman in 1948 for the New York Central Railroad, it was that most common of sleeping cars, a 10-6 (10 single rooms [roomettes] and 6 rooms to sleep two [doubles]) named *Scioto River*. Sold to Canadian National in 1965 and renamed *Hay River,* it next went into service on VIA Rail Canada in 1978, and eventually wound up on the New Georgia Railroad, an early

Nanette Casanova greets her guests as they enter the Palmetto State dining room. Bill Kcenich

dinner train operating in Atlanta, Georgia. Purchased from them in 1995, it was converted into a sleeper-lounge-diner, then completely renovated in 1997.

Cooking duties on board often fall to Chef Nanette Casanova, a South Carolina native who lives in Charleston. She got into the rail-car world via a friend. "Tom Whitted, the *Palmetto State*'s owner, was my college roommate's brother. He knew of my experience cooking on yachts, so he recruited me to cook on his railcar several years ago. That job led to meeting Matthew Gipson on board the *Belle Vista* (see pages 63–64). As a result, I've also enjoyed many trips with him and car owner John Kirkwood."

Of her work Chef Nanette says, "I enjoy cooking. At home, in Charleston, I work a great deal with a local caterer. However, I have no desire to cook full time, but do love that I can travel the rails seeing the country, and use my cooking skills to get paid to do it. I have met some wonderful people from all over the country on my charters, including the 'foamers' (an expression used by railroad people to describe avid rail fans), and can honestly say I have never had a bad trip.

"Cooking on a train," she says, "can be challenging. You just have to remember, when you open the oven to check your pie, to check the motion of the train. And then, if the train lurches and your pie falls out of the oven, if you can catch it you can always have cobbler for dessert instead.

"At breakfast, this is always a crowd-pleaser," says Chef Nanette. "I make it up the night before, so my mornings become easier."

Upside-Down Apple French Toast

1 cup brown sugar
½ cup butter
2 Tbsp. light corn syrup
2 large tart apples, peeled, cored, sliced
3 eggs
1 cup milk
1 tsp. vanilla extract

10 slices day-old French bread, cut ¾-inch thick
1 cup applesauce
1 10-oz. jar apple jelly
½ tsp. cinnamon
whipped cream (optional)

Before You Begin

You'll need: small saucepan, 9" × 13" baking dish, medium bowl, aluminum foil

Preheat oven to 350°F.

Prep: 15 minutes (plus 8–10 hours to refrigerate)

Cook: 40 minutes (plus 30 minutes before baking to allow to reach room temperature)

Yield: 5 servings

In a small saucepan over medium-high heat, combine brown sugar, butter, and corn syrup. Bring just to a boil, reduce heat, and simmer until thickened, about 5 minutes. Pour mixture into a 9" × 13" baking dish and arrange apples on top. Combine eggs, milk, and vanilla in a bowl and mix well. Soak the bread slices in the egg mixture for 1 minute, then arrange them over the apples. Cover with foil and refrigerate for 8 to 10 hours. Remove from refrigerator 30 minutes before baking. Place in a 350°F oven and bake, uncovered, until set, about 35 to 40 minutes. Meanwhile, in a small saucepan over medium heat, combine applesauce, apple jelly, and cinnamon and simmer until heated through. To serve, remove two slices per portion from serving dish and flip them over onto individual plates. Spoon sauce over. Serve with whipped cream, if desired, and accompanied by crispy thick-sliced bacon or sausage.

For brunch or a continental breakfast, these *Palmetto State* favorites are easy to prepare and perfect to serve on a buffet or at table.

Breakfast Frittata

Before You Begin

You'll need: 12-cup muffin tin, large skillet, large mixing bowl, medium mixing bowl

Preheat oven to 350°F.

Prep: 20 minutes

Cook: 20 minutes

Yield: 6 servings

Pam vegetable spray

1 lb. ground sausage, hot preferred

1 medium onion, chopped

2 cups frozen hash browns, thawed

4½ oz. cheddar cheese, shredded

3 Tbsp. flour

Lawry's seasoning salt to taste

pepper to taste

1 Tbsp. chopped parsley (or ½ Tbsp. bottled flakes)

6 eggs

1 cup ranch dressing

½ cup milk

salsa (optional)

Spray muffin tins with Pam and set aside. In a large skillet over medium heat, crumble sausage and mix with chopped onion to brown, about 3 to 5 minutes. Drain and transfer to a large mixing bowl. Add hash brown potatoes and cheese. Stir in flour. Add Lawry's seasoning salt, pepper, and parsley and stir to mix. In a medium bowl, lightly beat eggs. Stir in dressing and milk. Combine this mixture with sausage mixture. Spoon into muffin tins, filling to about ¾ full. Bake at 350°F until set and golden brown, about 15 to 20 minutes. To serve, for individual portions serve two frittatas with salsa ladled on top, and for self-service, line a platter with endive, arrange frittatas on top, and place a bowl of salsa at the end of the platter.

For appetizers, two easy-to-prepare selections:

Plum Tomato Sandwiches

10 slices Pepperidge Farm sourdough
   sandwich bread
1 cup mayonnaise

4 Tbsp. fresh basil, chopped
5 plum tomatoes, cut into ¼-inch slices
salt and white pepper to taste

Before You Begin

You'll need: 2-inch round cookie cutter, sheet pan, small bowl

Preheat oven to Broil.

Prep: 10 minutes

Yield: 10 servings

Using a 2-inch round cookie or biscuit cutter, cut two rounds out of each slice of bread. Arrange rounds on a sheet pan, place under broiler, and watch closely to lightly brown one side only, about 1 minute. Set aside to cool. In a small bowl, combine mayonnaise and basil. Spread mixture on untoasted side of bread rounds. Top each round with a tomato slice, and sprinkle with a mixture of salt and white pepper.

Brie Cheese with Brandy Topping

¼ cup packed dark brown sugar
¼ cup broken nuts, walnuts or pecans
1 Tbsp. brandy

14-oz. round of Brie cheese
ginger snaps or thin-sliced baguette

Before You Begin

You'll need: microwave oven, glass microwave-safe bowl, ovenproof pie plate

Prep: 5 minutes

Cook: 3 minutes

Yield: 8 servings

In a glass microwave-safe bowl, mix together sugar, nuts, and brandy. Place Brie in ovenproof pie plate. Cook sugar mixture at 100-percent power for 1 minute or until melted. Pour over Brie and place back in microwave at 50-percent power for 2 minutes, until cheese is heated but not melting. Serve with ginger snaps or thin-sliced baguette and a serving knife.

For the main course:

Pan-Seared Grouper over Spinach, topped with Seared Scallops and Tomatoes

Before You Begin

You'll need:
medium bowl, heavy-bottomed sauté pan, small saucepan, small bowl, large stockpot, heavy-bottomed sauté pan

Prep: 20 minutes

Cook: 30 minutes (elapsed time for all items)

Yield: 4 servings

2 eggs

flour to coat

salt and pepper to taste

4 6-oz. grouper filets (substitute: any meaty white fish)

clarified butter

Asiago cheese, grated (when serving)

In a medium bowl, beat eggs until of uniform lemon color. Combine flour, salt, and pepper, and scatter on a flat surface. Dredge fish in flour, immerse in egg wash, then dredge in flour again. Meanwhile, in a heavy-bottomed sauté pan over medium-high heat, melt clarified butter and heat until hot. Sear both sides of fish, allowing about 2 minutes per side, depending on thickness. Make sure fish is cooked through but be careful not to overcook or burn. Set aside to keep warm.

Tomato Sauce

1 14½-oz. can diced tomatoes (Italian style is good)

½ cup white wine

1½ Tbsp. fresh basil

½ tsp. Italian seasoning

In a small saucepan over medium heat, simmer all ingredients until most, but not all, of the liquid is reduced, about 20 minutes, stirring occasionally.

Spinach

1 bag fresh spinach, well washed, stems removed

1 clove garlic, minced

2 Tbsp. butter, room temperature

salt to taste

In a small bowl, mix garlic and butter, and add salt. In a large stockpot over medium heat, melt butter mixture. Add spinach and sauté until wilted, about 3 minutes. Set aside to keep warm.

Scallops

12 large sea scallops   **clarified butter**
salt and white pepper to taste

Sprinkle scallops with salt and pepper. In heavy bottomed sauté pan over high heat, melt butter. When pan is hot, sear scallops, about 1 minute on both sides.

To serve, place a bed of spinach on an individual serving plate, top with grouper, then with three scallops, and finish with tomato sauce and a sprinkle of Asiago cheese. Accompany with wild rice.

Wild Rice

¾ cup wild rice   **½ cup onion, diced**
2 cups rich beef stock (see pages 246–247)   **¼ cup green bell pepper, diced fine**
½ cup butter, divided
1 cup sliced mushrooms (substitute
  stems and pieces)

Before You Begin

You'll need:
3-quart saucepan, medium skillet

Prep: 10 minutes (plus overnight for soaking)

Cook: 30 minutes

Yield: 8 servings

In a 3-quart saucepan, place wild rice and beef stock and allow to stand overnight. To finish, in a medium skillet over medium heat, melt 2 tablespoons butter and sauté mushrooms, onion, and green pepper until tender, about 3 minutes. Add sautéed vegetables and remaining butter to wild rice and bring just to a boil. Reduce heat, cover lightly, and simmer until tender but crunchy, about 10 to 15 minutes. Add water if necessary during cooking so rice does not dry out.

Blueberry Nut Crème Pie

Before You Begin

You'll need: small mixing bowl, electric mixer or food processor, 9-inch pie pan (shallow, not deep dish)

Prep: 10 minutes (plus time to bake a pie pastry) (allow at least 3 hours to chill)

Yield: 1 9-inch pie

4 oz. cream cheese, room temperature

1 cup confectioners' sugar

1 pre-baked 9-inch pie shell, cooled (see page 82)

½ cup chopped walnuts

½ can blueberry pie filling (use 21-oz. can)

Cool Whip

In a small mixing bowl, using an electric mixer or food processor, blend cream cheese and confectionerrs' sugar together until smooth. Spread mixture in bottom of a baked pie shell. Sprinkle chopped nuts on cream cheese and top with blueberry filling. Apply a layer of Cool Whip on top of filling and finish with sprinkle of walnuts. Refrigerate 3 hours or longer to set.

Scottish Thistle

www.scottishthistle.com

Built in 1959 for use by executives of the Canadian National Railway, the *Scottish Thistle* is one of the newest private rail cars in operation today. A product of Canada throughout, the car body was produced by National Steel Car, and the interior completed at CNR's Montreal Shops. Because it was designed for use in a northern climate, it is well insulated for warmth in winter, air-conditioned for cool summer running, and quiet any time. Purchased from the Canadian National in 1994, updated and modernized, now headquartered in Santa Ana, California, the *Scottish Thistle* has been in continuous service since it was built.

Scottish Thistle dining room.
John H. Kuehl

Chef Shaun Murphy, who is in constant motion and who talks even faster than her hands work, began her culinary career with a degree from the New York Restaurant School ("Top of my class," she points out). To start, she worked at a four-star French restaurant in the city, then switched to a three-star American restaurant. "I worked every station in the kitchen," she says, "and I didn't have a life." To get a life, she took up acting and found herself in California. There she reentered the culinary arts by working for a caterer. "I was helping a friend on a private rail car when they discovered I was actually a chef, certified." In possession of that rare ability to cook well in a moving kitchen, she has been in demand by both Dean McCormick, owner of the *Scottish Thistle,* and an "A" list of private individuals who charter the car. Her distinctive style is captured in some of her cooking instructions and tips here.

Fresh Tomato, White Wine, and Basil Soup

2 Tbsp. olive oil

8 to 10 ripe field tomatoes, chopped

⅓ cup chopped fresh garlic

½ cup white wine

⅓ cup chopped fresh basil

3 oz. heavy cream

salt and pepper to taste

Before You Begin

You'll need: 2-quart saucepan

Prep: 20 minutes

Cook: 15 minutes

Yield: 8 servings

In a 2-quart saucepan over medium heat, heat olive oil. Add tomatoes and sauté until soft and juicy, about 2 minutes. Add garlic and sauté 1 minute more, taking care that garlic does not brown. Add white wine, increase heat to medium-high, and simmer to reduce until moisture is nearly gone and tomatoes begin to disintegrate, about 5 minutes. (**NOTE:** You can continue cooking from here, or set aside to finish later by bringing the tomato mixture back up to temperature.) Add basil and stir. Add just enough heavy cream to "take the corners off." Season to taste and serve hot.

Field Salad with Fresh Balsamic Vinaigrette

⅓ cup golden raisins

¼ cup pine nuts

4 cups mesclun lettuce

4 oz. goat cheese, crumbled (when serving)

Before You Begin

You'll need: small bowl, baking sheet, food processor

Preheat oven to 350°F.

Prep: 20 minutes

Cook: 5 minutes

Yield: 4 servings

In a small bowl, soak raisins in water to cover until plump, drain, and set aside. Spread pine nuts on a baking sheet and place in a 350°F oven until golden brown, not dark, about 5 minutes (Chef Shaun warns: "Watch closely because if you can smell them, it's too late"). Set aside.

Balsamic Vinaigrette Dressing

2 Tbsp. Dijon mustard

1 tsp. chopped fresh garlic

¾ cup olive oil

2 Tbsp. balsamic vinegar (or to taste)

juice of ½ lemon

½ tsp. fresh thyme, finely chopped

salt and pepper to taste

In a food processor, emulsify mustard and garlic. Reduce setting to Mix, and drizzle olive oil in. Thin to taste with balsamic vinegar. Add lemon juice and thyme, and season to taste.

To serve, toss greens, raisins, and pine nuts with sufficient dressing to coat nicely and pile on individual serving plates. Top with crumbled goat cheese.

CHEF'S TIP: This dressing recipe can be doubled, and then some, as it holds for a long time.

Sliced Beef Tenderloin with Red Wine Mushroom Sauce

Before You Begin

You'll need: cast-iron skillet, baking pan, aluminum foil, 2-quart covered saucepan, small saucepan

Preheat oven to 350°F.

Prep: 30 minutes

Cook: 45 minutes

Yield: 6 servings

4 lbs. beef tenderloin, butt end, silverskin removed

olive oil

kosher salt

Rub tenderloin with oil and sprinkle lightly with kosher salt. In a cast-iron skillet over high heat, sear tenderloin until crusty but not blackened on all sides, about 4 minutes per side. Transfer to a foil-lined baking pan and roast in a 350°F oven until internal temperature reaches 135°F to 140°F. Remove from oven, cover with foil, and let stand 10 minutes before slicing. Slice ¼ inch to ½ inch thick, three slices per portion.

Red Wine Mushroom Sauce

2 large portobello mushrooms

¼ cup olive oil

kosher salt

⅓ cup chopped fresh garlic

1 750-ml. bottle Hearty Burgundy (see CHEF'S TIP)

3 Tbsp. butter

3 Tbsp. flour

salt and pepper to taste

2 Tbsp. chopped fresh thyme (no stems)

¼ cup heavy cream

With a spoon, scrape and discard gills from mushrooms. Break mushrooms in half and slice ½ inch thick. In a 2-quart saucepan over medium-high heat, heat olive oil. Add mushroom slices and toss immediately to coat. Sprinkle lightly with kosher salt to draw out moisture. Add olive oil as needed to moisten, but don't allow mushrooms to get greasy. Reduce heat to low and sweat until soft and moist, about 5 minutes. Add garlic and continue to simmer for about 1 minute, stirring occasionally, taking care not to allow garlic to brown. Increase heat to high and add Hearty Burgundy. Bring to a boil, reduce heat to simmer, and reduce by ⅔. Meanwhile, as reduction nears completion, in a small saucepan over medium heat, melt butter. Stirring constantly, gradually add flour to make a blond roux, about 3 minutes. Add roux to mushroom/wine mixture and stir to thicken. Season with salt and pepper. Add thyme. Add sufficient heavy cream to smooth the flavor. Set aside to serve hot.

To serve, place a portion of mashed potatoes in the center of individual serving plates. Fan sliced beef tenderloin in front of potatoes and ladle sauce over. Place spinach at the back of the plate and garnish with a thyme sprig.

CHEF'S TIPS: (1) Use cheap, inexpensive, cost-conscious, price-sensitive, screw-top Hearty Burgundy and boil it silly. Do not use Cabernet Sauvignon or Merlot as the reduction will cause any tannins present to intensify and make the sauce bitter. Burgundy will sweeten as it reduces. Cabernet will make you wonder why you bothered. (2) The sauce can be made one day in advance and reheated. (3) When slicing the tenderloin, add any juice to the sauce to bump the flavor.

Roasted Garlic Mashed Potatoes

¾ **cup whole cloves garlic, peeled**
olive oil
kosher salt
20 baby white potatoes, scrubbed,
    quartered (NOTE: Do not peel)

½ **cup butter**
½ **cup half & half**
salt and pepper to taste

Before You Begin

You'll need: pie tin, aluminum foil, 4-quart saucepan, colander, potato masher, 9" × 13" baking pan

Preheat oven to 375°F.

Prep: 15 minutes

Cook: 1 hour 15 minutes

Yield: 4 servings

Line a pie tin with foil, add garlic, and toss with sufficient oil to coat. Sprinkle lightly with kosher salt, cover with foil, and roast in a 375°F oven until golden but not dark, about 45 minutes. (**NOTE:** This may be done several days in advance.) Reduce oven temperature to 350°F. Mash roasted garlic or puree in a food processor. Meanwhile, place baby potato quarters in a 4-quart saucepan with sufficient unsalted water to cover. Bring to a boil, reduce heat slightly, and boil until tender, about 10 minutes. Drain in a colander and allow to steam until dry. Return potatoes to pot and add mashed/pureed roasted garlic, butter, and half & half. Mash by hand with a potato masher. Season aggressively to taste. Transfer potatoes to a greased 9" × 13" baking pan and cover with foil, taking care foil does not touch potatoes. Place in a 350°F oven until very hot and slightly souffléd, about 30 minutes. To serve, remember, "There is very little worse in this world than cold mashed potatoes."

Creamed Spinach

Before You Begin

You'll need: stock pot, potato ricer, 2-quart saucepan, whisk

Prep: 5 minutes

Cook: 20 minutes

Yield: 12 servings

3 lbs. fresh spinach, thoroughly washed

¼ cup whole milk or half & half

¾ cup cream cheese

nutmeg

salt and cracked black pepper to taste

In a stockpot bring ½ cup water to a boil. Add spinach and turn continuously until just wilted. Squeeze dry in a potato ricer, or by hand if allowed to cool. In a 2-quart saucepan over medium heat, warm milk. Add cream cheese and whisk until smooth. Sprinkle with nutmeg and season aggressively with salt and pepper. Stir in wilted spinach to coat thoroughly and heat through.

NOTE: This can be made up to 1 hour in advance and reheated to serve.

Apple Blossoms

Before You Begin

You'll need: small saucepan, 6-cup muffin tin, pastry brush, large sauté pan

Preheat oven to 325°F.

Prep: 30 minutes

Cook: 20 minutes

Yield: 12 servings

4 layers phyllo dough (see NOTE)

6 Tbsp. butter, divided

3 large Granny Smith apples, peeled, cored

¼ cup dark brown sugar

¼ cup white wine

1 tsp. candied chopped ginger

juice of ½ lemon

cinnamon

½ tsp. pure vanilla extract

vanilla bean ice cream

mint leaves (for garnish)

NOTE: Small size box of phyllo in double roll is recommended.

Defrost phyllo dough according to package directions. Meanwhile, in a small saucepan over medium heat, melt 4 tablespoons butter. Unwrap phyllo dough and cover pile with a dry cloth. Working one layer at a time, brush melted butter on top, apply another layer, and repeat for total of four layers. Cut buttered phyllo into 4-inch squares and press into muffin cups. Bake at 325°F until light gold and dried crisp, 8 to 10 minutes. Stand to cool. (NOTE: Can be made up to 3 days in advance if held airtight.) Meanwhile, prepare apples, rub with lemon juice to prevent browning, and cut lengthwise into 14 wedges per apple. In a large sauté pan over medium-high heat, melt 2 tablespoons butter, add apples, and toss to cook until the apples begin to brown, taking care not to let the butter burn. Add brown sugar and continue to sauté for 2 minutes. Add white wine, ginger, and lemon juice, and continue to cook until mixture thickens. Sprinkle with cinnamon, remove from heat, and stir in vanilla extract. (NOTE: Can be made ahead and reheated to serve.)

To serve, place one phyllo blossom on a dessert plate at room temperature. Fill blossom with a scoop of ice cream and ladle hot gingered apples over. Garnish with fresh mint.

Railroad Art: Tex Wilson's "Workin' on the Railroad"

www.texwilson.com

Railroad/Western artist and graphic illustrator Tex Wilson grew up in Slaton, Texas, a community sixteen miles south-east of Lubbock that was shaped by the farm, ranch, and railroad life that prevailed there. In a tribute to the industry that engaged his father, and many others in the town that was once a division point on the Atchison, Topeka & Santa Fe Railway, he has created a

series of artworks he calls "Workin' on the Railroad." Fittingly, two of the twelve pieces depict significant developments in the history of rail dining. One identifies and portrays the work of dining car personnel. The other celebrates the famous Harvey Girls, the thousands of young women hired by Fred Harvey to serve as waitresses in his eating houses along the route of the Santa Fe beginning in the 1870s.

ABOVE: *Tex Wilson's "Dining Car."*
Tex Wilson.
RIGHT: *Tex Wilson's "Harvey Girls."*
Tex Wilson

The Survivor

www.aaprco.com/cgi-bin/cardisplay.pl?survivor:name

The Survivor offers a unique, eclectic mix of period authenticity, owner preferences, and railroad memorabilia. Built in 1926 by American Car & Foundry Company as the private car of the F. W. Woolworth family, and named *Japauldon,* it was most often used by actress and Woolworth heiress Barbara Hutton. (It is thought to be the site of a courtship between Ms. Hutton and the actor Cary Grant.) The interior is of rare golden heart oak. Privately owned until 1941, then acquired by the Baltimore & Ohio Railroad as business car number 902, and subsequently the Monon 3, and Louisville & Nashville 350, it returned to private service in 1982. Today, headquartered in Atlanta, Georgia, Dante S. Stephensen, president and chairman of Dante's Down the Hatch, a popular jazz club and restaurant in the city's Buckhead section, owns *The Survivor.*

Chef Gay McClelland's first reaction to being asked to share her secrets for preparing a fine meal fast was to express gratitude for the interest. "Before I start, though," she went on, "you ought to know a little bit of my culinary history. I trained at the London Cordon Bleu, with additional classes taken at the Sorbonne in Paris. I took master classes with Paul Prudhomme, Jacques Pépin, and Julia Child. Last year I was chef at the Ritz Carlton for their club level. In almost twenty years as a rail chef, I have worked many train cars, some of which are the *Virginia City, Northern Sky, Sierra Hotel, Intrepid,* and the *Dagney Taggert.* I consider *The Survivor* my 'home' car."

What followed is a typical evening dinner on the train, à la McClelland. First up, this easy and beautifully elegant appetizer. "But remember," says Gay McClelland, "presentation is paramount."

Classic Champagne and Caviar Service

Before You Begin

You'll need: small bowl, fine grater, decorative serving pieces (see instructions)

Prep: 20 minutes (plus 2–3 hours for crème fraîche to thicken and chill)

Yield: 6–8 servings

½ cup whipping cream
1 Tbsp. fresh lemon juice
6 slices Pepperidge Farm thin white bread

3 oz. caviar, osetra
2 eggs, hard-boiled
¼ cup sweet onion, finely chopped

In a small bowl, create crème fraîche by combining whipping cream and fresh lemon juice. Allow to sit at room temperature until thick, about 2 hours, depending on room temperature. Refrigerate until ready to use. Meanwhile, trim crusts from bread, then lightly toast, taking care not to brown. Cut toast into triangles and set aside. To prepare for service, gather together five of your most unique small bowls or sherry or martini glasses, as well as a silver tray on which to arrange them. Shave ice into a small bowl and nestle an opened jar of caviar, tilting lid for prominent display. Separate egg whites from yolks, finely grate each separately, and place each in one of the decorative bowls or glasses you've selected. Place onion in another bowl or glass. Spoon ¼ cup crème fraîche into another bowl or glass. Arrange all on the silver tray with serving pieces and toast. (**NOTE:** Caviar spoon cannot be metal.) Serve with the finest ice-cold champagne.

Next, an incredibly smooth, velvety soup, with wonderful chunky bits of Camembert, builds on the champagne theme.

Champagne and Camembert Crème Soup

10 Tbsp. butter, divided
1 Tbsp. flour
1 cup chicken broth
½ pint heavy cream

5 oz. milk
4½ oz. Camembert cheese, cubed with rind
5 oz. champagne

Before You Begin

You'll need: 2-quart saucepan, whisk

Prep: 10 minutes

Cook: 20 minutes

Yield: 4 servings

In 2-quart saucepan over medium heat, melt 4 tablespoons butter. Stirring constantly, add flour and blend until golden, about 3 minutes. Add chicken broth and whisk until just boiling. Remove from heat and add cream and milk. Return to heat and bring to just boiling. Remove from heat and add remaining butter, Camembert, and champagne. Return saucepan to medium heat and stir until cheese melts. Serve immediately.

Baby Greens Crowned with Warm Goat Cheese, Dried Cherries, and Pancetta Vinaigrette

4 oz. dried cherries
½ cup sherry
¼ cup olive oil
½ pound pancetta, cut into ⅛" wide × 1" long strips

1 Tbsp. garlic, finely chopped
1 Tbsp. thyme, finely chopped
6 Tbsp. sherry vinegar
8 cups baby greens
6 oz. goat cheese, cubed, softened

Before You Begin

You'll need: small bowl, small strainer, medium skillet

Prep: 20 minutes

Yield: 8 servings

In a small bowl, combine cherries with sherry and microwave on Medium power 1 minute to reconstitute. Let stand until plump, then strain off sherry.

Meanwhile, in a medium skillet over medium heat, heat olive oil and sauté pancetta until done, about 5 minutes. Remove pancetta to paper towels to drain. Retain 3 tablespoons of fat in the skillet and add garlic to sauté gently, about 1 minute. Add thyme, and vinegar. Increase heat to medium-high and boil 1 minute. Remove from heat and keep warm. To serve, arrange greens attractively on serving plates. Place goat cheese in center and scatter pancetta strips and cherries over. Drizzle with warm vinaigrette and serve.

Roasted Salmon with Fresh Corn Sauce and Black Bean Salsa

Begin by preparing the Black Bean Salsa so that it can rest and blend. Next, complete the Fresh Corn Sauce and let stand while you cook the salmon.

Before You Begin

You'll need: large skillet, small bowl, 2-quart saucepan, hand-held mixer.

Preheat oven to 350°F.

Prep: 20 minutes, plus 1 hour to chill salsa)

Cook: 30 minutes

Yield: 6 servings

6 7-oz. salmon steaks

¼ cup butter, melted

6 tsp. Cajun seasoning

Brush salmon steaks with butter and dust with Cajun seasoning. Preheat a large skillet over medium heat. Place salmon in skillet, raise heat to medium-high, and carefully brown each side, about 1 to 2 minutes per side. Remove skillet from burner and place in 350°F oven to cook salmon to desired temperature, allowing about 10 minutes.

Fresh Corn Sauce

2 Tbsp. butter

1 cup sweet onion, diced

1 bay leaf

3 cups fresh corn off the cob

1 tsp. salt

1¼ tsp. white pepper

1¼ tsp. cayenne

1¼ tsp. cumin

1 cup heavy cream

In a 2-quart saucepan over medium heat, melt butter in saucepan, add onion and bay leaf, and stir until onion is soft and clear, about 3 minutes. Reduce heat to medium-low, add corn, and stir occasionally until corn is tender, about 10 to 15 minutes. Add salt, white pepper, cayenne, and cumin, and stir well. Add heavy cream and bring to just to a boil. Reduce heat to simmer and cook about 5 minutes. Using hand-held mixer, blend the sauce until corn is coarsely chopped but not pureed.

Black Bean Salsa

1 cup black beans, cooked and chilled

¼ cup green onions, thin-sliced to
    include white and green

¼ cup red bell pepper, diced

2 Tbsp. fresh lime juice

1 Tbsp. olive oil

2 Tbsp. coarsely chopped cilantro

salt and pepper to taste

Combine all ingredients in small bowl and refrigerate 1 hour to chill and infuse.
    To serve, place salmon on individual plates. Spoon corn sauce over top
and top with 1 tablespoon black bean salsa.

French Quarter Bananas Foster

¼ cup butter

¼ cup brown sugar

½ cup fresh orange juice

1 tsp. cinnamon

2 Tbsp. bourbon

3 bananas, medium ripe

vanilla ice cream

Before You Begin

You'll need: 1-quart saucepan, whisk

Prep: 5 minutes

Cook: 12 minutes

Yield: 8 servings

In a 1-quart saucepan over medium heat, melt butter, add brown sugar, and
stir until dissolved and thick. Whisk in orange juice and continue to whisk
until smooth. Add cinnamon and bourbon. Adjust to personal taste. Meanwhile, cut bananas in ½-inch slices and carefully fold into sauce to coat. Simmer until bananas are soft. Mixture is ready to serve, or can be removed from
heat and reheated when ready to serve. To serve, scoop vanilla ice cream into
wine goblet and top with Bananas Foster.

Tamalpais

www.generalrail.ouzo.com

The owners of *Tamalpais,* out of Walnut Creek, California, describe it as "a classic
vintage time machine." That is fitting for a heavyweight (pre-streamliner era) executive car built in 1923 for the Atchison, Topeka & Santa Fe Railway. Care has been
taken to restore the car as closely as possible to its original condition, especially in
preserving the oak paneled interior and brass decorations and fixtures. Now named
after Marin County's famed "sleeping maiden" mountain (railroad business cars
had numbers, not names), today the car is operated by Key Holidays in charter and
Amtrak excursion service.
    In an echo of the Pullman Company's extensive and detailed manuals of proce-
dure for on board personnel, Key Holidays has set down instructions for the staff,
entitled "Guidelines for Private Railcar Waiters." Thirteen situations are covered,

from "Boarding the Passengers" to "End of the Trip" procedures. They end with this admonition: "*Never* harass or give a bad time to the chef."

That would likely be Chef Connie Luna, who recalls that as a little girl growing up in Burlingame, California, she watched passengers taking breakfast in the dining car on the Southern Pacific's *Lark* as it raced by on its way to San Francisco. "Now that I'm inside looking out," she says, "I realize just how much those early experiences influenced my life." She credits her mother with teaching her to cook, but got experience working in restaurants as well. "Like Fred Harvey," she says, referring to the legendary founder of the Harvey Houses along the route of the Atchison, Topeka & Santa Fe Railway and of dining car service on that railroad, "I started out washing dishes." When the possibility of opening her own restaurant came about, she and her husband became concerned about its effect on their life together. "So I compromised," she says, "and I started cooking on private railcars. I consider it a privilege to be part of the way vintage car travel brings alive an era lost in time, of sharing the gracious style of living that bygone era offered."

Of her meals, she says "I don't emulate Wolfgang Puck, I emulate Fred Harvey. Railroad recipes offer a straightforward approach to cooking. I try to follow railroad tradition and serve good old-fashioned tasty food, and plenty of it." A respected and legendary seventeen-year veteran of private rail car service, Chef Connie has never before shared her secrets and recipes.

Grand Marnier French Toast

Before You Begin

You'll need: small bowl, rolling pin, baking pan, blender, deep-fryer or large skillet, paper towels, baking sheet

Preheat oven to 200°F.

Prep: 20 minutes (plus overnight to chill)

Cook: 10 minutes (plus 20 minutes for deep-fryer to warm oil)

Yield: 8 servings

½ cup cream cheese, room temperature
¼ cup orange marmalade
16 slices white bread
8 eggs, beaten
⅓ cup orange juice
½ cup Grand Marnier

½ cup half & half
1 Tbsp. sugar
½ tsp. vanilla extract
¼ tsp. salt
vegetable oil
confectioners' sugar (for garnish)

In a small bowl, cream the cream cheese with marmalade and spread on bread to make sandwiches. Roll lightly with a rolling pin to ensure the sandwich is stuck together, and cut off crusts. Cut sandwiches in half diagonally, arrange pieces in a single layer in a baking pan, and refrigerate overnight. In a blender, combine eggs, orange juice, Grand Marnier, half & half, sugar, vanilla, and salt, mix well, and pour over bread. Allow to soak 10 minutes. Meanwhile, warm sufficient oil, about ⅔ full, in a deep-fryer to 350°F (see NOTE). Place 4 sandwich triangles in the fry basket and submerge in hot oil until golden brown, watching carefully not to over cook, about 4 minutes. Drain on paper towels and place in warm oven until ready to serve. Before serving, sprinkle with confectioners' sugar. May be served with syrup, but these are sweet enough to eat without it.

NOTE: Alternative cooking method: In a large skillet over medium-high heat, warm ¼-inch vegetable oil. Fry sandwiches in hot oil until golden brown, about 2 minutes per side.

Spinach Salad

½ cup olive oil
¼ cup brown sugar
1 Tbsp. balsamic vinegar
1 Tbsp. garlic red wine vinegar
1 Tbsp. red raspberry vinegar
¼ tsp. Lawry's garlic salt
⅛ tsp. pepper
pinch ground cloves

2 oranges
1 6 oz. bag baby spinach
½ cup sliced mushrooms
¼ cup sliced red onion
¼ cup dried cranberries
basil and tomato feta cheese
Sugared Pecans

Before You Begin

You'll need: blender, 1 cup covered container, 1-gallon freezer bag, large bowl, small saucepan, cookie sheet

Preheat oven to 300°F.

Prep: 15 minutes (plus overnight to chill)

Cook: 20 minutes (plus time to cool)

Yield: 8 servings

In a bowl, mix oil, brown sugar, vinegars, garlic salt, pepper, and cloves in a blender, put in container with lid, and refrigerate up to one day. Wash spinach well, remove stems, spin or pat dry, place in a 1-gallon freezer bag, and refrigerate. Peel oranges, then section, removing all strings, and cut sections in half. In a large bowl, toss spinach, dressing, oranges, mushrooms, onion, and cranberries in large bowl. Serve on chilled salad plate, topped with feta cheese, sugared pecans sprinkled around outside of salad, accompanied by a chilled salad fork.

Sugared Pecans

4 Tbsp. butter
½ cup brown sugar

⅛ tsp. nutmeg
1 cup chopped pecans

In a small saucepan, melt butter and add brown sugar and nutmeg. Stir occasionally until sugar is dissolved. Add pecans and stir until coated. Spread on a cookie sheet and bake in 300°F oven until slightly darkened and crisp, about 20 minutes. Cool and place in sealed container to use as needed.

✳ ✳ ✳

Prime Rib

Before You Begin

You'll need:
roasting pan, meat thermometer, 2 medium mixing bowls, whisk, electric beater

Preheat oven to 325°F.

Prep: 10 minutes (plus 1½ hours to make horseradish sauce)

Cook: 2–2¼ hours

Yield: 8 servings

5 lbs. commercial prime rib, bone
   loosened, retied
vegetable oil

kosher salt
pepper
horseradish sauce

Rub vegetable oil on ends of rib. Sprinkle kosher salt and pepper over top and place in roasting pan. Roast in a 325°F oven, using a meat thermometer to determine when done (an internal of 135°F to 140°F for "rare," 160°F for "medium," and don't even think about "well done"). Trim off the bone and tail, slice and serve with horseradish sauce.

CHEF'S TIPS: (1) The secret to great prime rib is to buy the best piece of meat you can afford. (2) On a moving train, one must remember to remove some of the hot grease from the pan with a baster to prevent it sloshing into the oven.

Horseradish Sauce

1 3-oz. pkg. lemon Jell-O
½ cup boiling water
1 Tbsp. vinegar
¼ tsp. salt

¾ cup prepared horseradish
⅛ tsp. hot sauce
1 cup whipping cream

In a medium mixing bowl, dissolve Jello-O in water. Whisk in vinegar and salt. Chill until of an egg-white consistency, about 20 minutes. (**NOTE:** Watch closely to ensure mixture does not set solid.) Stir in horseradish and hot sauce. Meanwhile, whip cream until stiff peaks form when beater is lifted. Fold whipped cream into horseradish mixture and chill until firm, at least 1 hour.

CHEF'S TIP: Spray an ice cube tray with vegetable oil, then pipe horseradish mixture into cubes, refrigerate overnight, and pop out to serve.

Parsley Potatoes

8 large potatoes, peeled
1 cup sour cream
¼ cup minced parsley

¼ lb. butter, divided
Lawry's garlic salt
pepper

Before You Begin

You'll need: 2 large pots, one to fit down inside the other to resemble a double boiler

Prep: 15 minutes

Cook: 15 minutes

Yield: 8 servings

Cut peeled potatoes in large chunks and put in a large pot of salted cold water to cover. Bring to a boil, then simmer until soft, about 15 minutes. Drain and return to pot. Add sour cream, parsley, 4 tablespoons of butter, and garlic salt and pepper to taste. Stir together until consistency reaches that of half mashed with chunks of potatoes. Place pot in larger pot holding hot water to resemble a double boiler. Cut remaining butter into spears and push into potatoes. Cover until ready to serve.

Squash Medley

4 zucchini squash
4 yellow crookneck squash
3 chayote squash

¼ lb. butter
Lawry's garlic salt to taste
pepper to taste

Before You Begin

You'll need: vegetable peeler, large pot, large skillet

Prep: 15 minutes

Cook: 10 minutes

Yield: 8 servings

Cut ends from zucchini, peel lengthwise in an alternating striped pattern, then cut in 1-inch pieces. Cut end from crookneck squash, leave peel on, and cut in 1-inch pieces. Peel chayotes, cut lengthwise into quarters, remove ends and white pit area, and cut into 1-inch chunks. In a large pot with water to cover, parboil squash in salted water. (**NOTE:** Start with chayote to boil 5 minutes, adding zucchini and crookneck squash for last 3 minutes.) This can be done ahead of time. To finish, in a large skillet over medium heat, melt butter, add garlic salt and squash, and stir to mix and heat through, about 5 minutes. Add pepper and stir to mix. Serve hot with slotted spoon.

Peach Bread Pudding

Before You Begin

You'll need: large mixing bowl, nonstick vegetable spray, 2 large (3½"–4") muffin tins, spatula, large baking sheet (optional), 1-quart saucepan

Preheat oven to 350°F.

Prep: 20 minutes

Cook: 1 hour

Yield: 8 servings

Here is another example of that staple of the railroad chef: the planned-over. The crusts trimmed from the morning's French toast are put to use in the evening's dessert, the model of efficient use of space in stocking the car and in minimizing waste and cleanup.

1 loaf French bread	28 oz. can peaches, drained, cut in bite-
crust trimmings from French toast	size pieces
(optional)	2 Tbsp. vanilla extract
1 qt. half & half	1 tsp. cinnamon
1 cup sugar	1 tsp. nutmeg
½ lb. butter, melted	½ cup dried cranberries
3 eggs, beaten	Bourbon Sauce
1 cup peach schnapps	peach ice cream

Quarter French bread lengthwise, and cut in thin slices. (**NOTE:** Bread should be stale or baked at very low temperature until fairly dry.) If using, cut French toast trimmings into 1-inch-long pieces. Combine all ingredients in large mixing bowl, stirring after each addition. Spray cups in large muffin tin with nonstick spray. Fill each tin ¾ full with pudding mixture. Bake at 350°F for 1 hour. When cool enough to handle, carefully remove cakes from pan with spatula.

To serve, place a bread pudding cake in individual serving bowls and ladle Bourbon Sauce on top. Add a small scoop of peach ice cream alongside.

CHEF'S TIP: You can also prepare the bread pudding cakes in advance; to warm them for service, place them on baking sheet and heat in a warm oven while eating dinner.

Bourbon Sauce

¼ lb. butter	½ cup bourbon
1 cup brown sugar	2 large scoops vanilla ice cream

In a 1-quart saucepan over medium heat, melt butter. Add brown sugar and stir until dissolved. Add bourbon and vanilla ice cream. Whisk until ice cream is melted. Keep warm until ready to serve.

One of the unique challenges faced by private car operators is to pleasantly and efficiently get guests, with their luggage, on board during the two minutes Amtrak typically allows for station stops along its routes. Chef Connie Luna of the private car *Tamalpals* solves this problem by announcing that drinks are waiting in the lounge. There, passengers will find a tray with inviting glasses of Mimosa, Bloody Marys, and something known as a "Luna Fizz." "Most people know it as 'Connie Luna's Gin Milkshake,' " she says.

Luna Fizz

Fill a blender ⅓ full of ice. Add three scoops of vanilla ice cream, ¾ cup orange juice, 1½ cups Sweet & Sour drink mix, ¾ cup half & half, and gin. When asked "How much gin?" Chef Connie replies, "I tip the bottle up and count to seven." A test revealed that to be about 1 cup. Blend until of the consistency of a milkshake. Garnish with a slice of orange and serve immediately.

In another awkward situation, if there is an unexpected delay on the trip, to divert attention, a variation of this drink is served. Call it the "Luna Alexander." Substitute 1 cup brandy and 2 cups Kahluá for the OJ, Sweet & Sour mix, and gin.

All those in favor of taking a siding to await an oncoming freight train, raise your hand.

Virginia City

www.vcrail.com

With its stunning interior and illustious pedigree, the *Virginia City* could arguably be called the best-known private rail car in the world. Built by Pullman Standard Company in 1928 as an open-platform observation-lounge car with sleeping for ten, a ladies' lounge, and shower, it was originally named *Crystal Peak* and assigned to the Chicago-Oakland (California) *Overland Limited*. Over the course of its operation it was updated, renamed, and assigned to various trains, only to be retired in the 1950s as a common Pullman pool service car. Then things got interesting.

The car was acquired from Pullman by Lucius M. Beebe, one of America's genuine characters, in 1954. Beebe was a journalist for the *New York Herald Tribune* and the *San Francisco Chronicle,* a writer for *The New Yorker, Gourmet,* and *Town & Country* magazines, and author of more than thirty books. His accomplishments included the rare distinction of being kicked out of both Harvard and Yale, being named one

Virginia City
dining room.
John H. Kuehl

of the ten best-dressed men in America, and appearing on the cover of *Life* magazine. His literary output was characterized by acerbic wit, his lifestyle most conveniently described as extravagant, and his tastes in food as gourmet. All of this found expression in the *Virginia City*.

With his collaborator and longtime companion Charles Clegg, Beebe had the car overhauled in the shops of the Western Pacific Railroad in Sacramento, California. The interior was remodeled by the Hollywood set designer Robert Hanley (whose work included the set for *Auntie Mame*), reportedly at the cost of $350,000, into what present owners Wade and Julia Pellizzer label "Venetian Renaissance Baroque." Surround by opulence, with kitchen and crews quarters installed, Beebe and Clegg were spotted traveling all across the United States in the *Virginia City* until Beebe's death in 1966 at age 65. The car was eventually acquired by a group that included Wade Pellizzer in 1984. Wade and his wife Julia took sole title to the car in 1992, and have been working ever since to restore it to the ornate appearance of the Beebe-Clegg years.

Virginia City chef Katherine Mitchell says, "It seems I was born with the love of food and travel, and came to prize the knowledge that one could support the other." She put her passion and knowledge to work first in Alaska, where she cooked on fishing boats at a time when women were still a rarity in that industry. Her ambition fueled, she enrolled in the Western Culinary Institute in Portland, Oregon, and while there went onto work as a private live-in chef. Upon graduation, Kathy spent three years as chef on the private yacht *Kritter II,* where she earned the title "Queen of Utilization" for being able to use what was local and available in a variety of situations while sailing in the waters off South America and in the Caribbean. Now, after years as the owner and operator of a restaurant and resort, she has begun a new chapter in her culinary traveler's life, that of chef on *Virginia City*. "I enjoy plying my trade for a smaller, more intimate audience," she says. Lucius Beebe would no doubt approve.

Raspberry Vinaigrette

⅓ cup raspberry vinaigrette dressing
½ cup salad oil
1 scant tsp. Dijon mustard
1 Tbsp. sugar

salt to taste
2 tsp. poppy seeds
6 cups mixed greens

Before You Begin

You'll need: small bowl, whisk

Prep: 10 minutes (plus 1 hour to stand)

Yield: 6 servings

In a small bowl, combine first six ingredients and whisk to blend. Let stand 1 hour or more before using. Serve at room temperature. On individual plates, arrange greens and drizzle dressing over.

CHEF'S TIP: This dressing also goes well drizzled over or tossed with fresh fruit.

Pistachio Crusted Salmon

1½ lbs. boneless skinless salmon fillet
¼ cup salad oil
2 Tbsp. lemon juice
2 cloves garlic, minced
2 Tbsp. chopped fresh parsley, divided
2 tsp. chopped chives

salt and pepper to taste
1 cup unsalted pistachio nuts
½ cup plain bread crumbs
2 Tbsp. butter, melted
oil spray for sheet pan
Braised Cream Leeks (for service)

Before You Begin

You'll need: 1-gallon freezer bag, food processor, sheet pan

Preheat oven to 425°F.

Prep: 20 minutes (plus 1 hour 15 minutes to marinate)

Cook: 10 minutes

Yield: 8 servings

Cut salmon across grain into 2-inch fingers. Put oil, lemon juice, garlic, 1 tablespoon chopped parsley, chives, salt, and pepper in a 1-gallon freezer bag, and massage to mix. Add salmon pieces and gently turn to coat. Marinate at room temperature for 15 minutes, then refrigerate for 1 hour. Meanwhile, in a food processor, combine pistachios, bread crumbs, and parsley, and pulse until evenly chopped and combined. (**NOTE:** Texture can range from coarse to fine, depending on personal preferences.) Coat salmon pieces with nut/crumb mixture and place on oil sprayed sheet pan. Drizzle with melted butter. Place in a 425°F oven to bake 10 minutes. To serve, arrange a bed of Braised Creamed Leeks and place salmon on top. Garnish with fresh dill or lemon twist.

CHEF'S TIPS: (1) This recipe can also serve as an entrée. Cut salmon into 4- to 6-ounce filet portions, and bake 15 to 20 minutes instead of 10 minutes. (2) "At home and on the train, I line my sheet and roasting pans with foil, then spray with cooking oil. Cleanup is a snap, and you use less water."

Braised Creamed Leeks

Before You Begin

You'll need: 12-inch sauté pan with cover

Prep: 20 minutes

Cook: 30 minutes

Yield: servings.

8 leeks, 1½" diameter

1 cup chicken stock

½ cup white wine

2 oz. butter

sugar to taste

salt and pepper to taste

½ cup heavy cream

Trim leeks using white and light green parts only, julienne, and wash well. In a 12-inch sauté pan over medium-high heat, bring stock, wine, and butter to a boil, and season with sugar, salt, and pepper to taste. Reduce heat to simmer, add leeks, and cover to cook until leeks are just tender, about 30 minutes. Remove leeks, raise heat, and simmer uncovered to reduce liquid by ½. Adjust seasonings, add cream, and cook until sauce thickens.

CHEF'S TIP: If burner space is at a premium, use an ovenproof pot and put leeks in seasoned liquid in a preheated 350°F oven to cook for 30 minutes.

Pork Tenderloin Roulade with Lemon Sage

Before You Begin

You'll need: plastic wrap, mallet or cleaver, food processor, linen towel, twine or skewers, large skillet, 3-quart saucepan

Preheat oven to 200°F.

Prep: 30 minutes (plus 1 hour to chill roulades)

Cook: 40 minutes

Yield: 8 servings

3 cups clean, dry spinach

4 lbs. pork tenderloin

¼ cup fresh sage, chopped

zest of 2 lemons

4 cloves garlic, chopped

salt and pepper

1 cup dry white wine

oil to coat skillet

1 14½-oz. can chicken stock

2 tsp. lemon juice

Carefully wash spinach, pat dry, and set aside. Slice tenderloin lengthwise, cutting to, but not through, the opposite side. Lay flat, again cut each half in the same manner, and lay open. With the tenderloin opened flat, cover with plastic wrap and pound with a meat mallet or the flat side of a cleaver to ½-inch thickness. Remove plastic and sprinkle with salt. Combine spinach, sage, lemon zest, and garlic in food processor. Pulse until chopped fine and well combined. Put mixture in clean linen towel and twist to remove excess liquid. Spread mixture over the surface of the pounded tenderloin, leaving ½ inch border around edge. Roll "jellyroll" style, starting on long side. Tie roulade at 2-inch intervals or weave with skewers to secure closure. If possible, chill roulades for 1 hour. Then, in a large skillet over medium-high heat, heat oil. Brown roulades, turning until all sides are well browned, about 3 minutes per side. Add wine and stock and bring to a boil. Reduce heat, cover, and simmer

20 minutes. Remove roulades to warm oven. Simmer pan juice until reduced to ¾ cup. Add lemon juice, and adjust seasoning. To serve, remove string or skewers from pork and slice at ½-inch intervals on slight diagonal. Arrange on Golden Orzo. Drizzle with pan juice. Accompany with asparagus (see pages 240, 248, and 258).

Golden Orzo

1 16-oz. pkg. orzo
½ tsp. turmeric (substitute: pinch of saffron)

1 red bell pepper, diced fine

Cook orzo according to package directions, but add turmeric or saffron to water while cooking to achieve color. Add red bell pepper and stir to mix and heat through.

Chocolate Kahlúa Mousse Torte

12 oz. chocolate chips
4 oz. butter
6 eggs, separated
½ cup granulated sugar, divided
pinch cream of tartar
¾ cup whipping cream

1 envelope unflavored gelatin
¼ cup water
1 cup + Kahlúa, divided
2 boxes Trader Joe's Ladyfingers (or similar)

Before You Begin

You'll need: large mixing bowl and saucepan to hold it over boiling water, 2 small mixing bowls, electric mixer, small saucepan, pie tin, 10-inch springform pan

Prep: 45 minutes (plus 4+ hours to chill and set)

Yield: 12–16 servings.

In a large heat-proof mixing bowl over water simmering in a saucepan large enough to support the bowl, add chocolate chips and butter to melt. Stir to mix, then set aside to cool slightly. In a small mixing bowl, beat egg whites with ¼ cup sugar and pinch of cream of tartar until solids dissolve and the mixture is firm, then set aside. In another small bowl, beat cream with remaining sugar until firm. In a small saucepan over low heat, dissolve gelatin in ¼ cup water and heat until clear. Stir egg yolks into cooled but still liquid chocolate. Add gelatin. Fold in one-half of meringue to lighten. Fold in whipped cream and remaining meringue until all are incorporated. Refrigerate while preparing crust. To finish, pour Kahlúa in a pie tin, about ½ inch, and roll ladyfingers in liqueur until moist. Using a 10-inch springform pan, trim ladyfingers so they are even with the top edge of pan. Line sides of pan with ladyfingers standing vertically. Use trimmings and remaining ladyfingers to line bottom of pan. Fill pan with mousse and chill until firm, 4 hours minimum. To serve, drizzle individual slices with Kahlúa and garnish with whipped cream and mint.

Everyone's Favorites

Chefs everywhere have a specialty that draws raves. The favorable reaction of guests can take the form of empty plates being returned to the kitchen, praise uttered more as a murmur than a sentence, or a request for the recipe. Here are a handful of such menu items, ones encountered "in the cars," from prize-winners to a presidential candidate's request.

This item from *My Old Kentucky Dinner Train* (page 155) proved so popular that it was printed up on a card to be picked up by passengers departing the train. Highly seasoned, these croutons go great with soups or salads.

Hearty Croutons

Before You Begin

You'll need: small pan, small bowl, large bowl, cookie press

Preheat oven to 350°F.

Prep: 10 minutes

Cook: 10–15 minutes

Yield: 4 cups

3 Tbsp. garlic salt

1 tsp. celery seed

2 Tbsp. basil, chopped fine

1 Tbsp. parsley flakes

2 tsp. oregano

½ tsp. black pepper

¼ tsp. cayenne pepper

¼ cup butter, melted

1 loaf French or Italian bread, coarsely broken into ½" pieces

In a small bowl, combine the first seven (dry) ingredients and mix. In a small pan over medium heat, melt butter. Place bread pieces in a large bowl, drizzle butter over, and toss to coat. Continue tossing lightly and sprinkle with dry ingredients. Spread the pieces on a cookie sheet and bake at 350°F until brown and crisp, about 10 to 15 minutes.

Paul's Special Salad Dressing

The beauty of this recipe, a creation of Paul Goodmundson while on board the Montana Daylight *(see page 23), is that it calls for ingredients you no doubt have on hand. Use it for planned, and unplanned, events. "It never fails to draw compliments and requests for the recipe," says Chef Paul.*

CHEF'S TIP: Try to stay one meal ahead prep-wise. Use downtime during cooking for one meal, say as you wait while a reduction simmers, to begin preparing items for your next meal.

Before You Begin	1 apple of any variety, pared, cored	1 cup rice vinegar
You'll need: food processor	1 onion, whatever is on board	3 cups canola oil
Prep: 5 minutes	1 clove garlic, peeled	2 Tbsp. curry powder
Yield: 1 quart +		salt and pepper to taste

Place all ingredients in a food processor and blend until smooth.

BNSF: A Prize-Winning Adaptation

Good chefs will always look for ways to adapt the work of others to their own unique situation and style. So it is with Dave Nixon, whose work can usually be found on the business cars of the Burlington Northern Santa Fe Railroad. There, he has converted the company's Roasted Tenderloin of Beef (see page 239) into a main course that won him the blue ribbon at the Kansas State Barbecue Contest. "The key," he says, "is to replace the flavor lost when you trim the fat off of the tenderloin. I use the highest quality olive oil for this. And don't be concerned about the finished appearance. You're going to look at the charred surface and say, 'Oh my God, what have I done?' But when you slice the tenderloin, you will find a beautiful, rare, flavorful piece of beef that invites and pleases everyone who samples it."

Roasted Tenderloin of Beef

Before You Begin	¾ cup teriyaki sauce	olive oil
You'll need: 1-gallon freezer bag, roasting pan rack, aluminum foil	¾ cup Worcestershire sauce	4 cloves garlic, minced
	4 lbs. beef tenderloin, silverskin removed	1 Tbsp. black pepper, ground
Preheat electric grill or charcoal coals to hot.		1 Tbsp. Lawry's seasoned salt
Prep: 15 minutes (plus 4 hours to overnight to marinate)		
Cook: 60 minutes		
Yield: 8 servings		

In a 1-gallon freezer bag, combine teriyaki sauce and Worcestershire sauce. Immerse the tenderloin in the marinade and rotate to ensure it is coated on all sides. Set aside at least 4 hours to marinate, overnight if possible. Remove tenderloin and set on a roasting rack to drain, rub with olive oil, then season heavily with garlic, pepper, and seasoned salt. On an electric or charcoal grill warmed to hot, place tenderloin and cook for 5 minutes per side (allowing four sides, a total of 20 minutes). Remove tenderloin, wrap loosely in aluminum foil, and let stand 5 minutes before slicing. To serve, slice tenderloin using three medallions per serving and place the medallions over bordelaise sauce. Garnish with sprig of fresh rosemary. Serve hot.

RailCruise America's Executive Chef, Michael Slay, reports this to be the most requested recipe on his train (see pages 169–170). He reminds guests that it is a substantial portion. On the train, one order is usually adequate for a party of four:

Chicken Phyllo Enchiladas

Before You Begin

You'll need: 2
1-quart saucepans,
strainer, medium
skillet, paper towels,
2 medium bowls,
heavy large skillet,
wide pastry brush,
sharp knife, sheet
pan

Preheat oven to
375°F, then 350°F.

Prep: 2 hours (plus
1 hour for filling to
cool)

Cook: 15 minutes

Yield: 4 servings

½ cup fine diced, peeled carrot

1½ cups medium diced,
    peeled yellow potato

¼ cup whole milk

⅓ cup + 3 Tbsp. olive oil,
    divided

1 cup medium diced white
    onion

1 cup medium diced red bell
    pepper

1 tsp. balsamic vinegar

2 tsp. granulated sugar,
    divided

2 lbs. boneless, skinless
    chicken breasts

3 Tbsp. fresh lime juice

1½ tsp. fine sea salt

1½ cups shredded Monterrey
    Jack cheese

½ tsp. ground black pepper

1½ tsp. chili powder

1½ tsp. paprika

1½ tsp. granulated garlic

½ cup chopped fresh cilantro

⅔ cup butter, melted

1 pkg. #2 thick sheets phyllo
    dough (See NOTE)

NOTE: #2 thick phyllo is much easier to work with than the thin phyllo usually found in supermarkets. It can be purchased at a Greek import store or specialty market.

In a 1-quart saucepan over high heat, bring 2 cups water to a boil, add diced carrot, and simmer until tender, about 4 minutes. Strain and set aside. In another 1-quart saucepan, bring potatoes in water to cover to a boil, reduce heat, and cook until soft through, about 10 minutes. Drain liquid from potatoes, add milk, mash as for mashed potatoes, and set aside to cool. In a medium skillet over medium heat, heat 1 tablespoon of olive oil and add onion and red bell pepper to sauté, turning frequently with a spatula, for about 3 minutes. Add balsamic vinegar and 1 teaspoon sugar and continue to sauté until nicely browned and caramelized, about 5 more minutes, then set aside. Pat chicken dry with paper towels and place in a medium bowl. Add 2 tablespoons olive oil, then lime juice, and gently toss. Add 1 teaspoon sugar, the salt, black pepper, chili powder, paprika and garlic, toss to coat, and let rest 10 minutes. In a heavy large skillet over medium-high heat, heat ⅓ cup of olive oil. Add the marinated chicken breasts and cook on both sides until dark brown and slightly caramelized, about 5 to 6 minutes per side. Transfer chicken to an ovenproof dish, discard marinade, and place chicken in a 375°F oven to cook through, about 7 minutes. Let chicken rest 15 minutes, then dice in ¾-inch cubes and place in a medium-size bowl. Add diced cooked carrots, shredded cheese, and cilantro, and toss lightly. Then add cooled mashed potatoes to bind all ingredients and refrigerate 1 hour to firm up.

Remove phyllo from refrigerator. On a large work surface, unroll phyllo and lay out two sheets side by side, narrow edge facing you. With a wide pastry brush lightly coat both sheets with melted butter. Place one more sheet over each buttered sheet and lightly cover with butter again. Continue this process until you have two stacks of phyllo four sheets thick. Remove filling from refrigerator. With your hands make a firm roll of filling about 1¼ inches in diameter across the edge of phyllo facing you. Repeat this process halfway up the phyllo sheet giving you a total of four rows of filling. With the tip of a small knife slice the phyllo across just in front of the inside row of filling. Sprinkle caramelized peppers and onions next to the filling. Roll each one tightly to form four logs. Brush with melted butter and cut each in half forming eight rolls. Cut each one in half again, this time on a sharp angle (bias). Place rolls seam side down on a sheet pan and bake at 350°F until golden brown, about 15 minutes. (**NOTE:** Can be grilled or smoked with cherry chips.) Remove from oven for assembly.

To serve, place one piece of enchilada in the center of a 9-inch plate. Lean a second piece across the first with the tip of the bias pointing up. Ladle about 1½ ounces Ancho Chili Cumin Cream Sauce over the top. Garnish with your choice of diced green onion, fresh cilantro sprigs, fine diced tomato diamonds, toasted shelled pepitas (green pumpkin seeds), and/or fried thin flour tortilla strips.

Ancho Chili Cumin Cream Sauce

Before You Begin

You'll need: heavy skillet, small bowl, strainer, aluminum foil, 2-quart saucepan, blender

Prep: 35 minutes

Cook: 25 minutes

Yield: 3 cups

1 dried ancho chili	2 cups heavy cream, divided
½ cup hot water	1 tsp. paprika
1 fresh poblano chili	1 tsp. ground cumin
2 Tbsp. canola oil	½ tsp. chili powder
¼ cup diced onion	½ tsp. fine sea salt
1 Tbsp. crushed fresh garlic	1 Tbsp. cornstarch
⅓ cup white wine	2 Tbsp. cold water

Remove stem, seeds and membranes from ancho chili and coarsely chop. Over medium-high heat in a dry heavy skillet, toast the ancho chili, stirring and turning, for 1 minute. In a small bowl, add toasted chilies to hot water and soak 30 minutes, then drain and set aside, reserving liquid. On an open gas flame or under a broiler, char poblano chili, turning frequently, until skin blisters and turns black on all sides. Wrap in aluminum foil for 15 minutes, then, under cold running water, remove burnt skin, stem and open to wash out seeds of chili, then dice and set a side. In a 2-quart saucepan over medium heat, heat canola oil and add onions to cook until translucent, about 3 minutes. Add garlic and stir for 1 minute more. Add white wine and ancho chili, then simmer for 3 minutes. Remove from heat and pour mixture into a blender. Add 1 cup cold heavy cream, reserved ancho chili liquid, diced poblano chili, paprika, cumin, chili powder, and salt. Blend until smooth. Return blended chilies to the saucepan, add second cup of cream, and bring sauce to a simmer. In a small bowl, dissolve cornstarch in cold water and whisk mixture into simmering sauce. Remove from heat.

Milwaukee Road Deluxe Muffins

Before You Begin

You'll need: 12-cup muffin pan, large mixing bowl

Preheat oven to 425°F.

Prep: 10 minutes

Cook: 20 minutes

Yield: 12 muffins

There was a time, up until 1971, when the Class I railroads wooed passengers to their trains with unique food offerings. This specialty of the Chicago, Milwaukee, St. Paul & Pacific Railroad was one enticement. A whole-grain muffin, it also met Southern Pacific Executive Chef Paul Reiss's suggestion for a successful menu for long-distance travelers (see page 218).

1 cup sifted enriched flour

½ tsp. salt

3 Tbsp. baking powder

¼ cup brown sugar

¼ cup shortening

1 cup Pettijohn's cereal, uncooked (See NOTE)

1 egg, beaten

1 cup milk

NOTE: Today Pettijohn's cereal goes by the name "Mother's 100% Natural Whole Wheat Hot Rolled Wheat Cereal," available in supermarkets.

Grease muffin tin cups and set aside. Sift together flour, salt, and baking powder. Stir in brown sugar. Cut in shortening until mixture resembles cornmeal. Add Pettijohn's cereal and blend thoroughly. Add beaten egg and milk, stirring only until moistened. Fill greased muffin cups ⅔ full. Bake in a 425°F oven until done, about 20 minutes.

VARIATIONS: Nut Muffins: Add ½ cup chopped nut meats with Pettijohn's; Raisin Muffins: Add ½ cup raisins with Pettijohn's.

Max & Me Catering: From the Campaign Train

www.maxandmecatering.com

Max Hansen, chef and owner of Max & Me Catering in Doylestown, Pennsylvania, drew an unusual assignment for his staff during the 2000 United States presidential campaign: To work on the Bush-Cheney campaign train. Known as a whistle-stop tour, wherein candidates visit cities along a railroad's right-of-way, pausing for photo opportunities and to stump from the business car platform at the rear of the train, it is time-honored a part of the American political tradition. The close 2000 campaign made America's industrial heartland a battleground. To kick off his campaign, George W. Bush toured key Midwestern states by train following the Republican Convention in Philadelphia. While the candidates' own staffs prepared their meals, Max & Me Catering fed members of the print and broadcast media, Secret Service agents, the campaign staff, and railroad employees.

In the process, the thirteen-member Max & Me crew had to adjust to all the problems associated with cooking on a train: sudden, unexpected movements by the kitchen; narrow and cramped work space; twenty-hour work days; the absolute necessity to plan for, order, then pack everything to be used throughout the three-day assignment; and the ability to think fast and adapt to constantly changing circumstances.

From the experience, Max Hansen identifies this as a favorite of those he served during the trip, including, no doubt, the campaigners, who enjoyed some of his high speed cuisine at the rear of the sixteen-car train.

Jumbo Lump Crab Cakes with Mango Butter Sauce

Before You Begin

You'll need: food processor, medium mixing bowl, medium skillet, cookie sheet

Preheat oven to 350°F.

Prep: 15 minutes (plus 1 hour for mixture to chill)

Cook: 20 minutes

Yield: 30 "mini" or 6 large cakes

½ lb dry scallops (see NOTE)
½ cup heavy cream
¼ cup mayonnaise
1 tsp. Creole mustard
1 tsp. Worcestershire sauce
1 tsp. Tabasco, more if you like
kosher salt and fresh black pepper to taste

1 lb. jumbo lump crab, picked clean of shell pieces
1½ cups panko Japanese bread crumbs
3 oz. sweet butter
cilantro oil (to garnish)

NOTE: "Dry" scallops are fresh off the boat and unprocessed. Substitute the best fresh scallops you can find.

Combine scallops and cream in the bowl of a food processor and process until smooth. Place scallop mixture in a mixing bowl, add mayonnaise, mustard, Worcestershire sauce, and Tabasco, and mix well. Season with salt and pepper. Fold the crab into the mixture, being careful to leave the crab lumps on the large side. Chill mixture approximately 1 hour, then form into 30 small "mini" cakes or 6 large cakes, and cover with bread crumbs. In a medium skillet over medium heat, melt butter and sauté crab cakes in batches until golden brown, turning once, about 3 minutes per side depending on size. When all the cakes are sautéed, place them on a cookie sheet and heat in a 350°F oven until hot, about 7 to 10 minutes. Serve immediately.

NOTE: Crab cakes can be sautéed ahead of time, refrigerated, and reheated right before serving. Do not hold for more than 1 day.

Mango Butter Sauce

Before You Begin

You'll need: food processor, 1½-quart saucepan, 2-quart saucepan, strainer, blender

Prep: 15 minutes

Cook: 10 minutes

Yield: 3 cups

1 large or 2 medium mangoes, very ripe

1 large jalapeño, seeds and membrane removed, diced fine

1 small bunch cilantro, thoroughly cleaned

6 Tbsp. sweet butter

salt and pepper to taste

Reserve 6 beautiful cilantro sprigs for garnish, then chop remainder fine. Peel mango and remove pulp to a food processor, then pulse until completely smooth. In a 1½-quart saucepan over low heat, combine mango puree and jalapeño and heat through. Whisk butter into mixture until completely incorporated. Season with salt and pepper, and chopped cilantro, and stir to mix and heat through. To serve, place a spoonful of sauce on the plate, top with one large or five small crab cakes, and spoon a little more sauce around the cake(s). Drizzle warm Cilantro Oil around outer edge.

Cilantro Oil

1 bunch cilantro, thoroughly cleaned, large stems removed

1 cup olive oil

In a 2-quart saucepan bring sufficient water to cover cilantro to a boil. Blanch cilantro in boiling water 1 minute, strain to remove water, and place in a blender while still warm. Puree cilantro, then drizzle olive oil in and continue to puree until a smooth green color presents. Use warm.

Dinner Trains

When Amtrak took over the operation of passenger trains in the United States on May 1, 1971, an entrepreneur saw an opportunity to launch a new type of restaurant: the dinner train. Charles Crocker, a fourth-generation descendant of the Charles Crocker who was one of the "Big Four" who built the transcontinental Central Pacific Railroad, owned the Sierra Railroad Company, which operated ninety miles east of San Francisco. In 1972 Crocker granted the concession business on the line to one Richard R. ("Dick") Reynolds, who then launched the first dinner train. He promoted it with the catchy name *The Supper Chief*. Reynolds ran a mixed fleet of food service cars that could feed as many as 240 people out of Jamestown, California, to Oakdale on Saturday nights. There were two seatings on each run (diners out became passengers back, and vice versa). The first year saw six trains operate April to September. In 1973 there were ten *Supper Chiefs,* and that growth continued throughout the train's brief history. The end came in 1979, before most of today's dinner trains even started, when ownership and the priorities of the railroad changed. In that last year, twenty-nine *Supper Chiefs* ran.

Reynolds also innovated the "ride 'n' dine" concept with the *Twilight Limited,* a train that ran from Jamestown to Cooperstown and back from 1973 to 1979. Passengers were served drinks and hors d'oeuvres on board, then, when the train returned to Jamestown, were greeted by a roast beef dinner. The Sierra Railroad today operates the *Sierra Railroad Golden Sunset Dinner Train.*

Today, dinner trains can fall into one of several categories. Some operate year-round and on a regular schedule, such as every Saturday evening, or every Friday and Saturday for dinner and Sunday for brunch. Others operate year-round, but on a varying schedule, such as on Valentine's Day, Mother's Day, and the like. Still others operate on a seasonal basis, with either regularly scheduled or periodic trips. Food service varies, too. Some trains offer food cooked on board, others offer meals catered on to the train by a cooperating hotel, restaurant, or catering service, and still others take passengers to an eatery, where they detrain, eat, and reboard to return to the station. Here, in alphabetical order, is a sampling of the fine meals you can expect to encounter on today's dinner trains. Each train included here prepares and serves these and other dishes on board.

First stop, the *Café Lafayette Dinner Train*. Its operation is typical of dinner trains. The cuisine is a standout.

Café Lafayette Dinner Train

www.nhdinnertrain.com

"We want your meal to be a surprise," says Leslie Holloway, who, with Lance Burak, owns and operates the *Café Lafayette Dinner Train*. "Most people come to enjoy the train, but get their socks blown off by the food." Take it from one who has stood barefooted in New Hampshire, Leslie and Lance achieve that goal, and then some.

The *Café Lafayette Dinner Train* operates from a location on Route 112 in North Woodstock, New Hampshire, just off Interstate 93 at Exit 32, in the heart of the White Mountain National Forest. The train consists of three lovingly and elegantly renovated rail cars, an ex–New York Central 1924 Pullman Standard day coach rebuilt into the dining car *Indian Waters,* an ex–Missouri Pacific/Illinois Central 1952 Pullman Standard dome car rebuilt (see page 133) as the dining car *Granite Eagle,* and an ex–Canadian National long-distance coach rebuilt into the *Algonquin,* an open and flexibly configured car that serves corporate functions, weddings, and private parties. An ex–U.S. Army Kitchen car, built in 1953, and the ex–Canadian National/VIA Rail Canada sleeper *Enterprise,* now used as an entrance car, gift shop, and partial dining car, complete the set. The nearby Hobo Railroad, an excursion operation, contributes locomotives to power the train.

The boarding area is a siding off the ex–Boston & Maine right-of-way into Lincoln that once served a lumber mill. A twenty-mile round-trip excursion goes through the picturesque Pemigewasset River valley, past lush forests and open fields surrounded by mountains whose faces reveal the source of New Hampshire's nickname—the Granite State. But it is the food that makes this dinner train so exceptional.

"We want you to enjoy a restaurant experience, where you can walk in and see what's good," says Leslie. "We have our own herb garden and grow our own vegetables and edible flowers, so the emphasis is on what's fresh. We don't have a pre-printed menu." The five-course dinner menu changes regularly to feature a choice of three entrées. "Cooking on board and to order gives us the ability to assure high quality and outstanding presentation. We employ three to five chefs and four to eight waitstaff to carry that off." The train can accommodate as many as 152 guests. A wide assortment of companionable wines from Europe and California are available to accompany the meal.

How did two pleasant, personable, normal-appearing adults get involved in such an arduous and complicated undertaking? Lance answers, "Between us, Leslie and I have over forty years in the restaurant business. We wanted to open a restaurant near here. I grew up in Lincoln, and Leslie has lived here for twenty years." To which Leslie adds, "We both hired on with the former owner of the *Café Lafayette* as part time help. But as our scheduled hours expanded, and the owner began to burn out from the business, he offered to let us buy him out at a price that was too good to turn down."

The *Café Lafayette Dinner Train* is a seasonal operation that generally begins running on weekends in mid-May, expands to a four-days-a-week schedule, July through the end of October and the wrap-up of the fall foliage season.

For a gourmand, a rail fan, one who enjoys scenic travel, or an all-three-in-one, a visit to the *Café Lafayette Dinner Train* will not be forgotten. Just be sure to carry spare footwear. For it is entirely likely that part of the fond memory will be to have had one's socks blown off.

Café Pâté

Stage 1

2 oz. unsalted butter	1½ tsp. ground thyme
1 medium onion, diced	1½ tsp. dried basil
1 Tbsp. dry ground rosemary	½ tsp. ground nutmeg
1½ tsp. salt	1¼ lbs. chicken livers, fresh or frozen,
1½ tsp. white pepper	trimmed, rinsed, and patted dry

Before You Begin

You'll need: large ovenproof skillet, food processor, pâté molds

Preheat oven to 400°F.

Prep: 1 hour (plus 24 hours to chill)

Cook: 30 minutes

Yield: 2½ pounds

Melt butter in large ovenproof skillet over medium heat. Combine next seven ingredients and sauté until onion is tender and translucent, about 3 minutes. Increase heat to high, add chicken livers, and brown, stirring frequently, until well coated with seasonings, about 5 to 10 minutes. Place skillet in 400°F oven and bake until livers are barely pink in the center, about 10 minutes. Cool completely, then go to Stage 2.

CHEF'S TIP: Be sure chicken livers are well chilled. Even the slightest warmth will crack the butter.

Stage 2

14 oz. unsalted butter

2 Tbsp. Cognac or bourbon

2 Tbsp. dry sherry or dry vermouth

2 Tbsp. fresh parsley, chopped

2 Tbsp. fresh dried bread crumbs

cooked chicken livers from Stage 1

Whip butter in food processor until smooth and creamy. Add remaining ingredients and process until very smooth, but not "broken." Transfer to desired molds. Refrigerate twenty-four hours. Serve with croustades, crackers, or crostini, accompanied by sweet gherkins, slivered red onion, variously colored bell pepper, capers, and the like.

NOTE: Holds well and can be frozen.

Mushroom Turnovers

Before You Begin

You'll need: medium sauté pan, cookie sheet, parchment

Preheat oven to 425°F.

Prep: 45 minutes (plus time for filling to cool)

Cook: 15 minutes

Yield: 48 puffs

3 Tbsp. butter

1 medium onion, diced fine

½ lb. fresh mushrooms, diced fine

1 tsp. salt

¼ tsp. thyme leaves

¼ cup sour cream

2 Tbsp. flour

puff pastry sheets

1 egg beaten

2 tsp. water

In a medium sauté pan over medium heat, melt butter and sauté onion, then mushrooms until tender. Remove from heat and gently stir in salt, thyme, sour cream, and flour. Cool completely. Cut puff pastry into 3- or 4-inch squares. Make a wash of beaten egg and water. Spoon a generous teaspoon of mushroom mixture onto puff pastry squares, brush two edges with egg wash, fold into a triangle and crimp with a fork. Place on cookie sheet which is covered with parchment, brush tops with egg wash and bake at 425°F for 12 to 15 minutes or until golden brown.

Fresh Strawberry Sorbet

2 qt. fresh strawberry puree
1 bottle champagne
1 qt. water
¼ cup lemon juice

1 cup light Karo syrup (more or less to
  taste)
mint leaves (for garnish)

Before You Begin

You'll need: large bowl, ice cream machine

Prep: 30 minutes (plus time to chill and freeze)

Yield: 1 gallon

Blend all ingredients together in a large bowl. Chill completely, allowing 1 to 2 hours. Process mixture through an ice cream machine and rest in the freezer at least 1 hour before scooping to serve. Garnish with mint leaf.

Red Leaf and Mesclun Salad à la Café

red leaf lettuce
mesclun or spring mix greens
caramelized almond slices

3 whole segments Mandarin orange
red wine vinaigrette
croutons

Before You Begin

You'll need: lettuce spinner

Prep: 15 minutes

Yield: 1 serving

Wash and spin the greens. Rechill if not to be used immediately. Individually plate greens. Sprinkle with almonds. Garnish with Mandarin orange segments. Drizzle with red wine vinaigrette and top with croutons.

Red Wine Vinaigrette

3 cups olive oil
1 cup red wine vinegar
¼ cup finely diced onion
2 Tbsp. chopped chives
1½ Tbsp. dill weed, fresh or dried
1½ tsp. garlic, fresh chopped or dried
  minced

3 Tbsp. mustard seed
2 tsp. salt
½ tsp. white pepper
2 Tbsp. sugar (substitute: honey)

Before You Begin

You'll need: medium bowl, whisk

Prep: 20 minutes

Yield: approximately 1 quart

In a medium bowl, combine all ingredients, mix well, and allow to infuse for several hours before serving. Mix or shake well again before serving.

Caramelized Almonds

Before You Begin

You'll need: small sauté pan, parchment or waxed paper

Prep: 5 minutes

Cook: 15 minutes.

Yield: approximately 8 portions

3 oz. butter

½ lb. sliced almonds

½ cup granulated sugar

In a small sauté pan over low heat, melt butter and add almonds, stirring to coat. Slowly raise heat to medium to gently toast. When about half of the almonds are lightly golden, add sugar a little at a time, stirring or tossing often. Almonds are done when sugar has caramelized, about 3 minutes. Spread out onto parchment or wax paper to cool.

Pork Tenderloin with Blueberry Salsa

Before You Begin

You'll need: large plastic storage bag, roasting pan, meat thermometer

Preheat oven to 425°F.

Prep: 5 minutes (plus 4–12 hours to marinate)

Cook: 45 minutes

Yield: 6 8-ounce servings

4 lbs. whole pork tenderloin, completely trimmed

Pork Marinade

Blueberry Pecan Salsa

fresh sage leaves

In a large plastic storage bag, place tenderloin and pork marinade and fold to coat. Refrigerate 4 to 12 hours. Remove tenderloin from marinade, place in a roasting pan and roast, uncovered, at 425°F to desired degree of doneness (internal temperature of 145°F to USDA-recommended 160°F), about 45 minutes.

NOTE: Pork can be grilled. To serve, slice into medallions ¼ inch to ½ inch thick. Fan onto hot plate and top with Blueberry Pecan Salsa. Garnish with fresh sage leaf.

Pork Marinade

Before You Begin

You'll need: small bowl or jar, whisk

Prep: 15 minutes

Yield: approximately 2 cups

1 cup olive oil

½ cup Pinot Noir (or other red wine)

¼ cup fresh orange juice

2 Tbsp. orange zest

2 Tbsp. parsley, chopped

1 Tbsp. dried tarragon

salt and fresh ground pepper to taste

In a small bowl or jar, combine all ingredients. Allow to stand for 1 hour or more. Mix or shake before using.

Blueberry Pecan Salsa

¼ lb. butter
½ lb. pecan halves
dash salt

1 cup maple syrup (approximately)
1 pint fresh blueberries

Before You Begin

You'll need:
medium sauté pan

Prep: 15 minutes

Cook: 15 minutes

Yield:
approximately 1
quart

In medium sauté pan over medium heat, melt butter, add pecan halves, and toss to coat. Sprinkle with salt and lightly brown the pecans, about 5 minutes. While still hot toss with blueberries taking care to avoid crushing berries. Add maple syrup until mixture is of desired consistency and heated through. (**NOTE:** Chef recommends "loose," not thick, consistency.) Remove from heat. May be gently reheated (do not simmer or boil) or served at room temperature. (**NOTE:** Honey or honey and applesauce can be substituted for maple syrup to achieve desired consistency.)

Asparagus with Sauce Maltaise

5 pieces fresh, pencil-thin asparagus
salt and pepper

Sauce Maltaise

Before You Begin

You'll need:
asparagus steamer

Prep: 5 minutes

Cook: 2–3 minutes

Yield: 1 serving

Rinse asparagus and leave wet. Meanwhile, bring water in asparagus steamer to a boil. Place asparagus in perforated basket and season with salt and pepper. Steam, covered, 2 to 3 minutes until heated through but still crisp. Fan asparagus on the plate and drizzle with Sauce Maltaise. (**NOTE:** See page 240 if you do not have an asparagus steamer.)

Sauce Maltaise

3 large egg yolks
1 Tbsp. cold water
½ lb. clarified butter, melted

2 Tbsp. orange juice
2 tsp. orange zest
salt and cayenne pepper to taste

Before You Begin

You'll need:
stainless-steel bowl,
large bowl

Prep: 20 minutes

Yield: 2 cups

In a stainless steel bowl combine egg yolks and water and beat well. Place bowl over a hot (not boiling) water bath and beat mixture until thick and creamy. Remove from heat and continue beating while adding the butter very slowly. Use all the butter (thin with a little orange juice if necessary). Add orange juice and zest. Carefully add salt and cayenne to taste.

Polenta

Before You Begin

You'll need: large saucepan

Prep: 15 minutes

Cook: 30 minutes

Yield: 8 servings

1 Tbsp. butter or olive oil
¼ cup onion, minced
½ Tbsp. garlic, minced
1 cup milk
1 cup half & half or light cream
½ to ⅔ cup cornmeal (from less to more thick)

¼ cup Parmesan cheese
¾ cup red and green bell peppers, diced
2 Tbsp. parsley, chopped

In a large saucepan over medium heat, melt butter, add onion, and sauté until just tender, 2 to 3 minutes. Add garlic and sauté 2 or 3 minutes more. Add milk and half and half, and heat until scalded. Slowly add cornmeal, stirring constantly. Cook mixture over medium heat, stirring constantly until mixture thickens completely, about 15 to 20 minutes. Add Parmesan cheese, peppers, and parsley. Blend well and remove from heat.

NOTE: Polenta can be served as is or spread into a pan, cooled, then cut into shapes and reheated in a skillet or in an hot oven.

Chocolate à l'Orange Pie

Before You Begin

You'll need: beater, large mixing bowl, small mixing bowl

Prep: 30 minutes (plus 1 hour or more to freeze)

Yield: 18–24 servings

1 lb. cream cheese, softened
2 14-oz. cans Carnation sweetened condensed milk
2 cups semisweet chocolate chips, melted, cooled
1 cup evaporated milk

6 oz. orange juice concentrate, thawed
3 9-inch graham cracker pie crusts
½ pint whipping cream, whipped
orange slices and mint leaves (for garnish)

In a large mixing bowl, with beater set on Medium, beat cream cheese until smooth. Gradually add sweetened condensed milk, then chocolate, then evaporated milk, beating each time until smooth again. Add orange juice concentrate and continue beating for 1 minute at medium speed. Immediately pour into previously prepared graham cracker crusts. Place in freezer until frozen. Meanwhile, whip cream. Garnish each serving with an orange slice, mint leaf, and whipped cream.

The Making of a Dinner Train: Rebuilding the Granite Eagle

When Lance Burak and Leslie Holloway, the owners of the *Café Lafayette Dinner Train,* made a decision to acquire a dome car to enhance the rail dining experience they offer, they learned they faced a unique problem. "We needed a dome car that measured less than sixteen feet high," says Burack. "We travel over several short bridges along our route." Not to be denied, they searched for two and a half months, then found a privately owned Planetarium Car, formerly of the Missouri Pacific and Illinois Central railroads, in Kansas. Built by Pullman Standard in 1952, the rare car measured just 15 feet 8 inches. That was just the beginning of the adventure.

Lance traveled to Kansas to supervise the move of the car to Lincoln, New Hampshire, where he and a team that included Leslie Holloway, Chefs Scott Buckland and Doug Truson, and Tom Sabourn could restore it in the shops of the nearby Hobo Railroad, a tourist shortline. "It took us

TOP, LEFT: *Ex-Illinois Central dome car #2211, scheduled to become* Café Lafayette Dinner Train's *domed dining car* Granite Eagle, *sits forlorn—its windows broken out, the exterior corroded, the interior vandalized—on a siding in Kansas. Lance Burak* TOP, RIGHT: *The* Granite Eagle *awaits passengers after it emerges from the car shop in Lincoln, New Hampshire. Lance Burak* ABOVE, LEFT: *The interior of ex-Illinois Central dome car #2211 was heavily vandalized by intruders—stripped of its furnishings and appointments, its floor strewn with broken glass—before it was acquired by the* Café Lafayette Dinner Train. *Lance Burak* ABOVE, RIGHT: *The dining room of* Granite Eagle *today, ready for guests to sit down to a five-course dinner. Lance Burak*

six weeks to prep it for the move," says Lance. "We replaced air hoses, grab irons, steps, and re-lease levers, then lubricated the truck center pins and bearings. Finally, we had to weather- and vandal-proof it."

Arrangements were then made with seven different railroads to move it to Lincoln, New Hamp-shire. Lance went on, "I traveled ahead of it all the way. The freight haulers distrusted the couplers, so made it a rear-rider in case it came apart. I learned trainmasters weren't accustomed to dead-heading passenger cars, and car knockers weren't used to its length or brake system. I would arrive before the car to forewarn them. It made their life easier." Two weeks and some 1,500 miles later, it was delivered to Lincoln by the Springfield Terminal Railroad on December 20, 1995. Five and one-half months after it arrived, it emerged as the beautiful and stately *Granite Eagle*. "The only work we contracted was the carpet," he says with justifiable pride. Call ahead to make dinner reservations, and see if you can arrange with him to look over his photo albums of the project. These illustrations only hint at what it takes to restore a classic rail car to serviceable standards.

The Grand Traverse Dinner Train

www.dinnertrain.com

On arrival at the Traverse City, Michigan, depot at Eighth and Woodmere streets, built in 1926, one need not worry about missing *The Grand Traverse Dinner Train*. Graphic designer George Bartell, whose specialty is depicting things that go fast and whose fame is sufficient to have had a school of design—Bartellism—named after him, created the bold and distinctive color scheme. Richard Vartian, a noted creator of corporate logos—for Carnation, TRW, and Japan Disney, among others—conceived the emblem. The work of these men is displayed on a train set framed at each end by an F7A diesel locomotive. Each is followed by a pair of ex–Southern Pa-

Grand Traverse
Dinner Train
dining room.
Glen Graves
Photographs

cific Railroad articulated dining cars that seat fifty-six guests apiece. In the center, a baggage car converted into a kitchen car actually contains two complete kitchens to allow opening cars to guests as needed. Purchased as a set, the train has been completely restored from the floor up for dinner train service. Each dining car's name reflects the pleasing blend of predominate colors found in northern Michigan, from the dark and pale grays, cream, and silver in the *Silver Arrow* and *Moon Shadow,* to the dark and light greens in the *Emerald Velvet* and *Forest Magic.*

A year-round schedule of Saturday midday and evening departures is supplemented by additional trips that add up to as many as five dinner train departures each week in July and August. The Traverse City depot serves both as the headquarters for the train and as home to a Starbucks Espresso Bar in the waiting area. (Starbucks, open from 7:00 A.M. to 7:00 P.M., serves those waiting to board the train.) On departure, *The Grand Traverse Dinner Train* follows different routes through the scenic woods and waterways of the Grand Traverse Area at lunch and dinner. The ex–Chesapeake and Ohio and Pennsylvania Railroad lines are now owned by the Michigan Department of Transportation and operated by the Tuscola & Saginaw Bay Railway. Luncheon runs head east past Cherry Capitol Airport, turn north along the east arm of Grand Traverse Bay, and then east to Williamsburg and back for a two-hour, twenty-two-mile round trip. The thirty-three-mile, three-hour dinner run goes south along Boardman Lake, then east following the Boardman River and Pere Marquette State Forest to Kingsley, before returning.

A wine list at table, made up of twenty-two selections from premier vintners in Michigan, California, Washington, France, and Australia, hints at the unique dining experience ahead.

"The Orange and the Greens": Caesar Salad with Bacon Dressing

4 strips bacon, ⅛″ × 1″ julienne	1 Tbsp. light brown sugar	**Before You Begin**
2 Tbsp. Mandarin orange liquid	romaine lettuce	**You'll need:** small skillet, small mixing bowl, strainer, lettuce spinner, large mixing bowl
1 cup mayonnaise	baby spinach	
1 clove garlic, grated	1 11-oz. can Mandarin orange segments	
1¼ oz. Parmesan cheese	1 red bell pepper, roasted (see pages 170–171), ¼″ × 2″ julienne	**Prep:** 20 minutes
2 tsp. Dijon mustard		**Cook:** 5 minutes
2 Tbsp. red wine vinegar	36 salad croutons	**Yield:** 6 servings
½ tsp. finely ground black pepper	½ cup Parmesan cheese, freshly grated	
½ tsp. Worcestershire sauce		

In a small skillet over medium heat, gently render bacon to desired degree of doneness, and drain on paper towel. Strain Mandarin orange sections and retain liquid. In a small mixing bowl, combine first ten ingredients well. (**NOTE:** This dressing may be served immediately or held in refrigerator for up to 2 weeks.)

Wash lettuce and spinach well and spin dry. Shred romaine lettuce and mix with spinach in a large mixing bowl. Pour dressing over greens and toss to cover. Place salad portions on serving plates, top with Mandarin orange segments, pepper strips, croutons, and a sprinkle of Parmesan cheese.

Northwoods Spring Game Hen

Before You Begin

You'll need: baking sheet, parchment

Preheat oven to 450°F.

Prep: 10 minutes

Cook: 45 minutes

Yield: 8 servings

4 large Cornish game hens, halved, cleaned

Montreal seasoning for chicken

butter, softened

lemon juice

Rub hens with butter on all sides and sprinkle with Montreal seasoning and lemon juice. Place on a parchment covered baking sheet and roast in a 450°F oven for 15 minutes. Reduce oven to 350°F and cook until done, approximately more 30 minutes.

Sweet Potato, Portobello Mushroom Hash

Before You Begin

You'll need: cookie sheet with ½-inch sides, nonstick cooking spray, small mixing bowl, whisk, large mixing bowl

Preheat oven to 400°F.

Prep: 30 minutes

Cook: 60 minutes

Yield: 8 servings

½ cup olive oil

½ cup balsamic vinegar

½ cup maple syrup

2 tsp. Dijon mustard

½ cup fresh sage, chopped

1½ Tbsp. salt

2¼ Tbsp. black pepper

13 medium cloves garlic, minced

5 large leeks, halved lengthwise, rinsed, ½-inch dice

3 lbs. sweet potatoes, peeled, ½-inch dice

1½ lbs. portobello mushrooms, ½-inch dice

¾ lb. rutabaga, peeled, ½-inch dice

Spray cookie sheet with nonstick cooking spray. In a small mixing bowl, whisk together oil, vinegar, syrup, mustard, sage, salt, and pepper until blended. In a large mixing bowl, combine garlic and diced vegetables and toss with oil/vinegar mixture to coat each piece well. Spread vegetable mix over cookie sheet and roast until tender, approximately 1 hour, turning the sheet in the oven periodically to ensure even cooking.

"Golden Kisses": Dark Belgian Chocolate Cups Filled with Pumpkin Mousse and Drizzled with Caramelized Pears

Mousse

1¼ cups heavy cream, divided

5 eggs

¼ cup confectioners' sugar

1 cup solid-pack pumpkin

1¼ envelopes unflavored gelatin

½ Tbsp. pumpkin spice

¼ cup granulated sugar

2 Tbsp. light brown sugar

2 Tbsp. Kahlúa

8 large (2½" diameter × 1¾" deep) Belgian chocolate cups

Before You Begin

You'll need: medium mixing bowl, heat-proof glass bowl, whisk, large saucepan, large skillet

Prep: 20 minutes (plus 1½ hours for mousse to set)

Cook: 10 minutes

Yield: 6–8 servings

In a medium mixing bowl, beat 1 cup heavy cream until stiff, and set aside. Select a heat-proof glass bowl that will rest in a large saucepan of hot water over medium heat, with bottom submerged in water. In the glass bowl, whisk eggs and confectioners' sugar together and continue whisking until mixture forms soft peaks. Remove glass bowl from hot water and set aside. In heavy saucepan over medium heat, combine pumpkin, gelatin, spice, granulated sugar, brown sugar, ¼ cup cream, and Kahlúa. Stirring occasionally, heat until sugars have melted and mixture is well combined. Let mixture cool slightly and then turn it in to the egg/sugar mixture, beating lightly while doing so. Fold in whipped cream, blending fully. Refrigerate 1 to 1½ hours until mixture is set.

Caramelized Pears

1 Tbsp. butter

2 firm Bartlett pears, peeled, cored, cut into wedges

2 Tbsp. brandy

3 Tbsp. granulated sugar

1 Tbsp. light brown sugar

2 Tbsp. heavy cream

½ tsp. pure vanilla extract

In a large skillet over medium heat, melt butter and gently sauté pears until partially softened, about 3 minutes. Remove from heat, pour on brandy and, holding at arm's length, ignite and flambé until alcohol burns off. Return to heat. Add sugars and cook, stirring constantly, until sugar begins to caramelize. Stir in heavy cream and vanilla. Cook for 1 minute, then remove from heat and allow to cool slightly.

To serve, spoon chilled mousse into Belgian chocolate cups. (**NOTE:** This can be done in advance and refrigerated.) To finish, drizzle mousse-filled cups with warm pears and caramel sauce. Serve immediately.

Great Smoky Mountains Railroad

www.gsmr.com

The Great Smoky Mountains Railroad operates out of Dillsboro, North Carolina, on fifty-three miles of track that traverses two tunnels and fifteen bridges through the beautiful Carolina side of the Great Smoky Mountains. Dinner trains customarily run every Saturday evening year-round, except from late December to early January, Murder Mystery Trains run every other Friday night, and numerous special trains featuring jazz, a wine tasting, a Caribbean menu, or a local "celebrity chef" menu, even a Harley celebration run throughout the year.

For its passenger schedule, the railroad operates four diesel-electric locomotives and a Baldwin-built steam locomotive, Number 1702, which saw service in the Army during World War II. The train's club cars and dining cars have been beautifully restored to appear as they did when they ran in such famous trains as the *Silver Meteor* from New York to Miami, the *Dixie Flyer* between Cincinnati and Tampa, and the *Champion* from New York to Tampa. It also provides rail service to local industry, business, and agriculture. Today the line is becoming the "Hollywood Railroad of the East" for its role in major movies, including parts in *The Fugitive, My Fellow Americans, Digging to China, Paradise Falls,* and *Forces of Nature.*

Executive Chef Paul Swofford plans his menus for the coming year each December, including the fact that they change each month. The dinner train offers a four-course meal, while the Murder Mystery Train features a three-course dinner. That may sound daunting, but the advance planned provides plenty of time to take into account the techniques, ingredients, storage, and holding and heating that will be required for the various menus. One technique Chef Paul has perfected is having most items cooked ahead of time and either held at temperature for service, or chilled for eventual use at service. Space, he finds, is the biggest challenge and, like railroad chefs throughout history, he has learned to use every bit of it.

CHEF'S TIP: Use disposable aluminum pans, available at your supermarket, to hold food for service, then simply dispose of them rather than let them pile up around the kitchen.

Portobello Mushroom Napoleon

8 large portobello mushrooms

1 cup Marinade (see below)

½ lb. fresh spinach

2 8-oz. pkgs. Boursin cheese, each cut into 8 pieces

1 large yellow bell pepper, roasted, ½-inch julienne

1 large red bell pepper, roasted, ½-inch julienne

2 Tbsp. butter

2 cloves garlic, chopped

salt and pepper to taste

Before You Begin

You'll need: medium bowl, sheet pan, sauté pan

Preheat oven to 450°F.

Prep: 15 minutes (plus 1 hour to marinate)

Cook: 30 minutes

Yield: 4 servings

Using a teaspoon, remove gills and any stem from bottom of mushrooms. Place mushrooms in marinade and chill for 1 hour. Meanwhile, wash spinach well, spin or pat dry and set aside. Cut each package of Boursin into four equal pieces and set aside. Halve peppers, remove stem and seeds, place cut-side down on oiled roasting pan, place in a 450°F oven until lightly charred and tender (not burnt), julienne, and set aside. Remove mushrooms from marinade and place, inverted, on sheet pan. Pour extra marinade into each cap. Bake in 450°F oven until soft and starting to brown, 5 to 7 minutes. Remove and set aside (browned mushrooms can be chilled up to 24 hours before used). Meanwhile, in a sauté pan over medium heat, melt butter and heat until it starts to brown, about 3 minutes. Add garlic and stir until golden brown. Add spinach, salt, and pepper, and stir to wilt. Remove from heat (can be chilled overnight before used).

To assemble, place mushrooms inverted on clean sheet pan. Add layer of garlic-infused spinach. Then add layer of roasted yellow pepper to four caps and red pepper to four caps, followed by a layer of Boursin cheese. Close by placing mushroom caps with red peppers atop mushrooms with yellow peppers, mushrooms cap up. Bake at 375°F for 15 minutes or until Boursin cheese starts to turn brown on edges. Serve immediately.

Marinade

½ cup olive oil

⅓ cup soy sauce

⅓ cup Chablis or white cooking wine

2 shallots, chopped

In medium-sized bowl combine all ingredients and stir to mix well

Apple Blue Cheese Salad with Raspberry Vinaigrette

Before You Begin

You'll need: electric mixer, large bowl

Prep: 15 minutes

Yield: 6 servings

Raspberry Vinaigrette

½ cup frozen raspberries, defrosted

¼ cup honey

2 Tbsp. light brown sugar

1 cup salad oil

¼ cup raspberry vinegar

In an electric mixer set on low, in order, combine raspberries, honey, brown sugar, salad oil, and raspberry vinegar. Continue beating until well infused.

Apple Blue Cheese Salad

1 apple, peeled and sliced

1 sweet red or yellow bell pepper, cut in
    ½-inch dice

1 cup blue cheese, crumbled

1 medium red onion, sliced

½ cup croutons

1 lb. mixed greens

Toss all ingredients with 1 cup dressing and serve on chilled salad plates immediately. **NOTE**: Leftover dressing can be refrigerated for 2 weeks.

Roasted Cornish Hens with Cajun Cornbread Stuffing

Before You Begin

You'll need: small skillet or sauté pan, roasting pan,

Preheat oven to 375°F.

Prep: 15 minutes (plus 1 hour to make cornbread)

Cook: 45 minutes

Yield: 4 servings

3 Tbsp. olive oil, divided

½ cup diced yellow onion

½ cup diced bell peppers

 pound Andouille sausage

6 cloves garlic, chopped, divided

2 8½-oz. pkgs. Jiffy Corn Muffin Mix

Tabasco sauce

½ cup fresh herbs (rosemary, parsley,
    thyme), chopped, divided

4 12 to 16-oz. Cornish hens

salt and pepper to taste

In a sauté pan over medium heat, heat 1 tablespoon olive oil and sauté onions, peppers, and sausage until vegetables are tender, about 3 minutes. Add 3 tablespoons garlic for the last minute. Remove from heat and set aside (can be chilled up to 4 hours before used). Prepare Jiffy Corn Muffin Mix according to package directions, except stir in sauté mixture, a few drops of Tabasco sauce and half of the chopped herbs. Bake following directions and allow to cool.

To finish, coarsely crumble cornbread and stuff and truss hens. Rub hens with olive oil, then remaining herbs and garlic, and salt and pepper. Place in a roasting pan and bake at 375°F for 45 minutes or until golden brown and fluid runs clear when poked with fork or knife.

Grand Marnier Flan

½ cup sugar
3 Tbsp. Grand Marnier or other orange-
  flavored liqueur
3 eggs
3 egg yolks

2 tsp. pure vanilla extract
1 can sweetened condensed milk
1 cup heavy cream
5 oz. cream cheese, softened

Before You Begin

You'll need: small saucepan, 9-inch flan pan or 1-quart mold, blender or food processor, large baking pan

Preheat oven to 350°F.

Prep: 30 minutes

Cook: 45–60 minutes

Yield: 6 servings

In a small saucepan over low heat, combine sugar and Grand Marnier, stirring constantly until sugar melts and liquid is golden brown, about 20 to 30 minutes. Pour into 9-inch flan pan or a 1-quart mold, quickly tipping pan to spread caramel evenly over bottom, and set aside. In a blender or food processor on a low setting, combine eggs, egg yolks, vanilla, sweetened condensed milk, heavy cream, and cream cheese. Blend until smooth and pour over caramel mixture. Place flan pan in a large baking pan and pour hot water into the larger pan until it comes halfway up on side of the flan pan. Bake in center of a 350°F oven 50 to 55 minutes, or until knife inserted comes out clean. Cool at least 4 hours, or for up to 2 days, then run knife along the inside edge of the pan and invert to release flan.

CHEF'S TIPS: Chef Paul Swofford keeps a supply of the following on hand at all times: (1) olive oil for sautéing, marinating, or making dressings; (2) balsamic vinegar for its versatility and flavor; (3) Japanese bread crumbs, which are more coarse and lighter than ordinary bread crumbs and thus are great for crumb toppings, fillers for many items like crab cakes, and for breading.

Michigan Star Clipper Dinner Train

www.michiganstarclipper.com

The *Michigan Star Clipper,* departing tiny Coe Rail Depot in Walled Lake, Michigan, just west of Detroit, offers guests two distinctive features. First, Larry Coe, the owner and operator of regional short line Coe Rail, and his wife Judy have restored two sleeping cars and added them to the dinner train to create the nation's only moving bed-and-breakfast. These attractive and comfortable cars—the *Cleveland* and the *Vista Cavern*—offer a total of eight suites with private dining and dancing. Each car features its own attendant, a sound system that reaches each room, and the opportunity to enjoy a meal of specially prepared foods and fine wines and liquors served in the drawing room, or to join other patrons of the dinner train in the dining cars.

The other distinctive feature of the *Michigan Star Clipper* is that it is made up of the only remaining passenger cars from the original Pennsylvania Railroad "Keystone" train, built in 1956 by the Budd Company. The Keystone cars feature a depressed well between the trucks that creates a low center of gravity, for an extremely smooth ride. Historically significant for having innovated technology still in use today on Amtrak's newest cars, they provide an initially unsettling sensation as you

Michigan Star Clipper Dinner Train *dining room. Courtesy* Michigan Star Clipper Dinner Train

look out a train window to discover you are no further off the ground than you would be when driving a minivan. The Keystone cars have been restored and converted into a pair of dining cars, each of which seats seventy-two. Mirrored panels on the upper walls, as well as seating on the platforms over the wheels, give the cars a pleasant sense of spaciousness. A kitchen car separates the two dining cars.

Michigan Star Clipper General Manager Michael Beckham began his culinary career at age fourteen, washing dishes at Howard Johnson's. By age nineteen he was the assistant manager. His passion for food was then interrupted by a five-year stint in the automobile industry. But he returned to food, first with the Sonic chain, and eventually as the owner of the Lone Oak, a restaurant in Gladwin, Michigan, where he spent eight years "doing everything." Michael eventually sold the restaurant. He'd been working at a country club for two years when a friend called to ask him to go to work for Gulf City Seafoods, a large seafood processing company, where he developed new product lines, specializing in soups and entrées. After five years in that position, he returned to Michigan and, for the past eight years, has overseen the operation of the *Clipper*. Once again, he's doing everything.

Crab-Stuffed Artichoke Bottoms

Sauce

Before You Begin

You'll need: 1-quart saucepan, sheet pan, strainer

Preheat oven to 400°F.

Prep: 20 minutes

Cook: 10 minutes

Yield: 4 servings

2 cups port

1 cinnamon stick

1 bay leaf

1 Tbsp. whole black peppercorn

In a 1-quart saucepan over medium heat, place all sauce ingredients and bring just to a boil. Reduce heat and simmer to reduce liquid by half, about 10 minutes. Once the sauce is reduced, strain it and place it back on the stove to keep warm.

Crab-Stuffed Artichoke Bottoms

12 artichokes bottoms, fresh, or canned, drained

8 oz. Boursin cheese

8 oz. fresh crabmeat

4 oz. Italian bread crumbs

4 oz. fresh grated Romano cheese

salt and pepper to taste

Season artichoke bottoms and stuff with crabmeat. (**NOTE:** If using fresh artichokes wash thoroughly.) Be generous but do not overstuff. Then, using a soup spoon, place Boursin cheese on the crab meat. Do this by dipping the spoon in a glass of lukewarm water, then placing the cheese on the spoon to soften, and in a sweeping motion, starting in the center of the artichoke, work out to the edge, repeating this until an even amount of cheese is on the artichoke. Place artichokes on a sheet pan, coat them with bread crumbs and sprinkle with Romano cheese, then bake in a 400°F oven to heat through, approximately 8 to 10 minutes. To serve, cover the bottoms of individual serving plates with sauce, remove the artichokes from the oven, season to taste and place them on the sauce, three per plate.

Fresh Oyster Bisque

Before You Begin

You'll need: 2-quart saucepan, large bowl, large skillet

Prep: 10 minutes

Cook: 30 minutes

Yield: 4 servings

2 russet potatoes, peeled, ½-inch cubed
16 fresh oysters (see NOTE)
¼ cup fine-diced carrot
¼ cup fine-diced onion
6 cups heavy cream

½ cup sherry
2 Tbsp. butter
salt and white pepper to taste
1 oz. fresh chives, chopped

NOTE: Safety considerations, time, and the need to clean fresh oysters thoroughly may make substituting canned or frozen oysters preferable.

In a 2-quart saucepan over high heat, bring sufficient lightly salted water to cover potatoes to a boil. Add potatoes and cook until softened, about 10 minutes. Remove potatoes from the water and place in a large bowl filled with ice water to arrest cooking. Over a large skillet, shuck the oysters, reserving the juice in the pan. Remove and clean oysters and keep them chilled until needed. Add carrot and onion to oyster juice in skillet and, over medium heat, sauté until tender, about 10 minutes. Use a slotted spoon to remove vegetables, stir in heavy cream and sherry, and bring to just steaming, but do not boil. Add oysters and potatoes and again bring to just steaming. Remove from the heat and allow to cool slightly. Add butter, salt, and white pepper, and stir to blend and heat through. Garnish with fresh chopped chives.

Corn Relish–Stuffed Tomato

2 Tbsp. butter

4 ears yellow sweet corn

salt and pepper

1 lb. sugar snap peas

1 Tbsp. olive oil

1 red bell pepper, minced

1 red onion, minced

18-oz. bottle balsamic vinegar

4 vine-ripened tomatoes of similar size

1 Tbsp. chopped fresh basil

Before You Begin

You'll need: small pan, aluminum foil, 3-quart saucepan, mixing bowl

Preheat oven to 350°F.

Prep: 50 minutes (includes 30 minutes for corn to roast)

Yield: 4 servings

In a small pan over medium heat, melt butter and drizzle over corn. Lightly salt and pepper ears, wrap separately in aluminum foil, and bake at 350°F until slightly browned, approximately 30 minutes. Meanwhile, in a 3-quart saucepan, bring sufficient lightly salted water to cover sugar snap peas to a boil. Add sugar snap peas to blanch for 1 minute, then drain and plunge into ice water to arrest cooking. Set aside. In a 10-inch skillet over medium heat, heat oil and sauté onion and red pepper lightly, trying to keep them firm, about 2 minutes. Set aside. To finish, cut corn from the cob and place in a mixing bowl. Stir in onion and pepper sauté and basil. Drizzle lightly with a balsamic vinegar and refrigerate. While corn relish is chilling, cut the tops off tomatoes. Trim a small portion of the tomato bottoms off to enable them to sit upright. Hollow out the tomatoes, leaving enough meat to hold stuffing securely. Spoon corn relish into tomatoes, mounding the top. Work the snap peas between the relish and tomato standing in an upright position. Then angle to leave them in a swirling position. Drizzle with balsamic vinegar to serve.

CHEF'S TIP: Have corn relish left over? Use it as a bed to serve the tomato on, much like the sauce for the artichoke. Or, chill it overnight and use it next day as an accompaniment to, say, a char-grilled burger or as a side dish for a ham sandwich. Still have some left? Top a grilled chicken breast or tuna steak with the relish; or put it, along with some sour cream and Jack cheese, through a processor or blender, and add chopped tomato and green chilies for a great dip.

✳ ✳ ✳

Seared Pork Medallions

Before You Begin

You'll need: medium bowl, mixing bowl, electric mixer, 1-gallon freezer bag, large skillet, 4 ovenproof serving plates 1-quart saucepan, strainer, whisk

Preheat oven to 400°F.

Prep: 90 minutes (includes 1 hour to bake sweet potatoes)

Cook: 10 minutes

Yield: 4–6 servings

4 large sweet potatoes

2 8½-oz. pork tenderloins

2 Granny Smith apples

6 oz. sugar, divided

2 oz. honey

2 oz. butter, melted

salt and pepper to taste

lemon juice

Place sweet potatoes in a 400°F oven to bake until soft throughout, approximately 1 hour, then cool to handle. Meanwhile, clean and cut pork tenderloin into about 1½ inch diameter and cut into ½-inch-thick medallions. Place the medallions on a plate and refrigerate until ready to use. In a medium bowl, dissolve 2 ounces of sugar in 4 cups cold water. Peel and core apples, rub with lemon juice to prevent browning, and soak in cold sugar water. Peel baked sweet potatoes, place in a mixing bowl, add honey, butter, and salt and pepper to taste. With an electric mixer, whip potatoes on medium speed until smooth. Pipe mashed sweet potatoes onto the center of individual ovenproof serving plates and set aside.

Slice apples ¼ inches thick. Pour 4 ounces sugar in 1-gallon freezer bag, add apple slices, and toss lightly to coat. Place apple slices in a large skillet over high heat and caramelize, turning once, about 2 minutes per side. Arrange caramelized apples evenly around the sweet potatoes on plate. Salt and pepper the pork medallions and sear in the same skillet that was used for the apples, about 1½ minutes per side. (**NOTE:** Check for doneness prior to serving, the meat should show no signs of redness, nor even pinkness.)

Place the medallions on the plate, alternating between the apples. Place the entire plate in the oven at 350°F for approximately 10 minutes. Remove the plate, drizzle the sauce over the pork and potatoes, and serve accompanied by a simple salad.

Sauce

2 cups Calvados brandy

1 cinnamon stick

1 Tbsp. black peppercorn

1 cup heavy cream

salt and pepper to taste

In a 1-quart saucepan over medium-high heat, bring brandy, cinnamon stick, and peppercorn to a boil. Season to taste, reduce heat, and simmer until reduced by ½. Strain and set aside. At 10 minutes prior to service, place sauce back in saucepan over medium heat. When warmed through, drizzle and whisk heavy cream into the sauce and allow to heat through. Do not boil.

Chocolate-Stuffed Pear

4 ripe Bartlett pears

1 cup mixed fresh berries

½ cup plain yogurt

8 oz. semisweet chocolate, grated coarse

1 tsp. butter

¼ cup heavy cream

4 mint leaves (to garnish)

Poaching Liquid

12 oz. port

1 cinnamon stick

1 Tbsp. black peppercorns

Before You Begin

You'll need: large saucepot, small bowl, double boiler, whisk

Prep: 30 minutes (plus 1 hour for poached pears to cool)

Cook: 15 minutes

Yield: 4 servings

Place poaching liquid ingredients in a saucepot large enough to eventually hold the four pears and bring just to a boil. Reduce heat and allow to simmer. Meanwhile, trim and wash berries. In a small bowl, fold berries and yogurt together and refrigerate. Peel and core pears, place them in simmering poaching liquid, and keep them submerged, stirring occasionally to ensure they poach evenly. When soft to the touch and a fork penetrates easily, in about 10 to 15 minutes, remove pears from liquid and refrigerate until cool. Stuff chilled pears with berry/yogurt mixture, stand upright on individual serving plates, and return to refrigerator.

Meanwhile, in a double boiler over high heat, bring water to a boil, taking care the water does not touch the bottom of the upper pan. Reduce heat to allow water to simmer, and place semisweet chocolate and butter in the upper pan. When chocolate begins to melt, slowly whisk in heavy cream. Continue to whisk until chocolate is melted and sauce is of a smooth consistency. Drizzle sauce over pears and return to refrigerator until ready to serve. Garnish with fresh mint leaf.

Mt. Hood Dinner Train

www.mthoodrr.com

The *Mt. Hood Dinner Train* boards at the Craftsman-style Hood River Depot, in Hood River, Oregon, where the railroad began in 1906. Built in 1911, the station hints at the trip back in time a ride on the Mt. Hood Railroad offers. Completed in 1910, the line is a twenty-one-mile feeder railroad that still provides vital freight operations to businesses along its route. At milepost 1.0, pass Powerdale, site of a 1904 Oregon power plant (the one there today was erected to replace it in 1923). At milepost 2.5, enter one of the few remaining revenue-service switchbacks in the country as the train climbs the Hood River Gorge. While crossing Oregon Route 35, Mt. Hood is visible to the south and Mt. Adams can be seen to the north. Then follows a number of sites important in the region's fruit-growing business: Sears at milepost 4.0, Pine Grove at milepost 5.6, Mohr at milepost 6.8, and Lentz at milepost 7.5, all bear traces of the railroad once serving orchards in the region. Elsewhere reminders of the area's equally important lumber industry appear, including Dee at milepost 15.5, Camp Number 1 at milepost 18.5, and Woodworth Park at milepost 19.5. Milepost 21 marks Parkdale, end of the line in 1910 and today. It was once home to McIsaac's store and Community Center, a station that included a twelve-room hotel, train servicing facilities, and the Anne Reis house, built in 1900 and the only building standing both then and now.

Executive Chef Jacob DeLeon, who joined the line in 2002, works both on the train and in the Railroad's Rail's End Cafe in Parkdale. A sixteen-year veteran of the kitchen, he credits his skill to the many fine chefs he worked with coming up. "I was working in Hood River when I was referred to the Railroad by a friend," he says, echoing the timeless explanation of how one comes to work on trains. DeLeon went right to work revamping the menu, and the entire operation with it. "When I came on board, everything was purchased, even the cooked rice," he says. "Now we prep everything at the Cafe, then move it on to the train and cook meals to order there." The Cafe, incidentally, also serves hungry excursion passengers, who lay over in Parkdale for one hour, and caters other events the railroad hosts.

Mt. Hood Dinner Train *logo. Mt. Hood Railroad*

Chef Jacob's menu echoes the region's bounty, with specialties made of huckleberries, salmon and Hood River pears. He changes the menu yearly, but like any tinkering chef, he alters his sauces all the time.

Huckleberry Vinaigrette Dressing

1 lb. huckleberries
¼ cup cornstarch
2 Tbsp. water
1½ cups granulated sugar

2 cups white wine
2 cups red wine vinegar
salt and pepper to taste

Before You Begin

You'll need: large saucepan, small bowl, large mixing bowl

Prep: 5 minutes (plus 1 hour to cool for use)

Cook: 45 minutes

Yield: 1 quart

In a large saucepan over medium-high heat, cover huckleberries with water, bring to a boil, reduce heat, and simmer for 30 minutes. In a small bowl, mix cornstarch and water to form a paste. Stir paste into simmering berries to thicken. Remove from heat and let cool. Pour berry mixture into a large mixing bowl. Slowly whisk the sugar, white wine, and red wine vinegar into the berries. Season, stirring to mix, cover, and refrigerate at least 1 hour.

Herbed Fillet of Salmon with Chardonnay Lime Sauce and Risotto

4 7-oz. salmon fillets, skinless
1 Tbsp. dried dill
1 Tbsp. dried parsley

2 tsp. paprika
1 tsp. garlic powder
salt and pepper to taste

Before You Begin

You'll need: sheet pan, small bowl

Preheat oven to 350°F.

Prep: 5 minutes

Cook: 12 minutes

Yield: 4 servings

Lightly grease sheet pan and place salmon fillets on pan. In a small bowl, mix remaining ingredients together and sprinkle on salmon. Place in 350°F oven to bake 12 minutes

Chardonnay Lime Sauce

1 cup chardonnay
1 shallot, chopped
1 tsp. whole black peppercorns
2 bay leaves

¼ cup white wine vinegar
2 cups heavy cream
juice of one lime

Before You Begin

You'll need: 2-quart saucepan, strainer

Prep: 5 minutes

Cook: 30 minutes

Yield: 2½ cups

In a 2-quart saucepan over medium-high heat, place first five ingredients and bring to boil. Reduce heat and simmer to reduce mixture to ¼, stirring occasionally. Add cream and lime juice, and simmer until thick and creamy. Strain sauce before serving.

One of the most common re-uses of railroad passenger stations is to turn them into restaurants. Because many of them are located adjacent to still-active rail lines, many of the eating establishments are popular with train-watchers. And because the stations are often spacious, they're great for microbreweries as well. Fittingly, many of these establishments celebrate their historic setting by honoring the railroads and trainmen who once worked on the premises. Here is a sampling.

LEFT: *Titletown Brewing Company label. Titletown Brewing Company* RIGHT: *Flossmoor Station Restaurant and Brewer label. Flossmoor Station Restaurant and Brewery*

LEFT: *B&O Station label. B&O Station Brewery & Restaurant* RIGHT: *Walter Payton's Roundhouse label. Jason Ascher / www.thinkmango.com*

Risotto

¼ **cup olive oil**
¼ **cup minced onion**
¼ **cup minced red bell pepper**
1 **cup arborio rice**
1 **tsp. minced garlic**

2½ **cups chicken stock**
pinch of saffron
½ **cup shredded Asiago cheese**
2 **Tbsp. dried parsley**
salt and pepper to taste

Before You Begin

You'll need: 3-quart saucepan, small saucepan

Prep: 10 minutes

Cook: 30 minutes

Yield: 6 servings

In a 3-quart saucepan over medium heat, warm olive oil, add onion and red pepper, and sauté for 30 seconds. Stir in rice and garlic, and sauté 3 additional minutes. Meanwhile, in a small saucepan over medium heat, warm chicken stock with saffron. Add stock/saffron mixture to rice, bring to boil, lower heat, and simmer, stirring every 5 minutes, until no liquid remains, about 20 minutes. Stir in Asiago cheese, parsley, salt, and pepper, and warm through.

White Chocolate Raspberry Cheesecake

Crust

2½ **cups graham cracker crumbs**
⅓ **cup granulated sugar**

⅓ **cup butter, melted**

Before You Begin

You'll need: food processor, 10-inch springform pan, double boiler, large bowl, small saucepan

Preheat oven to 350°F, then 300°F.

Prep: 15 minutes

Cook: 60 minutes

Yield: 10–12 servings

Using a food processor, reduce graham crackers to course crumbs. Mix with sugar and butter and press firmly onto bottom of 10-inch springform pan. Bake at 350°F for 10 minutes. Place in refrigerator to cool while filling is prepared. Reduce oven temperature to 300°F.

Cheesecake

6 **oz. good-quality white chocolate**
3½ **8-oz pkgs. cream cheese, softened**
½ **cup granulated sugar**

½ **tsp. vanilla extract**
3 **eggs**

In a double boiler over simmering water, melt white chocolate. Meanwhile, in a large mixing bowl, combine cream cheese, sugar, and vanilla, mixing at medium speed until well blended. Add eggs, one at a time, beating well after each addition. Blend in melted white chocolate and mix well. Pour into springform pan, bake at 300°F until firm and light golden brown on top, 45 to 60 minutes. Remove from oven and allow to cool before removing springform. Run a thin knife around edge of crust to loosen from pan base before lifting to serve.

Raspberry Sauce

2 cups fresh or frozen raspberries	**2 Tbsp. cornstarch**
½ cup granulated sugar	**¼ cup water**

In small saucepan over medium heat, place raspberries and sugar and bring to boil, stirring occasionally. Reduce heat to simmer to reduce. Meanwhile, in a small bowl, dissolve cornstarch in water and stir until smooth. Add cornstarch to sauce, stir, and continue to simmer until thickened sufficiently to adhere to the back of a spoon. Remove from heat, strain, and let cool. To serve, splash and swirl sauce on individual plates, top with cheesecake portion, then drizzle decoratively over cheesecake.

Poached Hood River Pears with Almond Meringue and Chocolate Mousse

Before You Begin

You'll need: large saucepan, 2 medium bowls, parchment paper, sheet pan, cups or glasses to mold meringue, double boiler, 2 large mixing bowls, pastry bag

Preheat oven to 375°F.

Prep: 30 minutes (plus 1 hour for pears to cool)

Cook: 45 minutes (plus 3 hours to chill)

Yield: 3 servings

This special treat is for those celebrating a birthday on board the train.

2 cups granulated sugar	**2 bay leaves**
4 cups water	**pinch of thyme**
4 cups Flerchinger Vineyards Riesling Blush, or similar	**3 Hood River Bosc pears, peeled, cored, stem left on**

In a large saucepan, mix first five ingredients, add pears, and bring to a boil. Poach pears for 30 minutes. Remove from liquid and cool.

Almond Meringue

4 large egg whites	**½ cup toasted almonds**
½ cup granulated sugar	

To toast almonds, spread in a shallow baking pan and place in a 375°F oven, stirring occasionally, until lightly browned, about 10 minutes. In a medium bowl, whip egg whites with sugar until stiff peaks form. Gently fold in toasted almonds. Line a sheet pan with parchment paper and deposit meringue in small mounds placed 4 inches apart. Bake at 375°F until lightly browned, about 10 minutes. Remove from oven and, while still warm, drape over inverted cups or glasses to form cups big enough to hold pears.

Chocolate Mousse

1 lb. high-quality semisweet chocolate	½ cup granulated sugar
(see NOTE 1 on page 237)	½ cup Grand Marnier
5 eggs, separated	4 cups whipping cream

In a double boiler over simmering water, melt chocolate and remove from heat. Whip egg yolks with sugar until light in color, then whisk into the chocolate. Add Grand Marnier, blend well, and pour into large bowl. In another large bowl, whip cream until fluffy, then fold into the chocolate mixture. In a medium bowl, whip egg whites until stiff peaks form, then fold into the chocolate/whipped cream mixture. Chill until set, about 3 hours.

To assemble, use a pastry bag to pipe mousse into the center of poached pears. Set pears upright in meringue cups. Cap with a dollop of mousse.

Hobo Stew

Close your eyes. Then, in a loud whisper, repeat the phrase "movin' on," making sure to employ the contraction and emphasize the syllable "in'." Ready? Go: "mov-IN-on, mov-IN-on, mov-IN-on, mov-IN-on. . . ." Can you hear it? It's the sound a steam locomotive makes—a sound that for more than 125 years was said to call those who engaged in a uniquely American phenomenon: the hobo life.

The relationship between hobos and railroads goes back to the beginnings of the industry in the 1830s. By the late 1800s and in to the early 1900s, as the nation's track mileage reached its peak, drifters increasingly rode the rails. Hobos allege they were standouts among the drifters. One, Hobo Skeets Simmons, explained it this way: "A hobo is a man who works and travels, a tramp is one who travels but don't work, and a bum neither travels nor works, he's just a bum." In his book *Railroad Avenue,* noted railroad writer Freeman H. Hubbard traced the term hobo to a shortening of the construction worker's greeting—"Hello, boy!"

Railroad managements, especially the detectives and yard "bulls" charged with chasing free riders off the company's trains and property, failed to appreciate Simmons's romantic distinctions. Their adherents think the term "hobo" derived from the call of railroad police—"Ho, boy!"—to roust the traveling man from his place on a train. To the company, the men who hopped trains, regardless of their motive, were a constant source of disruption, petty thievery, and vandalism.

In any event, food was right there with rumors of work, and knowledge of train schedules, for the travelin' man. It made an otherwise desolate spot a mile east of the Oregon Short Line's yard near Salt Lake City, Utah, popular in the 1930s because water from a natural hot spring there, with a little salt added, tasted amazingly like chicken soup. And railroad construction managers knew that well-provisioned work camp cars on their projects attracted the best traveling workers.

The menu item most often associated with the hobo life is Mulligan stew. Of course Mulligan stew, by definition, is made up of any available ingredients. Here is one recipe, attributed to legendary hobo "A No. 1," perhaps the most well known of all "travelin' men" (see the gritty 1973 movie *Emperor of the North,* starring Lee Marvin as "A No. 1," and Ernest Borgnine as a ruthless freight train conductor, for but one episode said to be drawn from his life).

A No. 1 Mulligan Stew

Before You Begin

You'll need: large pot

Prep: 20 minutes

Cook: 1 hour 45 minutes

Yield: 8 servings

2 cups water

1 cube chicken bouillon

2 lbs. lamb for stew

2 lbs. potatoes, cubed, divided

1 lb. onions, chopped

1 lb. turnips, cubed

1 tsp. salt, or to taste

½ tsp. pepper, or to taste

2 Tbsp. malt vinegar

In a large pot over medium-high heat, bring water to a boil. Add bouillon cube to dissolve. Add lamb and return to the boil. Add half the potatoes, reduce heat to medium, cover, and simmer 45 minutes. Stir in onions, turnips, and remaining potatoes, cover, and simmer for 30 minutes. Add salt, pepper, and malt vinegar, then simmer, uncovered, for 10 more minutes. Serve hot.

Of course this is Mulligan stew, so substitute ingredients are welcome. It'll still be an authentic hobo stew.

And if you want to try a second variety of hobo stew, head to Britt, Iowa. There, in mid-August every year, join today's hobos, retired hobos, and those who have what is called a "hobo's heart," to celebrate the National Hobo Convention. Britt's recipe for Hobo Stew, though, serves ten thousand, and starts with nine hundred pounds of beef. For more information, go to www.brittchamberofcommerce.com/Hobo/.

My Old Kentucky Dinner Train

www.rjcorman.com/dinner

Talk about handicaps. Try this: Launch a dinner train forty miles out of town. Run it on no particular schedule. Depart each evening at just about the time potential customers are getting out of work. Serve the same menu for an entire year. That just about sums up the operating philosophy behind *My Old Kentucky Dinner Train* in Bardstown, Kentucky. The creation of Rick Corman, the man behind the R. J. Corman Railroad Companies, headquartered in nearby Nicholasville, this long-running train has, since 1988, drawn guests to central Kentucky.

The remote but easily accessible location is dictated by the fact that the Bardstown Line, originally the Bardstown & Louisville Railroad that dates from 1860, and today the route of *My Old Kentucky Dinner Train*, is one of R. J. Corman's holdings. Train boarding occurs at the Bardstown Depot, also built in 1860. Constructed of native limestone, the Depot is the last remaining "dry-laid" railroad station in Kentucky, a distinction that has earned it a spot in the National Register of Historic Places. A thirty-five-mile round-trip along what was once the Louisville & Nashville Railroad's Bardstown Branch passes the Jim Beam distillery, home to the world's #1 selling bourbon, over the 310-fort Jackson Hollow trestle, through tobacco country, past two more historic depots, in Deatsville and Limestone Springs Junction (seen in the movie *Stripes*); and through a portion of the 14,000-acre Bernheim Forest and Arboretum, a research forest featuring every tree and many of the plants native to Kentucky.

The operating schedule and early departure time are built around the fact that many visitors are drawn to historic Bardstown to see a performance of *Stephen Foster: The Musical,* at My Old Kentucky Home historic site. The amphitheater's curtain goes up at 8:00 P.M.

General Manager and Corporate Chef Robert R. Perry, Jr., is a chef by profession. "I learned in Boy Scouts that the cook didn't have to do dishes," Bob says. "That's what got me started." A native Kentuckian, when he joined the train he quickly brought his years of restaurant experience to bear on the menu. "On a dinner train," he says, "you have to work with a limited menu, in a limited time, all while moving. In spite of that, I want to change the menu on a seasonal basis and include lighter fare through out the meal. I want to offer variety in the side dishes that accompany the entrees." He also makes use of local ingredients—Kentucky Bibb lettuce and bourbon in the recipes here—to enhance the uniqueness of his menu.

My Old Kentucky Dinner Train *logo. Courtesy* My Old Kentucky Dinner Train

Kentucky Beer Cheese

Before You Begin

You'll need: grater, electric mixer (see NOTE), large mixing bowl

Prep: 10 minutes (plus 6–12 hours to induce stale beer, 6–12 hours to blend, and 1 hour to come to room temperature)

Yield: 12 servings

1 lb. sharp cheddar cheese
½ lb. cream cheese
1 tsp. garlic powder

1 tsp. onion powder
1 tsp. Tabasco sauce, or more if desired
12 oz. stale beer (see NOTE)

Grate cheddar cheese cold, then let both cheeses warm to soften. Place seasoning ingredients and ½ of the beer in a mixing bowl and mix with an electric mixer set on Mix. Add cheeses and continue to mix until well blended. Add sufficient remaining beer to get a smooth consistency. Pack mixture into a serving bowl and cover tightly. Refrigerate at least 6 hours or overnight, until hard. Before serving, allow to come to room temperature. Serve accompanied by celery and carrot sticks and crackers.

NOTES: (1) This is easier to make in a standing mixer with a paddle attachment rather than with a hand-held mixer. (2) To make beer stale, open and let sit out overnight, or pour into a shallow container and let sit for a couple of hours.

Tomato Basil Bisque

Before You Begin

You'll need: 3-quart saucepan or soup pot, blender

Prep: 10 minutes

Cook: 60 minutes

Yield: 6 servings

2 Tbsp. butter
1 medium onion, coarsely chopped
½ cup white wine
1 28-oz. can whole tomatoes
1 cup tomato juice

pinch ground cloves
¼ cup packed fresh basil leaves
½ pint heavy cream, or more to taste
salt and white pepper to taste

In a 3-quart saucepan or soup pot over low heat, melt butter and add onion. Cover and sweat the onion until clear, about 5 minutes. Turn heat on high and deglaze with white wine. Add whole tomatoes, breaking them up with a spoon, and tomato juice. Reduce heat to medium-low and simmer for 20 minutes. Add pinch of ground cloves and remove from heat. Stir in fresh basil leaves and let the residual heat cook them. Put into a blender, in batches if necessary, and puree until smooth. (**WARNING:** Only fill blender ½ full and pulse to get started as hot liquids can be explosive in blenders.) Put pureed mixture back on stove over medium-low heat, stir in heavy cream, and simmer another 20 minutes. Season with salt and white pepper. Serve hot.

Soft Lettuce Salad with Champagne and Roasted Beet Vinaigrette

3 to 4 red beets, ends removed
olive oil
½ cup champagne vinegar
1 tsp. salt
pepper to taste

1 Tbsp. Dijon mustard
2 shallots, chopped
1 cup olive oil, good, but not extra-
    virgin as it is too strong
Bibb lettuce

Before You Begin

You'll need: aluminum foil, blender, medium bowl

Preheat oven to 350°F

Prep: 20 minutes (plus 30 minutes to stand)

Cook: 45 minutes (plus 1 hour to cool)

Yield: 1 quart

Rub beets with olive oil, wrap loosely in foil, and place in a 350°F oven to roast 45 minutes. When cool, peel and finely dice beets. (**NOTE:** Your hands and anything you have on are likely to be red at this point, so dress appropriately.) In a blender, put champagne vinegar, salt, pepper, mustard, and shallots. Pulse a couple of times to blend, then set on High and slowly drizzle olive oil in and emulsify. Pour dressing in a bowl and stir in diced roasted beets. Let stand 30 minutes before using. To serve, break lettuce onto individual serving plates and pour dressing over.

Crown Roast of Pork au Lait

½ rack of pork, or a 2- to 3-lb. bone-in
    pork roast, or ½ boneless pork loin
kosher salt
herbes de Provence
olive oil
3 carrots, large dice
2 celery ribs, large dice

1 onion, large dice
3 to 4 whole cloves garlic, peeled
salt to taste
1 cup white wine
3 cups milk
pepper to taste

Before You Begin

You'll need: covered heavy Dutch oven or roasting pan, meat thermometer, blender

Preheat oven to 350°F.

Prep: 20 minutes

Cook: 1½ hours

Yield: 6 servings

Season pork with kosher salt and herbes de Provence and rub with olive oil. In heavy Dutch oven or roasting pan over high heat, sear pork in olive oil. Remove pork from pan and add vegetables, including garlic cloves. Salt lightly and cook until vegetables begin to brown, about 5 minutes. Add white wine and deglaze pan, scraping any brown bits off the bottom. Cook off alcohol and return pork to pan. Pour milk over pork into pan and cover with lid or aluminum foil. Bake at 350°F for approximately 1½ hours, depending on cut and size of pork, until internal temperature reaches 140°F (rare) or 160°F (medium), depending on preference for doneness. Remove meat from pan and keep warm. Meanwhile, pour all remaining ingredients from roasting pan into a blender container and puree. (**NOTE:** See "Warning" on page 156 about hot ingredients in a blender.) Adjust with salt and pepper to taste. Serve over pork with Rice Pilaf (see page 70) and vegetable of choice.

Booker's Crème Brûlée

Before You Begin

You'll need: heavy saucepan, double boiler, rubber spatula, fine screen strainer, small bowl, 4 4- to 6-ounce ramekins, 9" × 13" roasting pan, propane torch (optional)

Preheat oven to 325°F.

Prep: 30 minutes (plus at least 6 hours to cool and set)

Cook: 30 minutes

Yield: 4 servings

1 pint heavy cream
2 oz. Booker's bourbon
5 egg yolks

½ cup sugar
confectioners' sugar

In heavy saucepan over medium heat, bring cream and bourbon to a simmer, but do not boil. Meanwhile, whip egg yolks and sugar until smooth and pale yellow, and place in a double boiler over simmering water. Slowly add the bourbon/cream mixture a little at a time, mixing constantly. Continue to stir with rubber spatula until mixture will coat the back of a spoon, 10 to 15 minutes. Strain through a fine screen into a clean container, then divide into 4 ramekins. Put the ramekins in a 9" × 13" roasting pan and fill pan with hot water to halfway up the sides of the ramekins. Bake in a 325°F oven for 30 minutes. Remove ramekins from pan and let cool for a few minutes and then put in refrigerator for at least 6 hours or overnight. Dust with confectioners' sugar and brown with propane torch or under broiler.

In Bourbon Country

www.straightbourbon.com

Ed O'Daniel, President of the Kentucky Distributor's Association, is fond of saying that "bourbon doesn't have to be made in Kentucky, but if you want to sell it, it does." With its departure from Bardstown, Kentucky, *My Old Kentucky Dinner Train* is at the very heart of bourbon country. In fact, en route during dinner the train passes much of the reason why, as another pundit put it, "while only 98 percent of all Bourbon comes from Kentucky, 100 percent of good Bourbon comes from Kentucky": Limestone formations. Water is the critical starting point of any distilling process. With central Kentucky positioned on the Highland Rim of the Pennyrile Plateau, the unique limestone formations found there filter iron, the enemy of distilling, out of the water while they lace it with minerals, an aid to the fermentation process. The result is "sweet," or hard water. Little surprise, then, that Jim Beam, Maker's Mark, Heaven Hill, Wild Turkey, in fact all the good bourbon makers have addresses in and around Bardstown.

Little surprise, too, that one popular item from the menu of *My Old Kentucky Dinner Train* is a Southern classic that includes bourbon.

Bread Pudding with Butter Bourbon Sauce

Before You Begin

You'll need:
9" × 9" baking dish, large mixing bowl, whisk

Preheat oven to 350°F.

Prep: 15 minutes

Cook: 90 minutes

Yield: 8 servings

8 cups day-old bread, broken into pieces

butter at room temperature for pan

6 eggs

2 Tbsp. cinnamon

6 cups warm water

2 14-oz. cans sweetened condensed milk

¼ cup melted butter

4 tsp. vanilla extract

1 tsp. salt

Butter a 9" × 9" baking dish and fill with bread pieces. In a large bowl whisk all other ingredients together and pour over bread. Cover baking dish with foil and bake at 350°F until knife inserted comes out clean, about 90 minutes. Let stand to cool. Spoon individual portions into serving bowls and drizzle with warm Butter Bourbon Sauce.

Butter Bourbon Sauce

Before You Begin

You'll need:
2-quart saucepan

Prep: 5 minutes

Cook: 10 minutes

Yield: 3 cups

½ cup melted butter

1½ cups brown sugar

1 cup heavy cream

¼ cup bourbon

½ cup chopped walnuts

In a 2-quart saucepan over medium-high heat, combine all ingredients, and bring to a boil. Reduce heat and stir occasionally at a slow-boil for 6 minutes, watching constantly that mixture does not boil over.

Napa Valley Wine Train

www.winetrain.com

Deep in the continuously-busy-but-not-cluttered Napa Valley, California's most famous wine-growing region, just off the main drag in the town of Napa, lies the McKinstry Street Station, home to the *Napa Valley Wine Train*, the most widely known private dinner train in America. Arrive there early on a hot summer afternoon and you may find the station's expansive parking lot nearly empty. Inside the station, however, activity abounds. Attendants make ready at their ticket windows. The Wine Emporium's manager eyes his display of over two hundred fine Napa Valley wines. In Baubles and Beads, jewelry vies with assorted unique gifts for a shopper's attention. More upscale merchandise awaits at Unique Gift Express. Paintings and sculptures by Napa Valley artists decorate an art gallery. The Artist's Corner Cafe and, of course, a wine-tasting bar complete the scene. The train can accommodate as many as 260 passengers, so by departure time the scene resembles the midway of a moderate-sized passenger station at peak.

As the scheduled departure nears, a blaring whistle announces the train's arrival from the Commissary. One can see immediately why some have labeled it the "Ori-

Napa Valley Wine Train *logo.*
Courtesy Napa Valley Wine Train

ent Express of the West." Beautifully restored heavyweight passenger cars, joined recently by a full-length dome car from the 1950s, are neat from the ground up in bands of burgundy, champagne gold, and grape leaf green, to be led by a pair of ALCO FA4's in compatible livery. The appearance of the cars has been backdated during restoration—the heavyweights were built between 1915 and 1917 by the Pullman Company as coaches and sleepers—by the addition of faux stained-glass arches to the windows. The effect of all this leads to just one complaint: The incongruous look. "Turn-of-the-century" rolling stock being pulled by diesel/electric locomotives built in the 1950s, is unsettling. If ever a train set cried out to be pulled by a steam locomotive, this is the one.

Inside, the luxurious cars feature wood paneling, spacious seating, and clean wide windows. Large ovals of glass in the bulkhead, etched gracefully along their left side with pods of grapes on a leafy vine, provide an inviting view of the dining rooms. There, layers of burgundy velvet frame the windows. Graceful chairs, their subdued rose and blue velvet upholstery set off by dark wooden arches, provide a fitting backdrop for place settings of linen, crystal, silver, and china. Gold fixtures against a cream-colored clerestory crown and accent the room. J. Pierpont Morgan would feel at home on this train. In the observation car, a pleasing combination of intimate tables and large overstuffed armchairs recreate what had to be one of the most pleasing aspects of earlier passenger trains, the parlor-lounge car. Here you can step out onto the platform and enjoy the scenery or become lost in thought as the rails recede to meet in the distance.

From the kitchen car, outfitted with a row of windows along a mahogany-lined passageway so guests can watch the chef and the crew at work, meals fit for a mogul are served up to order. A wine master—the train has its own—assists in pairing an appropriate wine from the region with menu selections.

A favorite among railfans, tourists, and gourmands alike, the *Napa Valley Wine Train* offers Chefs Tours, holiday excursions, and themed lunches and dinners, including jazz excursions and the twice-monthly *Murder on the Wine Train Express*. The most distinctive of these is the extensive schedule of Vintner's Luncheons. On Fridays, a winemaker from one of the Napa Valley's boutique wineries—from Far Niente Winery perhaps, or the Raymond Cellars, Merryvale Vineyards, Domaine Chandon Winery, or Grgich Cellars, to name just a few—greets passengers, offers insights into the intricacies of producing fine wines, and arranges for appropriate paired wines to accompany the menu.

Each year the Napa Valley Mustard Festival showcases another important crop of the valley. Each recipe here has been taken from menus found on the *Napa Valley Wine Train* during that celebration. Open with a Mustard Festival People's Choice Award winner:

California Crab Stack on Japanese Pickled Cucumber-Mâche Salad Dressed with Tarragon Dijon Dressing

Before You Begin

You'll need: 2 medium bowls, nonstick 12-inch sauté pan, 2 small bowls, whisk

Prep: minutes (plus 1 hour for dressing to chill)

Cook: 5 minutes

Yield: 4 servings

6 oz. Dungeness crabmeat, picked clean

2 oz. sourdough bread crumbs

1 egg, slightly beaten

1 Tbsp. Maui onion, finely diced
   (substitute sweet onion)

1 Tbsp. parsley, coarsely chopped

2 tsp. Dijon mustard

1 tsp. Worcestershire sauce

2 Tbsp. mayonnaise

olive oil

In a medium bowl, combine sourdough, bread crumbs, and Dungeness crabmeat and set aside. In a second medium bowl, combine remaining ingredients and mix thoroughly. Gently fold in crab/bread crumb mixture. Shape into patties approximately ½ inch thick. Coat a nonstick 12-inch sauté pan with olive oil over medium heat. Cook crab cakes over to a golden brown, turning once, about 2 minutes per side. Set aside.

Japanese Pickled Cucumber Salad

1 cup Japanese cucumber, peeled,
   julienne

¼ cup Maui onion, julienne

1 cup mâche lettuce (or other seasonal
   "soft" lettuce)

3 Tbsp. champagne vinegar

2 Tbsp. olive oil

salt and pepper to taste

flower petal confetti (optional garnish)

In a small bowl, combine all ingredients except flower confetti, cover, and refrigerate.

Dijon-Tarragon Vinaigrette

½ cup red wine vinegar

¾ cup olive oil

2 Tbsp. Dijon mustard

2 Tbsp. honey

2 Tbsp. light brown sugar

1 tsp. dried tarragon

salt and pepper to taste

In a small bowl, whisk together all ingredients, cover, and, refrigerate.

To serve, place ¼ cup of salad mix in the center of individual plates. Place a crab cake on top of each salad. Drizzle with Dijon-Tarragon Vinaigrette, and sprinkle with a garnish of flower petal confetti.

Smoked Sonoma Range Chicken on Crispy Wonton with Mustard Cream Sauce and Maui Onion–Apple–Mustard–Red Pepper–Sweet Corn Chow Chow

Mesquite Smoked Sonoma Free-Range Chicken Breast

1 cup mesquite chips

1 cup water

2 12- to 14-oz. boneless breast of
   chicken, skin on

BBQ grill and briquettes

Before You Begin

You'll need:
covered grill, 1-quart saucepan, whisk, small bowl, large skillet, 1-gallon freezer bag, 3-quart covered saucepan

Preheat grill and allow coals to burn to an even gray color.

Prep: 15 minutes

Cook: 1 hour

Yield: 4 servings

While coals are heating, soak mesquite chips in the water. When coals are ready, drain water from the chips and place them in an even layer over the coals. Place breasts on grill 12 inches above the coals, cover with lid, and smoke for 1 hour or until internal temperature of 160°F has been reached.

Mustard Cream Sauce

⅓ cup Chardonnay

3 Tbsp. finely chopped shallots

1 cup heavy cream

1 Tbsp. flour

dash of white pepper

1 Tbsp. Dijon mustard

Combine the Chardonnay and shallots in a 1-quart saucepan. Bring mixture to a boil, reduce heat, and simmer uncovered until liquid is reduced to 3 tablespoons. In a small bowl combine the cream, the flour, and the white pepper, and whisk smooth. Pour the cream mixture into the wine mixture and whisk to combine. Continue stirring and cooking until the sauce just begins to bubble. Remove from the heat and stir in the Dijon mustard. Keep warm until service.

Crispy Wontons

8 wonton skins, cut in half diagonally

canola oil

In a large skillet over medium heat, heat ½-inch-deep oil to 350°F. Separate wonton skins and place each skin in oil and fry to golden color. Drain and set aside until service.

Maui Onion–Apple–Mustard–Red Pepper–Sweet Corn Chow Chow

6 medium ears corn, blanched and
kernels cut from cob (substitute 2
cups fresh frozen or canned whole
kernel corn)

1 medium roasted red pepper (see pages
170–171), seeded, skinned, diced

1 medium carrot, finely chopped

2 medium onions, finely chopped

2 medium apples, peeled, cored, diced
juice of 1 lemon
1 cup sugar
1 cup cider vinegar
½ cup water
1 tsp. crushed red chili
2 Tbsp. whole-grain mustard
1 tsp. dry mustard

In a 1-gallon freezer bag, toss diced apple in lemon juice to prevent browning. In a 3-quart covered saucepan over medium-high heat, combine all ingredients except the dry and whole-grain mustard. Bring to a boil, reduce heat to low, cover, and simmer 45 minutes. Remove mixture from heat and let cool to room temperature. Stir in dry and whole grain mustards and refrigerate in an airtight container. (**NOTE**: Can be stored for up to 4 weeks.)

To serve, slice the chicken breasts on the bias in 2- to 3-inch long medallions. Pool the mustard sauce on individual serving plates. Placing first a piece of chicken over sauce, alternate wonton, chicken, wonton, chicken. Garnish with Maui Onion–Apple–Mustard–Red Pepper–Sweet Corn Chow Chow.

Crème Brûlée

12 oz. Grand Marnier

18 fresh strawberries, stemmed,
quartered

1¼ qts. heavy cream

½ split vanilla bean

8 oz. sugar, divided

8 oz. sugar, divided

1¼ cups egg yolks (approximately 9
eggs), beaten

12 crepes

granulated sugar

Raspberry Sauce (see page 152)

In a medium bowl, combine Grand Marnier and strawberries and set aside. In a 3-quart saucepan over medium-high heat, combine cream, vanilla bean, and 4 ounces sugar, and bring to boil. Meanwhile, in a medium mixing bowl combine egg yolks and remaining sugar and whisk until smooth and pale yellow. Slowly stir egg/sugar mixture into hot cream and cook until thick enough to coat the back of a spoon, about 10 minutes. Strain through fine sieve. Fill ramekins ⅞ full and place in a baking dish. Fill baking dish with hot water halfway up the sides of the ramekins. Bake in a 325°F oven until just barely set, approximately 45 minutes. Allow to stand in water bath until cool. Remove and refrigerate over night.

To serve, place ¼ cup crème brûlée in center of a crepe, fold square, and place in center of individual plate fold-side down. Sprinkle with granulated sugar. Circle crepe with raspberry sauce. Place 2 to 3 tablespoons of Grand Marnier–laced strawberries atop each crepe. Garnish with fresh mint. Serve at once.

Newport Dinner Train

www.newportdinnertrain.com

"We want to be one of the ten best dining experiences you have in your life," says Bob Andrews, president of the *Newport Dinner Train* in Rhode Island, which emerged anew under his management in 1997 from the old *Rhode Island Star Clipper.* "We are restaurant people who are proud of our food."

Bob Andrews is an affable fellow who makes passengers feel right at home. He greets them individually as they arrive at the train, one evening even serving as the parking attendant. He is in and out of the kitchen checking his crew's progress with the meal. On his way by a table, he straightens a place setting mysteriously knocked askew. He paid his dues in the dinner train industry running the *North Cove Express* in nearby Essex, Connecticut, for eight years. His enthusiasm and attention to detail shows throughout his newer operation.

Departing from an interpretation of the original Old Colony & Newport Railroad depot, put up adjacent to the Newport Convention and Visitor's Bureau and Gateway Center on America's Cup Avenue near the Marriott Hotel, the train makes an eighteen-mile round-trip north along the west side of Aquidneck Island, running along Narragansett Bay to pass the U.S. Naval Complex, once home to America's battleship fleet and a World War II training center for PT-boat crewmen, including John F. Kennedy. Four and one-half miles out, if the weather cooperates, the train pauses for ten minutes to allow dining guests to enjoy a beautiful Newport sunset. Passing marshes where, occasionally, a flock of Canadian Geese can grace guests with their presence, the train reaches milepost 9, the Melville Boat Basin, where the locomotive is run around the train set for the return to Newport.

Inside, the dining cars' decor is an attractive blend of past and present. The Victorian era is suggested by dried floral arrangements and gold-trimmed mirrors. The 1890s surely inspired the dark green velvet drapes drawn up with flourishes. The 1920s are reflected in the shaded candlesticks with simple Georgian-inspired gold bases. The postwar era is represented by the hard black ceramic mugs and sugar-packet holders. "Interior design and a high level of service are hallmarks of fine dining too," reminds Andrews.

Executive Chef Bob Cornett is, he says, "a Newporter, born and bred." He traces his love for cooking to his grandmother, who encouraged him to help her when he was a child. Trained in classic French technique, he entered the work of "professional cooking" at *Les Auteur,* the American Bistro in Royal Oak, Michigan, that was the brainchild of *Survivor II* contestant Keith Famie. After stints in country clubs and restaurants at various location around the country, he returned to Newport and joined the *Newport Dinner Train* as Executive Chef in 2001. He has a great mentor in Bob Andrews. They've teamed up to present a classic coastal-region dinner.

Blue Cheese Dressing

Before You Begin

You'll need:
medium bowl

Prep: 10 minutes

Yield: 1 quart

1 lb. blue cheese, crumbled

2 cups mayonnaise

1 cup sour cream

juice of 1 lemon

1 small onion, finely grated

In a medium bowl, combine ingredients and mix until creamy. Cover and refrigerate prior to service. Served on board over Bibb lettuce, it goes with any fresh garden salad.

Lobster Salad

Before You Begin

You'll need: large pot, shears or knife, large bowl, medium bowl

Prep: 15 minutes (plus 1 hour to chill)

Cook: 15 minutes

Yield: 6 servings

5 fresh 1½ lb. lobsters

1 cup French or Thousand Island dressing

2 cups celery, trimmed, minced fine

½ Tbsp. salt

¾ Tbsp. Minor's Lobster Base (see page 264)

½ tsp. ground white pepper

1½ cups mayonnaise

Bibb lettuce

roasted red bell peppers (see pages 170–171), julienne (for garnish)

green onions, chiffonade (for garnish)

In a large pot over high heat, bring to a boil enough salted water to immerse lobster(s). Plunge live lobster into boiling water, return water to a boil, then cook 12 minutes longer. Do not overcook. When cool enough to handle, pull tail section to remove from body. Using shears or knife, cut shell, remove tail, and chill until ready to serve. Remove and chop the meat from claws, knuckles, and legs, coarse. Remove any cartilage from the meat. In a large bowl, toss chopped lobster with dressing, cover, and refrigerate 1 hour. Meanwhile, in a medium bowl, blend celery, salt, lobster base, white pepper, and mayonnaise well. Add celery mixture to lobster/dressing mixture, toss lightly to mix, and refrigerate until service. To assemble, place Bibb lettuce on individual plates, top with lobster salad, and garnish with red peppers and green onions. Slice lobster tails into medallions and scatter on salad just before serving.

Fillet of Sole Stuffed with Crabmeat

4 Tbsp. butter, melted

juice of ½ lemon

½ Tbsp. salt

¼ Tbsp. ground pepper

6 5-oz. boneless sole fillets

¼ tsp. paprika

Before You Begin

You'll need: 2 small saucepans, large sheet pan, spray-on vegetable oil, 3 small bowls

Preheat oven to 450°F

Prep: 30 minutes (plus 1 hour to chill stuffing)

Cook: 12 minutes

Yield: 6 servings

In a small saucepan, melt butter and stir in lemon juice, salt, and pepper. Set aside. Spray large sheet pan with vegetable oil. (**NOTE:** Or use a nonstick sheet pan.) On a flat surface, place sole fillets flat. Divide and ball stuffing in portions equal to the number of fillets being prepared, and place on fillets. Wrap fillet around stuffing and set on sheet pan. Drizzle melted butter over each fillet and sprinkle with paprika. Place stuffed sole in 450°F oven for 12 minutes. Serve with drawn butter on side and a wedge of lemon, accompanied with Rice Pilaf (see page 70) and Asparagus Spears (see page 240).

Crabmeat Dressing

1 lb. crabmeat

6 Tbsp. butter, divided

3 oz. celery, chopped fine

3 oz. green bell peppers, chopped fine

3 oz. green onions, chopped fine

3 Tbsp. flour

1½ cups milk

1½ Tbsp. Worcestershire sauce

1 Tbsp. prepared mustard

1 Tbsp. Old Bay seasoning

dash of salt and pepper

1 egg beaten

1 cup plain bread crumbs

In a small bowl, clean and pick over crabmeat to remove bits of cartilage or shell and set aside. In a medium skillet over medium heat, melt butter and sauté celery, pepper, and onion until tender, about 10 minutes. Stirring constantly, gradually add flour and cook to form a blond roux, about 5 minutes. Meanwhile, in a small saucepan, warm but do not boil milk. Slowly stir warmed milk into sautéed vegetables and simmer to thicken, about 5 minutes. Remove from heat and set aside. In a small bowl, mix Worcestershire sauce, mustard, Old Bay seasoning, salt, and pepper, then stir into celery mixture. Add crabmeat and gently fold to mix. In a small bowl, mix beaten egg and bread crumbs until moist, add to crabmeat mixture, and mix lightly. Refrigerate until ready to use, at least 1 hour.

✳ ✳ ✳

Fresh Peach Pie

4 lbs. fresh ripe peaches
¾ cup cornstarch
¾ cup cold water
1½ cups water
½ lb. brown sugar
½ lb. granulated sugar
¾ tsp. salt

¾ tsp. ground cinnamon
⅜ tsp. nutmeg
1 Tbsp. lemon juice
2 Tbsp. butter
2 unbaked 9-inch deep-dish pie shells
 (see page 82)

In a large saucepan over high heat, bring sufficient water in which to float the peaches to a boil. Meanwhile, on the bottom of the peaches, slice a shallow "X," then drop into the boiling water for 3 minutes. Remove from water with a slotted spoon and plunge into ice water bath to arrest cooking. Peel, pit, and slice peaches ¼ inch thick. Set aside. In a small mixing bowl, dissolve cornstarch in ¾ cup cold water and set aside. In a large saucepan over medium-high heat, bring 1½ cups water to a boil. Stir in brown and granulated sugars, salt, cinnamon, nutmeg, lemon juice, and butter, and return to boil. Add cold water/cornstarch mixture, and stir until smooth. Add peaches, stir to mix, and allow to simmer 10 minutes, stirring occasionally. Remove from heat and allow to cool. Pour fruit mixture into the unbaked pie shells. Add the top crust and cut four 1-inch incisions to vent steam. Place in a 425°F oven until crust is golden brown and filling is bubbly, about 40 minutes. Serve warm with vanilla ice cream.

RailCruise America

www.railcruiseamerica.com

The *RailCruise America Luxury Dinner Train Excursion* is distinctive for operating out of a famous train station located in the heart of a major city: Union Station in St. Louis, Missouri. Also unusual: On selected days the train follows the route of Amtrak's *Texas Eagle* as it runs on the right-of-way of the Union Pacific Railroad. Two Class I railroads allowing a dinner train to be shoehorned among their trains is a tribute to the railroad savvy of RailCruise America's management. RailCruise America's Chairman and CEO Ed Boyce began the corporate excursion business in 1985 with one private car. Boyce came from a railroad family, his grandfather having been a switch and signal man at Union Station, and his father working off the Extra Board as a steward in the dining car department of the Wabash Railway. So it came easily to him to use a private car to entertain clients of his successful insurance business. As word of his unique meeting facility spread, he realized he had a new business on his hands. Fifteen years later he has his fleet of cars and locomotives offering a full-service meetings and events venue. Using the cars—eight meticulously restored smooth-side passenger cars from the 1950s, most built by Pullman, most for the Union Pacific, all now in green and gold livery—as a dinner train was a logical extension of the excursion business.

The order of the cars is typical of the large dinner trains: On the point is crew dormitory/power car *Current River,* followed by the executive sleeping car *Colorado River* (included in dinner train runs to save the expense of switching it in and out

of the train set), the diner/lounge car *Cuivre River,* dining car *Osage River* and dome dining car *Columbia River,* with their kitchens placed back-to-back, dome/lounge *Mississippi River,* party car *Charrette Creek,* and parlor/observation car *Missouri River.* Matching locomotives are set up in a push-pull arrangement.

On board, Executive Chef Michael Slay comes from an equally long line of St. Louis restaurateurs and food-service professionals. In 1911 his grandparents opened their first restaurant on Seventh and Gratiot in downtown St. Louis. Chef Michael began his culinary career making pizza dough after school at a small pizzeria at the end of his block. At

RailCruise America dining room.
Courtesy RailCruise America

sixteen he was in charge of the kitchen. While attending the Kansas City Art Institute he worked in a Welsh pub, an Italian restaurant, and a sushi bar. When he moved back to St. Louis, Slay studied Italian baking and pastry making for two years. Then, over the next eight years, he worked his way up the ranks to become Head Chef for the renowned Slay's Steakhouse of St. Louis.

"When I decided to branch out on my own," Slay says, "I went in to the catering business. My first job was on a private railroad dining car." Now, more than a quarter of a million miles later, he has toured the continental United States, Canada, and Mexico. He has served two U.S. presidents, several governors, numerous CEOs, and thousands of those wanting to experience a bygone era. In the process, Chef Slay has become widely known among private car owners for his magical execution of superb cuisine while running at seventy-nine miles an hour, be it for a party of two or for 182. "The experience has been incredible," he says. "From a culinary and cultural stand point, I have been able to sample and learn a lot about authentic regional cuisines in the places I've traveled. And the scenery I see by rail is just the icing on the cake."

Summer Tomato Salad with Fresh Mozzarella, Sweet Red Peppers, Roasted Shallot and Basil Vinaigrette

Before You Begin

You'll need: heavy aluminum foil, bowl, blender

Preheat oven to 350°F.

Prep: 30 minutes

Yield: 8 servings

2 bulbs shallot

1 cup + 1 Tbsp. extra-virgin olive oil, divided

2 red bell peppers

½ cup apple cider vinegar

1 tsp. sea salt

1 tsp. cracked black pepper

2 cloves garlic, crushed

½ cup coarse-chopped fresh basil leaves

2 tsp. granulated sugar

2 medium-to-large red beefsteak tomatoes

4 medium-to-large yellow beefsteak tomatoes

8 ounces fresh mozzarella

8 very thin slices red onion

4 cups mâche or micro greens

crusty Italian bread

Slice both ends off shallots, just enough to stand up and expose inside of bulbs, and place on a 5 × 5-inch piece of heavy aluminum foil. Coat the shallots with 1 tablespoon of olive oil and fold the edges of the foil up to form an enclosed pouch. Roast the shallots in 350°F oven for 30 minutes, remove pouch from the oven, and set aside without opening foil to cool. On an open gas flame or under a broiler, char the red bell peppers until skin blisters and turns black on all sides, about 1 to 2 minutes per side. Wrap peppers in aluminum foil for 15 minutes. Under cold running water remove burnt skin, stem, and open to wash out seeds, and place peppers in a bowl and chill. Lightly squeeze the cooled shallots out of their skins and place in a blender.

Add 1 cup olive oil, vinegar, salt, cracked pepper, crushed garlic, fresh basil, and the granulated sugar. Blend until smooth, about 10 seconds. Slice the red and yellow tomatoes about ½ inch thick to yield 8 slices of red and 16 slices of yellow. Slice mozzarella into 8 slices about ⅜ inch thick. Slice the cooled roasted red peppers into ¾-inch strips. To serve, place one slice yellow tomato on individual serving plate, lay a slice of red tomato ¾ of the way over the top of the yellow tomato. Repeat this process with one more slice of yellow tomato. Place roasted red pepper strip on each side of the tomatoes. Top tomatoes with one slice mozzarella, a few rings of red onion, and half a handful of mâche or micro greens. Drizzle shallot and basil vinaigrette over and accompany with fresh crusty Italian bread.

Black and White Sesame-Encrusted Halibut with Orange and Ginger Soy Glaze

4 Tbsp. black sesame seeds

4 Tbsp. white sesame seeds

1 cup all-purpose flour (approximate amount)

4 egg whites

8 6- to 7-oz. fresh Alaskan halibut fillets

1 Tbsp. fine sea salt

1½ tsp. cracked black pepper

1½ tsp. granulated garlic

½ cup peanut oil

Before You Begin

You'll need:
2 medium bowls, sheet pan, large nonstick skillet, holding platter, large ovenproof dish, 2 small bowls 2-quart saucepan, fine sieve

Preheat oven to 350°F.

Prep: 20 minutes

Cook: 15 minutes

Yield: 8 servings

NOTE: Black and white sesame seeds are reasonably priced and can be found at Asian grocers.

In a small bowl, mix black and white sesame seeds and set aside. Place flour in a medium bowl. In another medium bowl briskly whip egg whites until frothy, about 20 seconds. Pat fish fillets dry and season on both sides with salt, pepper, and garlic, pressing seasoning on to the flesh by hand. Pour enough flour into a medium bowl to measure 1 inch deep. Dredge fillets in flour, shake off excess, then dip in beaten egg white and place on a sheet pan. Liberally coat the top of the fish with mixed sesame seeds, pressing seeds on to flesh to adhere. In a large nonstick skillet over medium-high heat, warm peanut oil and add fish, seed-side down. (NOTE: It will likely take two batches to cook fillets.) Do not let the fillets touch each other in the skillet or they will bind together. Cook the fillets until seeds are toasted and golden brown. This will happen fairly quickly, depending on the heat and skillet, in about 1 to 2 minutes. Turn fillets and brown the other side, again 1 to 2 minutes. Remove fish from skillet and place on ovenproof dish large enough for all eight pieces. (**NOTE**: The fish will still be rare in the center.) Transfer to a 350°F oven until fish is cooked and still moist, about 7 more minutes. Remove from the oven, plate over Basmati Rice with Endamame, drizzle Orange Ginger Soy Glaze over fish, and serve with Fresh Sugar Snap Peas and Julienne Carrots.

CHEF'S TIP: You have a number of garnish options with this entree: Thin sliced orange segments, fresh daikon sprouts, julienne scallion that has been soaked in cold water for a few minutes before serving, or sprigs of fresh cilantro.

Orange Ginger Soy Glaze

¾ cup mirin (sweet sake)

1 Tbsp. minced fresh garlic

1 Tbsp. minced fresh ginger

1 tsp. grated orange zest

¾ cup orange juice

¾ cup lite soy sauce

1 Tbsp. cornstarch

1½ Tbsp. cold water

In a 2-quart saucepan over medium heat, combine mirin, garlic, ginger and orange zest and bring to simmer. Simmer very low for 10 minutes. Add orange juice and soy sauce and continue to simmer low for 10 more minutes. Strain through fine sieve. Return to pan and simmer. Meanwhile, in a small bowl, dissolve cornstarch in cold water. Add cornstarch to stained sauce to heat through and thicken sufficiently to stick to a spoon. Remove from heat.

Basmati Rice with Edamame

Before You Begin

You'll need: sieve, 3-quart saucepan

Prep: 45 minutes (includes 30 minutes to drain and to soak)

Cook: 15 minutes

Yield: 8 servings

1½ cups basmati rice

3 cups low-sodium chicken broth

1 bay leaf

1 tsp. ground allspice

1½ cups edamame (shelled soybeans)

In a sieve, wash the rice thoroughly in cold water until water is clear. Drain completely. Put rice in a 3-quart saucepan and add chicken broth, bay leaf, and allspice. Let stand for 15 minutes. Over high heat, bring rice to a boil, reduce heat to a simmer, cover and cook until broth is just absorbed, about 9 minutes. Remove from heat. Let stand for 2 minutes. Add edamame, fluff to heat through, and serve.

Fresh Sugar Snap Peas and Julienne Carrots

Before You Begin

You'll need:
3-quart saucepan, medium skillet

Prep: 5 minutes

Cook: 15 minutes

Yield: 8 servings

3 cups fresh sugar snap peas

1 large carrot, ¼" × 3" julienne

3 Tbsp. peanut oil

1 tsp. sesame oil

3 Tbsp. light soy sauce

fine sea salt to taste

In a 3-quart saucepan over high heat, bring 2 quarts of water to a boil and add sugar snap peas and carrots. Cook for 3 minutes, drain, and plunge immediately in a ice-water bath to cool. Drain and remove ice. In a medium skillet over high heat, heat peanut oil and the sesame oil. Add sugar snap peas and carrots and sauté, turning frequently, for 2 minutes. Add soy sauce and sea salt to taste, cook for 30 more seconds, and serve.

Chocolate-Laced Pastry Tulip with White Chocolate and Blueberry Mousse with Raspberry Sauce

Mousse

Before You Begin

You'll need:
5-quart capacity stainless-steel double boiler, 2 large stainless-steel mixing bowls, rubber spatula, food processor, fine sieve, 2 plastic squeeze bottles, small double boiler, 2 small bowls, nonstick cookie sheet pan, coffee cup or similar, ice cream scoop

Preheat oven to 350°F.

Prep: 45 minutes (allow 4 hours to chill mousse)

Cook: 7 minutes

Yield: 8 servings

½ Tbsp. unflavored gelatin

¼ cup Riesling wine

5½ oz. white chocolate, finely chopped

1 cup heavy cream

1 cup fresh blueberries

¼ cup granulated sugar

In a 5-quart stainless-steel double boiler over simmering water, dissolve gelatin in Riesling. Add white chocolate and sugar, and stir until blended smooth. Transfer to large stainless-steel mixing bowl, and refrigerate until cool but not set. Meanwhile, in another stainless-steel bowl, with a mixer, whip cream until stiff peaks form. Gently fold blueberries into the whipped cream. Using a rubber spatula, fold the whipped cream/blueberry mixture into the cooled white chocolate mixture. Chill 4 hours.

CHEF'S TIP: Stainless-steel bowls are preferred because they won't break if dropped.

Raspberry Sauce

2 cups fresh raspberries
2 Tbsp. light corn syrup
¼ cup sugar

2 Tbsp. Chambord liqueur
1 tsp. fresh lemon juice

In a food processor add all ingredients and process until smooth. Strain through a fine sieve, pour into a plastic squeeze bottle, and refrigerate to chill through, about 1 hour.

Chocolate Sauce

4 oz. semisweet chocolate
½ cup heavy cream

1 Tbsp. light corn syrup
1 Tbsp. sugar

In a small stainless-steel double boiler over simmering water, combine all ingredients and blend until smooth. Transfer to a plastic squeeze bottle and set aside.

Chocolate-Laced Pastry Tulips

⅔ cup sugar
½ cup egg whites, about 3 eggs
2 Tbsp. cocoa powder
¾ cup flour

½ cup unsalted butter, melted
fresh mixed berries and mint sprigs (for
    garnish)

Lightly butter a nonstick cookie sheet pan and set aside. In a small bowl, beat sugar and egg whites until sugar is dissolved. Add cocoa powder, flour, and melted butter, and blend until smooth. (NOTE: Batter will be very thin.) On the buttered cookie sheet, spread 3 tablespoons of batter to form a 5-inch circle. Make as many circles as will fit on the cookie sheet. Bake in a 350°F oven until the circles are dark brown on the edges, about 7 minutes. Remove from oven and let sit about 45 seconds to cool, then place individual circles on inverted coffee cups, gently pressing the circles down to form a tulip shape. Remove shapes and set aside to cool.

To serve, squeeze a little chocolate sauce on to the inside walls of the pastry tulip. On a 7-inch plate, squeeze raspberry sauce to form a flower pattern. Set the tulip on the plate. With an ice cream scoop, place one scoop of mousse into the tulip. Garnish with fresh mixed berries and a mint sprig.

NOTE: See pages 119–120 for the appetizer recipe Chef Michael Slay's passengers voted their favorite.

Scenic Rail Dining

This classy and popular train operated out of Milwaukee, Wisconsin, between 1988 and 1990. It was then sold to a tour operator in San Francisco. It is noteworthy for the high standards it set for both dinner train design and construction, and for food service.

Shrimp-Scallop-Asparagus Skewer on Tomato Butter Sauce

1 large raw shrimp

1 large raw sea scallop

1 thin asparagus spear

butter at room temperature

Before You Begin

You'll need: paring knife, asparagus skewers, sheet pan

Preheat oven to 350°F

Prep: 20 minutes

Cook: 30 minutes

Yield: 1 skewer (make 3 per serving)

Butter sheet pan and set aside. Peel, devein, and wash shrimp, leaving tail section attached. With paring knife, make small slit down through the top of the shrimp and across through the tail section adjacent, to hold asparagus skewer. Make slit through scallop at its widest part. Slice the stem of the asparagus spear at a sharp angle and to desired length of the skewer. Blanch asparagus 30 seconds in boiling water, and drain, before assembling, leaving asparagus stiff enough to work with. To assemble skewers, push asparagus spear through the top slit in the shrimp, through the entire width of the scallop, and lastly through slit in tail of shrimp. Snip the asparagus spear to desired length. Place on a buttered sheet pan sprinkled lightly with water, and bake at 350°F 20 to 25 minutes, or steam until tender, 10 to 15 minutes

Tomato Butter Sauce

⅓ cup dry vermouth

2 shallots, minced

¼ cup heavy cream

1 Tbsp. tomato paste

½ lb. sweet butter, chopped into pieces

salt and white pepper to taste

Before You Begin

You'll need: medium sauté pan, extrafine strainer

Prep: 5 minutes

Cook: 20 minutes

Yield: 4 servings

Over medium-high heat, place vermouth and shallots in medium sauté pan and reduce to nearly dry. Add cream and tomato paste. Whip mixture until smooth and reduce by half. Reduce heat to low. Whip butter in to the sauce one piece at a time. If the butter is added too quickly the sauce will break. Strain sauce through an extra fine strainer, and season with salt and pepper. To serve, place portion of Tomato Butter Sauce on individual serving plate. Arrange three Shrimp-Scallop-Asparagus Skewers on sauce.

Hungarian Mushroom Soup

Before You Begin

You'll need: 3-quart saucepan, two 2-quart saucepans

Prep: 30 minutes

Cook: 1 hour

Yield: 8 8-oz. servings

1 qt. chicken stock

4 oz. white button mushrooms

1 oz. shallots, minced fine

4 oz. butter

1 oz. paprika

½ oz. fresh dill

salt and pepper to taste

1 lb. butter, clarified

2 cups flour

1 qt. heavy cream

sour cream (for garnish)

dill sprigs (for garnish)

In a 3-quart saucepan, heat chicken stock to boil. Meanwhile, clean mushrooms and slice thin. Sauté shallots and mushrooms in butter. Add seasonings. In a 2-quart saucepan, clarify butter and slowly add flour, stirring constantly to avoid lumps, to make a blond roux, approximately 3 minutes. Thicken chicken stock to desired consistency with roux. Add sautéed shallots and mushrooms. In a separate 2-quart saucepan, heat cream, then add to stock/mushroom mixture. Simmer until taste of roux is cooked out, approximately 1 hour. Adjust consistency and seasoning if needed.

To serve: Whip sour cream with whisk. Place soup in a bowl and garnish with a dollop of sour cream and fresh dill sprigs.

Raspberry Vinaigrette Mixed Salad

Raspberry Vinaigrette

Before You Begin

You'll need: large mixing bowl, container with tight-fitting lid, serving bowls

Prep: 30 minutes

Yield: 3 quarts

2 cups raspberry vinegar

1½ cups raspberry puree

2 or 3 whole bay leaves, crushed

¾ tsp. thyme

1 oz. shallots, minced

1 oz. garlic, minced

salt and pepper to taste

½ cup walnut oil

1 qt. olive oil

1½ cups high-quality salad oil

Combine vinegar, puree, herbs, shallots, and garlic. Add oils and whip to mix well. Place in container with tight-fitting lid and refrigerate before serving. Stores refrigerated 2 months, frozen 6 months.

Mixed Salad

2 heads Bibb lettuce

1 head romaine lettuce

12 whole orange segments

8 whole grapefruit segments

12 whole strawberries, cut in half

1 oz. walnuts, chopped coarse (for garnish)

Clean and wash romaine lettuce, taking care that it is free of dirt and discolored areas, and tear into bite-size pieces. Remove root from Bibb lettuce. In serving bowls, assemble salads: 5 to 6 leaves of Bibb, portion of romaine to the right, fruit garnish (3 orange segments, 2 grapefruit segments, 6 strawberry halves) to the left. Apply Raspberry Vinaigrette. Garnish with chopped walnuts.

Roast Rack of Lamb Provençale

The main course is accompanied by boiled new potatoes trimmed to a mushroom shape, and by an assortment of fresh steamed vegetables of the season.

1 clove garlic, minced

¼ tsp. black pepper, freshly cracked

1 leaf rosemary, crushed

1 leaf thyme, crushed

salt to taste

1 hotel rack of lamb, giving 4 portions approximately 4" long each

3 Tbsp. olive oil

2 cups fresh bread crumbs, crust removed

Combine seasonings well. Rub rack of lamb with seasoning mix, taking care to coat all sides. Heat olive oil hot to smoking. Sear rack of lamb, top first, then bottom, then all sides. Cool, cover, and refrigerate until cool to touch, about 1 hour.

Before You Begin

You'll need: large skillet, roasting pan with roasting rack

Preheat oven to 450°F.

Prep: 30 minutes (plus overnight for spread to chill)

Cook: 1 hour (in two steps)

Yield: 4 servings

Mustard Spread

1 cup Dijon mustard

6 Tbsp. white wine

1 tsp. shallots, minced

1 tsp. garlic, minced

3 Tbsp. parsley, chopped fine

1 Tbsp. rosemary, chopped fine

1 cup olive oil

Before You Begin

You'll need: covered medium bowl

Prep: overnight

Yield: 2½ cups

In a bowl, mix all ingredients together, cover, and refrigerate overnight.

To finish: Spread seasoned mustard over cold seared lamb rack in a thin layer. Roll lamb rack in fresh grated bread crumbs to coat. Place on roasting rack, then in roasting pan, and in 450°F oven to roast 20 to 30 minutes. Internal temperature for medium rare service should be 110°F.

Natural Lamb Sauce

Before You Begin

You'll need: 2-quart saucepan

Prep: 10 minutes

Cook: 1 ½ hours

Yield: 1 quart

4 cups lamb stock or demi-glace

2 cups white wine

2 Tbsp. garlic, minced

6 oz. tomato puree

salt and pepper to taste

½ lb. butter, chopped into pieces

Place lamb stock, white wine, and garlic in a 2-quart saucepan over medium heat, bring to boil, lower heat to simmer and reduce by half. Add tomato puree, salt, and pepper, and simmer for 30 additional minutes. Strain through the strainer or cheesecloth, return to clean saucepan, and whip in butter one piece at a time. Serve immediately by pouring on individual serving plate and top with rack of lamb.

Chocolate Praline Pâté

Before You Begin

You'll need: double boiler, whisk, 10-inch springform pan, wax paper

Prep: 10 minutes

Cook: 30 minutes (plus overnight to cool)

Yield: 12 servings

1 lb. bittersweet chocolate

1 cup heavy cream

¼ cup unsalted butter

4 egg yolks

1 cup confectioners' sugar

½ cup praline liqueur

1 cup praline powder or almond paste (or more to taste)

2 cups chocolate wafers, crushed fine

¼ cup butter, melted

In a double boiler, over simmering water, combine the chocolate, cream, and unsalted butter. Cook over low heat, stirring occasionally, until chocolate is melted and mixture is smooth. Remove from heat. One at a time, whisk the egg yolks into the chocolate mixture until well blended. Gradually whisk in the confectioners' sugar, then the praline liqueur. Then fold in the praline powder.

Meanwhile, crush the chocolate wafers into fine crumbs and add enough butter to form a crust on the bottom of a 10-inch springform pan. Line the sides of the pan with a strip of wax paper. Pour the chocolate mixture over the crust. Let cool to room temperature, then cover and refrigerate overnight. Remove springform. Cut into wedges and serve cold.

Shasta Sunset Dinner Train

www.shastasunset.com

Late on a Saturday afternoon, driving northwest on state Route 89 from Susanville, California, through beautiful big-trees forest, the village of McCloud is just ahead. An historic, charming, unspoiled, and now restored company-built lumber mill town founded in the 1880s, McCloud is nestled on the southern slope of Mt. Shasta, and is home to the McCloud Railway Company and its *Shasta Sunset Dinner Train*.

After checking in on the depot platform, passengers enter the dining car to be greeted by a perfect evocation of America's first-class trains of the 1920s and '30s. Finished in Philippine mahogany throughout, with decorative touches carved by local artist Jess Hampton, each table is fitted with a wooden bracket holding a vase of fresh flowers. The lighting from brass fixtures and white glass shades is enhanced

Dinner trains offer spectacular views as part of their appeal, including the simultaneous view of Mt. Adams and Mt. Hood on the Mt. Hood Dinner Train, *of Mt. Rainier on the* Spirit of Washington Dinner Train, *or of Naraginsett Bay at sunset on the* Newport Dinner Train. *The* Shasta Sunset Dinner Train, *though, with its run along the base of Mt. Shasta, may be able to lay legitimate claim to having the most sustained vision of nature's glory offered by any rail dinning experience. Bob Morris*

Shasta Sunset
Dinner Train
dining room.
Bob Morris

by evening sunlight streaming across the room. Chairs and benches are upholstered with a floral fabric that emphasizes gold and burnt yellows, but with
splashes of pink and purple that blend imperceptibly with the carpet. Windows are
treated with cream damask curtains trimmed with bridal lace, and floral garlands
of the season run the length of the car at the roof line.

The meals are the creation of Executive Chef Edward Hines. When he joined the
Shasta Sunset Dinner Train in spring of 1998, he brought nearly thirty-five years of
culinary experience with him. He accompanies each run of the train to ensure
quality and service, and, in a manner that reflects his outgoing personality, takes
time to chat with guests.

Seafood with Pineapple-Mango Chutney

Seafood Salad

½ cup bay shrimp
½ lb. crabmeat
½ cup scallops
2 Tbsp. dill weed

½ Tbsp. cayenne pepper
¼ cup chopped green onions
1 cup mayonnaise

Before You Begin

You'll need:
1½-quart saucepan, strainer, medium bowl

Prep: 20 minutes (plus at least 1 hour to chill)

Yield: 4 servings

Shrimp and crabmeat are to come cooked. For scallops, in a 1½-quart saucepan bring 4 cups water to a boil. Add scallops and cook until white, about 5 minutes. Strain and set aside to cool. Coarsely chop shrimp and scallops and pick crabmeat clean of shell pieces. In a medium bowl, combine dill weed, cayenne pepper, onion, and mayonnaise. Add diced shrimp, scallops, and crabmeat, and mix well. Refrigerate to chill and blend.

Pineapple-Mango Chutney

½ cup ripe mango, peeled, chopped
   coarse
½ cup pineapple, chopped coarse

pinch saffron
¼ cup corn syrup
¼ cup brown sugar

Before You Begin

You'll need:
1-quart saucepan

Prep: 5 minutes

Cook: 20 minutes

Yield: 1½ cups

In 1-quart saucepan over medium heat, combine all ingredients and slowly bring just to a boil. Reduce heat and let simmer, stirring occasionally, until well blended and thickened, about 20 minutes. Remove from heat and let stand.

Grilled Prawns

¼ cup chopped cilantro
½ tsp. cayenne pepper

¼ cup sesame oil
12 medium prawns

Before You Begin

You'll need: medium bowl

Preheat oven to Broil or use barbecue grill on medium-high.

Prep: 5 minutes (plus 1 hour to marinate)

Cook: 5 minutes

Yield: 4 servings

In a medium bowl, combine cilantro and pepper, then add oil and whip to infuse. Add prawns, toss to coat, and marinate at least one hour. Toss shrimp on grill, or place under broiler, to cook until white with an orange cast, turning once, about 2½ minutes per side.

Smoked Salmon

Before You Begin

You'll need: small bowl, 1-gallon freezer bag, outdoor or stovetop smoker

Preheat smoker according to instructions.

Prep: 5 minutes (plus overnight to marinate)

Cook: 2 hours

Yield: 4 servings

4 6-oz. salmon fillets, skin removed
   optional
1 Tbsp. liquid smoke

½ cup brown sugar
¼ cup molasses

In a small bowl, mix liquid smoke, brown sugar, and molasses until smooth. Place salmon fillets in a 1-gallon freezer bag. Pour marinade over salmon and very gently massage to coat fillets without breaking them. Refrigerate overnight. Cook according to smoker instructions until salmon is firm, about 2 hours.

To serve, on individual plates spread a generous portion of pineapple-mango chutney. Place approximately ⅔ cup seafood salad in the center of the plate. Surround seafood salad with three grilled prawns. Position salmon fillet to one side.

Creamy House Caesar Salad

Before You Begin

You'll need: small pan, blender

Prep: 10 minutes (plus at least 1 hour to chill)

Yield: 3 cups

½ cup Parmesan cheese, grated
dash Worcestershire sauce
pinch of fresh garlic, minced
2 tsp. whole peppercorns
1 cup balsamic vinegar
½ cup buttermilk

1 anchovy fillet
2 cups Pomace olive oil (substitute: any high-quality olive oil)
1 egg
4 cups romaine lettuce, broken into 1-inch pieces

In a small pan over high heat, bring sufficient water to cover the egg to a boil and immerse the egg in the water for 1 minute. Meanwhile, combine first seven ingredients in blender and blend on high. With the blender running, carefully remove lid and slowly incorporate oil. Add coddled egg to dressing and pulse until well blended. Refrigerate before serving. To serve, toss with, or pour over romaine lettuce.

Beef Wellington with Sauce Béarnaise and Merlot Sauce

8 7" × 10" sheets Pepperidge Farm puff
    pastry
¼ cup Dijon mustard

2 cups pâté
8 10-oz. filet mignon

Before You Begin

You'll need: large baking sheet, 1-quart saucepan, blender

Preheat oven to 400°F.

Prep: 30 minutes (includes time to prepare pâté)

Cook: 30 minutes

Yield: 8 servings

For each portion, place a puff pastry on a flat lightly floured surface. Spread with 1 teaspoon mustard and approximately ¼ cup pâté. Center the filet mignon, trim pastry as needed, and fold to close around filet, overlapping edges and pressing to seal. Place with fold edges down on a large ungreased baking sheet and bake at 400°F to desired degree of doneness (about 25 minutes for rare to 30 minutes for medium-well). To serve, ladle small amount of Merlot Sauce on individual serving plates, set Beef Wellington in sauce, and ladle Sauce Béarnaise over.

Pâté

2 Tbsp. unsalted butter
4 cloves garlic, whole
2 shallots, chopped

4 oz. beef, chopped (see NOTE)
½ cup Dijon mustard
5 large button mushrooms, whole

(**NOTE:** Use trimmings from filet mignon or, if already trimmed when bought, buy sirloin or other very lean beef)

In a heavy 1-quart saucepan over medium-high heat, combine butter, garlic, shallots, and beef, and sauté until beef is fully cooked, about 5 minutes. Reduce heat, add mustard and mushrooms, and cook until mushrooms are soft, about 5 to 10 minutes. Remove from heat and allow to cool. Then, place mushroom mixture in a blender and pulse until of a consistency that can be spread on puff pastry.

Merlot Sauce

¼ cup unsalted butter, melted
3 cloves garlic, chopped
1 shallot, diced small

½ cup Merlot wine
2 cups beef stock (reduce by half)

Before You Begin

You'll need:
1-quart saucepan

Prep: 10 minutes

Cook: 20 minutes

Yield: 1 cup

In a 1-quart saucepan over medium heat, melt butter and sauté garlic and shallots until of a dark brown color, about 5 minutes. Deglaze pan with

Merlot wine and simmer for 5 minutes. Add beef stock and continue to simmer until reduced by half. Use a roux (see Cheese Sauce, below) to thicken if needed. Finished sauce should have the consistency of gravy.

Sauce Béarnaise

Before You Begin

You'll need:
2-quart saucepan, small saucepan, small sauté pan, heat-resistant medium mixing bowl, strainer

Prep: 15 minutes

Cook: 15 minutes

Yield: 1 cup

1 cup butter, melted

1 Tbsp. shallots, minced

1 Tbsp. fresh tarragon, minced

½ cup rice vinegar

3 egg yolks

warm water

pinch cayenne pepper

dash Worcestershire sauce

In a small saucepan over low heat, melt butter, skim to clarify, and set aside. In a small sauté pan over medium heat, combine shallots, tarragon, and rice vinegar, and reduce until liquid is about 2 tablespoons. Set aside. In a 2-quart saucepan over high heat, bring 4 cups of water to a boil. Meanwhile, in a heat-resistant medium mixing bowl, whisk egg yolks with 1½ tablespoons warm water. Whisk in cayenne and Worcestershire sauce. Place the mixing bowl on top of the boiling water, and whisk constantly until egg mixture thickens. Remove from heat. Slowly incorporate clarified butter while whipping. If sauce becomes too thick, add a little more warm water to thin. Whisk in the tarragon/shallots/vinegar reduction. Let stand for 5 minutes, then strain. Serve at room temperature.

Scalloped Potatoes

Before You Begin

You'll need: large pot, 2-quart ovenproof casserole, 1½-quart saucepan

Preheat oven to 400°F.

Prep: 30 minutes

Cook: 30 minutes

Yield: 8 servings

2 lbs. potatoes

3 cups Cheese Sauce

1 cooking onion, chopped, caramelized

Fill a large pot with water sufficient to cover potatoes and bring to a boil. Parboil potatoes to stiff, not soft, 15 to 20 minutes. Drain and place in cold water to arrest cooking. When cool to touch, peel potatoes and slice ⅛ inch thick. Layer in 8" × 12" baking pan, pour cheese over, and spread onions on top. Bake at 400°F until brown, about 30 minutes.

Cheese Sauce

2 Tbsp. butter

3 Tbsp. flour

2 cups heavy cream

¼ lb. medium cheddar cheese, grated

In 1½-quart saucepan over low heat, melt butter. Stirring constantly, blend in flour to make blond roux, about 2 minutes. Remove from heat, add cream, whip to mix well, and return to heat. Add cheese and cook, stirring frequently, until melted and blended.

NOTE: Extra cheese sauce is excellent mixed with cooked elbow macaroni, especially popular with children.

Green Beans Triple Sec

2 lbs. green beans
¼ cup butter
¼ cup chopped tarragon

3 oz. Triple Sec
½ cup toasted silvered almonds (see page 00)

Before You Begin

You'll need: large pot, colander, large bowl, cotton towel, large skillet

Prep: 15 minutes

Cook: 15 minutes

Yield: 8 servings

Trim beans of stem and tip. In a large pot, bring sufficient water to cover beans to a boil. Add beans and boil until bright green but not limp, about 10 minutes. Drain and plunge into large bowl of ice water to arrest cooking. Spread on a towel and pat dry. In a large skillet over medium heat, melt butter. Stir in tarragon and Triple Sec until blended. Add green beans and sauté, stirring occasionally, until heated through. Sprinkle individual servings with toasted almond slivers.

Mountain Berry Parfait

1 cup raspberry sauce
2 cups strawberries, halved

2 cups raspberries
2 cups blueberries

Before You Begin

You'll need: 4-quart saucepan, 2 large mixing bowls, whisk, small bowl, electric mixer

Prep: 30 minutes (plus overnight for custard mixture to set up)

Yield: 8 servings

Custard

10 egg yolks
3 cups heavy cream
1 cup sugar

2 Tbsp. unflavored gelatin
½ cup warm water
½ tsp. vanilla extract

Whipped Cream

2 cups heavy cream
2 oz. confectioners' sugar

½ tsp. vanilla extract

In a 4-quart saucepan over high heat, bring 2 quarts of water to a boil. Meanwhile, in a mixing bowl that will set in saucepan, prepare Custard. Mix egg yolks, cream, and sugar with a whisk until sugar dissolves. Put bowl of egg/cream/sugar mixture on top of pot of boiling water and stir constantly until thickened, about 20 minutes. In a small bowl, stir gelatin into the ½ cup warm water to dissolve, then slowly add mixture to custard while stirring. When mixture is hot to the touch, stir in vanilla. Take off water, cover, and chill overnight.

When ready to serve parfaits, prepare Whipped Cream. In large mixing bowl using a mixer, whip heavy cream on high speed, until semi-stiff (peaks form). Continue whipping and slowly add confectioners' sugar and vanilla. Mix well. Gently fold whipped cream into custard mixture.

To serve, in individual serving glasses, place a portion of raspberry sauce, layers of each berry, and custard, then repeat until glasses are full.

Spirit of Washington Dinner Train

www.spiritofwashingtondinnertrain.com

It's five-thirty on a summer's Friday evening near the Eastside Seattle community of Renton, home to Boeing, Kenworth, Paccar, and Microsoft. Swing off I-405, drive a short way, and arrive fifty years back in time.

Sitting along the platform of the restored Renton depot is the streamlined *Spirit of Washington Dinner Train.* Looking as though its about to set off across the nearby

Many dinner trains operate on working short line railroad rights-of-way that are themselves remnants of former Class I railroads. Here the Spirit of Washington Dinner Train *crosses the 975-foot-long, 102-foot-high Wilburton Trestle, built in 1891 in present-day Bellevue, Washington.* Courtesy *Spirit of Washington Dinner Train*

Cascade Range and race east to Chicago—flags aflutter on the point hint of sections to follow—it evokes memories of the glory days of American passenger railroading. For this train set is no eclectic mix of cars of varied eras and design. Led by a pair (or trio, depending on where the power car is placed) of flashily painted fire-engine red F-7A's sporting bold coal-black and snow-white striping, the seven-car consist, all silver sides built between 1937 and 1952, is accented with red, black, and white stripes. A matching "seahawk" logo identifies the train's parent, Washington Central Railroad.

Inside, each car is unique. The three domed cars—*Mt. Ranier, City of Renton* (a super dome), and *City of Seattle*—are the jewels of the fleet. Once under way, they afford magnificent views of the Seattle skyline, Lake Washington and Mercer Island, the historic towns of Bellevue and Kirkland, and the Sammamish River Valley (not for the faint of heart, though, is the view when crossing 102-foot high, 975-foot long Wilburton trestle, build in 1891).

The *Mt. Ranier* offers a private dining room that seats up to eight on request. For many, though, the lower level of the elegantly appointed *City of Seattle* is the place to eat. It is invitingly decorated, with dusty rose, grey, and green carpet; a fossiled seashell-pattern wallpaper; salmon, grey, green, and brown-upholstered chairs; dark green and rose satin drapes; fanned sea-shell art deco light fixtures; dark wood and gold metal detailing; and, overhead, a ceiling of backlit panels that contain hundreds of pin- and star-shaped holes, producing the effect of a spectacular night sky (one is reminded of the ceilings of rail baron Jay Gould's Lyndhurst mansion in Tarrytown, New York).

The *Spirit of Washington* even has a destination: At twenty-two miles north, a

The Spirit of Washington Dinner Train *dining room. Courtesy* Spirit of Washington Dinner Train

layover for a forty-five-minute diversion at the Columbia Winery in Woodenville. The oldest winery in Washington state, the Columbia wins international recognition for its eight premium varietals. A tour of the winery and a tasting in the gift shop is in order before heading back to the train for the return to Renton.

Whistling itself through grade crossings and back into Renton at 10:15 P.M., the *Spirit of Washington* places home sites along its route among that disappearing breed: urban settings haunted by the lonesome whistle of a train after dark.

Sweet Rosemary Rolls with Salmon Lox, Herbed Cream Cheese, and Honey Butter Spreads

Before You Begin

You'll need: medium mixing bowl, baking sheet, small bowl, pastry brush

Preheat oven to 400°F.

Prep: 2 hours (includes dough rising)

Cook: 20 minutes

Yield: 8 rolls

1 pkg. dry active yeast
¼ cup honey
1½ cups warm water
2 tsp. olive oil
1 tsp. salt

1 6-inch sprig fresh rosemary, finely chopped, or 2 Tbsp. dried
1½ cups whole wheat flour
2 to 3 cups unbleached white flour
1 Tbsp. cornmeal

Glaze

1 Tbsp. honey

1 Tbsp. water

In a medium mixing bowl, combine yeast, honey, and water. Cover and set aside in a warm place for 10 minutes or until foamy. Add oil, salt, rosemary, and whole wheat flour, and mix well. Stir in white flour ½ cup at a time until a stiff dough has formed. Turn dough out onto a lightly floured surface and knead for about 5 minutes, adding flour as necessary, until dough is smooth and elastic. Place in a lightly oiled bowl, cover with plastic wrap or a towel, and set in a warm place until doubled, about 1 hour. Then dust a baking sheet with cornmeal. Punch down dough and divide into 8 pieces. Form pieces into balls and place on prepared baking sheet at least 1-inch apart. Cover and let rise for 30 minutes. In a small bowl, combine honey with water and stir until dissolved. Brush rolls lightly with glaze and place in a 400°F oven to bake for 15 to 20 minutes, until golden brown.

Honey Butter

8 oz. butter, room temperature   ¼ cup honey

Using a food processor or mixer, in a small bowl, whip butter until smooth. Add honey and whip until well blended.

Before You Begin

You'll need: food processor or mixer, mixing bowl

Prep: 5 minutes

Yield: 1 cup

Salmon Lox Spread

4 oz. salmon lox, trimmed
½ lb. lightly salted butter, room
     temperature

8 oz. cream cheese, room temperature
1 Tbsp. lemon juice
1 Tbsp. ground black pepper

Using a food processor or mixer, put lox in a medium mixing bowl and run on high until smooth. Add butter and mix until blended. Add cream cheese, lemon juice, and pepper and mix until blended.

Before You Begin

You'll need: food processor or mixer, medium mixing bowl

Prep: 10 minutes

Yield: 2½ cups

Herb Cream Cheese Spread

8 oz. butter, room temperature
2 Tbsp. Herb Mix
1 tsp. chopped garlic

½ tsp. black pepper
2 Tbsp. chopped parsley
6 oz. cream cheese, room temperature

Herb Mix

1½ tsp. oregano, finely chopped
1½ tsp. basil, finely chopped

1½ tsp. tarragon, finely chopped
1½ tsp. thyme, finely chopped

Before You Begin

You'll need: food processor or mixer, small bowl

Prep: 10 minutes

Yield: 2 cups

NOTE: Fresh herbs are best, but dry herbs may be substituted.

Using a food processor or mixer, in a small bowl, whip butter until smooth. Add Herb Mix, garlic, pepper, and parsley, and continue to blend. Add cream cheese and whip until well blended.

For each serving, on individual bread or salad plates, arrange one roll and a portion of each spread, using either a melon baller, small scoop, or individual 2-ounce ramekins to present spreads.

Romaine, Grapefruit, and Toasted Almond Salad

Before You Begin

You'll need: small bowl, large bowl, blender

Prep: 20 minutes (plus 1 hour for dressing to chill and blend)

Yield: 6 servings

½ cup red wine vinegar

1 Tbsp. honey

6 thin slices red onion, separated into rings

2 heads of romaine, cleaned, cut into bite-size pieces

2 cups Mrs. Temple's Poppy Seed Vinaigrette Dressing

8 oz. sliced almonds, lightly toasted (see page 152)

1 grapefruit, peeled, cut into pieces

In a small bowl, mix red wine vinegar and honey well, and immerse red onion rings to marinate. Set aside. Peel and discard outer leaves from head of romaine. Remove remaining leaves from core, rinse, dry, and cut into bite-size pieces. In large bowl, combine lettuce with dressing and toss until evenly coated. Portion onto salad plates and top with toasted almonds and grapefruit sections. Garnish with sweet-and-sour red onions. Serve immediately.

Mrs. Temple's Poppy Seed Vinaigrette Dressing

¼ cup sugar

1½ Tbsp. onion juice

1 tsp. dry mustard

1 tsp. salt

⅓ cup cider vinegar

1 cup vegetable oil

1½ Tbsp. poppy seeds

In a blender, combine the first five ingredients and run on medium until well mixed. With the blender still running, gradually add vegetable oil and thoroughly infuse. Stir in poppy seeds and refrigerate for 1 hour before use. Stir to mix before serving.

Chicken Breast Stuffed with Wild Mushrooms and Smoked Gouda

6 8-oz. chicken breasts, skinned, butterflied

Wild Mushroom and Smoked Gouda Stuffing

4 Tbsp. olive oil

salt and pepper

beef gravy (optional)

Before You Begin

You'll need: meat-tenderizing mallet, 9" × 13" baking pan, large skillet, grater, meat thermometer

Preheat oven to 350°F.

Prep: 1 hour (includes preparing stuffing)

Cook: 30 minutes

Yield: 6 servings

Using a meat-tenderizing mallet, pound chicken breasts flat to ¼ inch thick. With breast lying flat, skin side down, place a ball of mushroom stuffing on breast, roll to close, fold ends under to secure. Drizzle with olive oil and lightly salt and pepper. Place in 9" × 13" baking pan and roast in 350°F oven until center temperature reaches 160°F, about 25 to 30 minutes.

CHEF'S TIP: This dish is best if topped with a good quality beef gravy. Serve with Rice Pilaf (see page 70) or Wild Rice (see page 97) and vegetables of the season.

Wild Mushroom and Smoked Gouda Stuffing

6 oz. crimini mushrooms

6 oz. portobello mushrooms

6 oz. shitake mushrooms

6 oz. oyster mushrooms

4 oz. lightly salted butter

4 oz. diced yellow onion

2 Tbsp. chopped garlic

2 cups red wine

2 cups beef broth

2 cups grated smoked Gouda cheese

Remove stems from mushrooms, clean, and slice about ⅛ inch thick. In a large skillet over medium heat, melt butter and sauté diced onion in until lightly browned or caramelized, about 5 minutes. Add mushrooms and garlic and continue to sauté until tender, about 10 more minutes. Add wine and beef broth and bring to a boil. Reduce heat to low and let simmer until liquid has reduced until almost dry. Remove and let cool. After mixture is completely cool, mix with smoked Gouda and portion into six balls.

Apple Crisp Topped with Cinnamon Whip Cream

Before You Begin

You'll need: medium bowl, 8" × 12" × 2" baking pan, food processor, large bowl, electric mixer

Preheat oven to 325°F.

Prep: 15 minutes

Cook: 35 minutes

Yield: 6 servings

½ cup flour
¼ cup sugar
1 Tbsp. ground cinnamon
⅛ tsp. nutmeg

pinch of salt
3 lbs. baking apples, cored, peeled, sliced ⅛ inch thick
Crisp Mixture

In a medium bowl, mix dry ingredients thoroughly. Dredge sliced apples in dry ingredient mixture to coat well and place in 8" × 12" × 2" baking pan. Cover apples evenly with Crisp Mixture and bake in 325°F oven until top is lightly browned, about 35 minutes.

Crisp Mixture

2 cups Quaker Quick Oats
1 cup brown sugar
1 Tbsp. cinnamon

½ cup butter
1 pinch of salt

Mix all ingredients in a food processor and pulse until well blended and of a coarse texture.

Cinnamon Whip Cream

2 cups heavy cream
¼ cup granulated sugar

2 Tbsp. ground cinnamon

Using an electric mixer, in large bowl, whip cream until soft peaks form. Continue to whip while sprinkling with granulated sugar and ground cinnamon. Continue whipping until stiff peaks form. Dollop onto finished apple crisp and serve.

The Passenger Railroads

"Trains are wonderful," noted Agatha Christie in her autobiography. "To travel by train is to see nature and human beings, towns and churches and rivers, in fact, to see life." She was speaking for many. Train travelers are alone among the traveling public for their stated view that a trip has begun when they depart the station, not when they arrive at a destination. The ride—through nature, over and along mountains and rivers, past human beings, towns, and churches, into and by the full range of human activity—is seen as an integral part of the trip, not something to be endured just to get somewhere else. In such a setting, to take a meal in a fine restaurant while en route to someplace you are looking forward to visiting, or while returning from a destination you found enjoyable, is arguably the most satisfying aspect of the ride.

Railcars equipped with a kitchen and cooking appliances and arrangements for serving meals were known as "restaurant cars" when they were introduced in the 1860s. Although such equipment has been referred to as a "dining car" since the late 1800s, that earlier moniker remains apt. A dining car does, after all, possess all the attributes of a fine restaurant: An inviting table set with linen, china, glass, and silverware, and fresh flowers; a charming and helpful host; a wide array of good food prepared to order by chefs and served hot; and pleasant companions around the table with whom to converse over the meal. All of that plus the truly unique aspect of "dinner in the diner," the varied beauty of North America's landscape passing your picture window as you sit enjoying your meal. Let's go eat!

Amtrak

www.amtrak.com

In May of 1971, the National Railroad Passenger Corporation, better known as Amtrak, came in to existence throughout the United States. It was created by an act of Congress—the Rail Passenger Service Act—in an effort to preserve and revive a national rail passenger system that was failing in the hands of the railroad industry. Since then, its on-board food service has experienced a cycle characterized by highs and lows.

Initially, the system relied on equipment from the railroads, supplemented by leased cars and locomotives. While nothing, from the outside color scheme to the rolling stock's electrical system, was standardized, Amtrak nonetheless launched an operating schedule that included short-haul trains—essentially day trips such as those between Washington and Boston—and long-haul trains, known as Intercity trains, linking major cities coast to coast. An equally varied array of food services was required for these operations, and usually consisted of snack bars and lunch stand/cafes on both short- and long-haul trains, and full dining cars on the long-haul trains.

As Amtrak matured in the late 1970s the organization ordered nearly 300 bi-level Superliner cars for its Intercity trains serving the West, and set about refurbishing what is known as Heritage equipment, those earlier cars inherited from previous operators, for the East. Typically, the types of cars found in a long-distance train in-

Amtrak's Washington-Chicago Intercity train The Capitol Limited, *its long line of two-story Superliners in tow, makes its way over the Allegheny Mountains in fall. Courtesy Amtrak*

The dining room on one of Amtrak's Superliner dining cars is ready to receive guests for dinner. Courtesy Amtrak

clude coaches that feature individual seating, lounge cars with seating at large windows that wrap up overhead so passengers can sightsee and a snack bar where one can purchase snacks, sandwiches, and other light fare, a dining car consisting of a kitchen on the lower level and a service preparation station and dining room on the upper level, and today the new single-level Viewliner and bilevel Superliner sleeping cars with both standard and deluxe bedrooms.

An *Amtrak Source Book* from the 1990s explains meal service on all long-distance trains in this way: "Complimentary meals are offered to first class travelers (those with sleeping compartments), but the dining car is also open to any passenger who desires a freshly prepared full-course meal at a reasonable price." While that characterizes the company's philosophy since its inception, the implementation of food service has varied. In 1981, for example, a directive from Congress, which partially funds the railroad's operation, required "cut(ting) the cost or providing food and beverages (and) forced a drastic reduction in staffing and amenities. . . ." Enter the era of plastic dishes and eating utensils.

Through the 1980s Amtrak substantially reduced its need for federal funding. This, in turn, brought about conditions favorable to improving on board services, including those found in the dining cars. By the early 1990s the corporation began once again to set tables with linen, china, and silverware, sent its chefs to the Culinary Institute of America for training, and undertook an extensive review and upgrade of its on-board offerings. One result was the publication in December 1994 of the *Amtrak Dining Service Chef's Cookbook*. Through the remainder of the decade, this rich source of menu items provided the basis of dishes coming out of the dining-car kitchen.

Meanwhile, a second corporate Amtrak decision, to divide the railroad into Strategic Business Units, resulted in greater freedom for the managers of individual trains, like the Chicago–New Orleans *City of New Orleans,* the Washington–Chicago *Capitol Limited,* and the Chicago–Seattle *Empire Builder,* to customize their services. One outcome was greater creativity on the menu, which led to chef's specialties and regional dishes.

In this environment, by 1996 a true star had emerged on the railroad's schedule. The *Coast Starlight,* an Amtrak original train, for the first time allowed passengers to travel between Los Angeles and Seattle without changing trains. On the *Coast Starlight,* passengers holding first-class tickets have exclusive access to the *Pacific Parlor,* a lounge car featuring a reading library, a small theater, games for kids and adults, a complimentary continental breakfast with fresh-baked pastries, and a wine tasting each evening that offers varietals from the vineyards along its route.

Today Amtrak's on-board food service continues to evolve with changing circumstances. Following the practices of businesses everywhere, food service has been outsourced, in this case to Gate Gourmet, a leading catering services company. There, under the direction of Gate Gourmet Executive Chef Tim Costello and others, menus have been redesigned, new recipes have been developed, and food items, from sauces to complete dishes, have been contracted out to sources that range from local establishments to specialty restaurant supply operations.

The recipes here showcase three variations of railroad cuisine Amtrak-style. First are dishes introduced on Intercity trains in 1994 with the publication of the *Amtrak Dining Service Chef's Cookbook.* Next are selections from the *Coast Starlight*'s interpretation of the Amtrak menu. Finally there are recipes from the first-class section of Amtrak's newest success story, the high-speed Washington–Boston *Acela Express.*

"And the Winner is . . ."

In 1992, Amtrak, in cooperation with the Culinary Institute of America, launched a "Chef of the Year" and "Food Specialist of the Year" competition to recognize the culinary contributions then being made by the men and women in the railroad's dining car kitchens. The distinction of being the first to receive these awards went to Chef Jerome White and Food Specialist Gerald Nocentino.

Jerome White, then twenty-nine, was introduced to the culinary arts by his mother, who sat him on the kitchen counter and let him help stir things as she cooked. By age thirteen White was doing all the cooking for his family of twelve. Little wonder, then, that after graduating from Los

Angeles Trade Technical College, he could adapt to the confines of an Amtrak Superliner kitchen on one of the company's premier trains, the Los Angeles–Seattle *Coast Starlight,* and prepare dishes like his award-winning Grilled Salmon Fillets in Dora Sauce.

Grilled Salmon Fillets

Before You Begin

You'll need: small bowl, shallow dish

Preheat grill to medium-high.

Prep: 5 minutes

Cook: 3 minutes

Yield: 6 servings

⅛ tsp. white pepper

¼ tsp salt

½ tsp. thyme

cooking oil

6 6- to 8-oz. salmon fillets

In a small bowl, combine white pepper, salt, and thyme with enough oil to bind. Wipe seasonings mixture on both sides of the fillets, then cover and refrigerate them 1 hour before grilling. Clean grill with burlap or similar material to prevent sticking. Place seasoned fillets over hot grill and cook 1½ minutes per side. Serve on a bed of Dora Sauce, accompanied by a medley of steamed vegetables and Rice Pilaf (see page 70).

Dora Sauce

Before You Begin

You'll need: large skillet, blender, small saucepan, 2-quart saucepan, cheesecloth or China cap

Prep: 15 minutes

Cook: 30 minutes

Yield: 2 cups

3 whole cucumbers, peeled

1 tsp. butter

1 tsp. shallots, chopped fine

1 cup chicken stock

½ cup heavy cream

1 bay leaf

1 whole clove

½ small onion

Cut cucumbers in half lengthwise, remove and discard seeds, then chop coarse. In a large skillet over medium heat, melt butter and sauté shallots and cucumber 3 to 5 minutes. In a blender, puree shallot/cucumber mixture and set aside. In a 1½-quart saucepan, combine chicken stock and heavy cream and heat slowly to a simmer. Peg bay leaf to onion with clove and add to stock/cream mixture. Simmer to thicken, about 5 minutes, and remove seasoned onion. Stir in pureed shallot/cucumber mixture and heat through. Strain through cheesecloth or China cap. Finished sauce should be of a light green color and with good cucumber flavor.

Food Specialist Gerald Nocentino began cooking in the eighth grade. He and three friends would select a recipe at random from a magazine, then compete to see who could do the best job creating it. He joined Amtrak after graduating from high school and from the Restaurant School of Philadelphia. Like many who work on the rails, he has family history there; his father and two uncles were Amtrak Conductors. At twenty-three he won CIA accolades for the following recipe.

Chicken in Burgundy Creole Sauce

Before You Begin

You'll need: large skillet, deep oven-safe braising pan, small saucepan

Preheat oven to 350°F.

Prep: 30 minutes

Cook: 1 hour 30 minutes

Yield: 6 servings

¼ cup butter

3 half-chickens, quartered

½ cup chopped carrots

½ cup chopped onion

½ cup chopped green pepper

½ cup chopped celery

2 cups Creole sauce

2 to 3 whole garlic cloves

¾ cup Burgundy wine, divided

salt and pepper to taste

In a large skillet over high heat, melt butter and sauté chicken pieces until nicely browned, 2 to 3 minutes per side, turning once. Remove chicken, reduce heat to medium-high, and add carrots, onion, green pepper, and celery. Sauté vegetables about 5 minutes to lightly brown, stirring occasionally. In a deep oven-safe braising pan, combine Creole sauce, sautéed vegetables, garlic, ½ cup Burgundy, salt, and pepper. Nestle chicken pieces into sauce. Cover pan with aluminum foil, sealing edges all around. Place in 350°F oven until vegetables are very soft, approximately 45 to 60 minutes.

Remove 2 cups sauce to a small saucepan. Cover and return chicken in remaining sauce to oven to cook a total of 1½ hours. Meanwhile, over medium-high heat, add ¼ cup Burgundy to removed sauce to create a deep red color. Bring just to a boil, reduce heat, and simmer to thicken until sauce sticks to the spoon. Strain thickened sauce one or two times, until clear.

To serve, pour ¼ cup thicken sauce on individual plate and arrange chicken pieces over. Accompany with roasted potatoes, and with medley of steamed green beans and diamond-cut yellow pepper to one side, and julienne-cut carrots and cauliflower florets to the other.

In the late 1920s, at the peak of American railroad passenger service, the call to dinner in the dining car was anticipated as a high point for train travelers. In that era, more than one hundred railroads made that call. Each railroad commonly had several, if not dozens of dining cars in operation on their system at the same time. One such line was the Louisville & Nashville Railroad—"Old Reliable."

The L&N connected Cincinnati, Ohio, through Louisville, Kentucky, Nashville, Tennessee, Birmingham, Montgomery, and Mobile, Alabama, with New Orleans, as well as with Atlanta, Georgia, St. Louis, Missouri, Memphis, Tennessee, and hundreds of points in between. With connections to other railroads, it operated trains from New York and Chicago to all points south. Among the L&N's own trains, the most famous of them included the flagship Cincinnati–New Orleans all-Pullman *Pan-American,* the streamliners *Humming Bird, Georgian,* and *South Wind,* the long-running *Dixie Flyer* and the short-lived *Dixiana*, the seasonal *Florida Arrow* and *Jacksonian,* and the *Dixie Flagler* and the *City of Memphis*. In addition, numerous special trains, to Mardi Gras and to the Kentucky Derby, for example, offered dining car service as well.

Dining cars were introduced on the L&N in October 1901, comparatively late for such a significant railroad. George Pullman had, after all, built the first railroad car to have food preparation and service facilities on board—the hotel car *President*—in 1866. Two years later Pullman wheeled out a rail car devoted exclusively to food service, the dining car *Delmonico,* named after the famous New York City restaurant. On the L&N, however, passengers were, until 1901, obliged to either bring a box lunch, purchase a basket meal provided by the railroad and loaded on the train at certain stations, or eat at selected station restaurants along the right-of-way where trains would stop to allow "20 minutes for refreshments." A few of the railroad's trains included a Pullman Buffet Car, where passengers who could afford the extra fare charged for riding Pullman equipment were offered limited meal service.

By 1901, however, pressure for on-board meal service, driven by competition, the demands of first-class passengers, and longer and faster through train schedules, was sufficient to compel the L&N to organize a dining car operation. Established in Louisville, the Dining Car Department started with a storeroom, three dining cars and their crews, a superintendent, and a chief clerk. Moved temporarily to Nashville in 1902 in anticipation of an increase in riders bound for the St. Louis Exposition in 1904, the Department returned to Louisville in 1905, and grew over the years with passenger traffic. Writing for *The L&N Employees' Magazine* in September 1927, P. A. Wagner, then Chief Clerk of the Office of Dining Cars, described the railroad's Dining Car Department at its peak:

> We now have 32 dining cars, 34 stewards, 142 waiters, and 100 cooks who have regular assignments, and it is necessary to hire additional men to operate the diners we so often place in service on special trains. . . .
>
> There are a number of reasons why dining cars do not show a profit. . . . A steel dining car such as we operate on *The Pan American* represents an investment of approximately $44,500

The classic view of a dining car kitchen, this one of an L&N dining car, with three cooks and the chef at their work stations. This scene would be recognizable to Pullman's first chef on the Delmonico in the 1860s, to Rufus Estes in 1900, to Robbie Williams in the 1950s, and to Warren McLeod and others today whose work is described in this book. Courtesy Association of American Railroads

for the car, to which must be added $4,500 for silver, linen, china, glass, and kitchenware. The napkins and tablecloths are imported Irish linens made especially for us with our "L & N" trade mark woven in each piece. Standard linen equipment for a diner on *The Pan American* consists of 1,000 napkins and 325 table cloths; their average life is ten months . . . The car must also be equipped with white jackets and aprons, canvas cloths in which fresh meats are wrapped, towels, etc. The annual cost per car of replacing linen and cotton goods is approximately $2,000; the silver, china, glass, and kitchenware, $700. Yearly it is necessary for the diners to be placed at South Louisville Shops for six weeks general overhauling and each of these visits costs our department in excess of $3,000 per car. Ice, water, coal, car cleaning, salaries of crew, provisions, mineral waters, laundry, stationery, and printing all grab at the dining car dollar.

Only the best of food supplies are purchased. . . . Staple supplies such as canned goods, flour, sugar, etc., are shipped to all cars from the Louisville commissary, while perishables such as fruits, vegetables, milk, cream, butter, bread, etc., are purchased at the different layover points.

A steward, chef, three cooks, pantryman, and five waiters constitute a full dining car crew. Each diner must carry an adequate crew at all times, even though there are instances when the trains are not heavily loaded or connections are missed and the train operated in two sections, thus dividing the dining car patronage. At the different terminals, rooms with baths are provided for the stewards, cooks, and waiters, for the men must keep themselves clean and present a neat and pleasing appearance to our patrons. . . .

The steward is in full charge of the entire dining car crew and is held responsible for the enforcement of all instructions; for the condition of the car enroute; for the supplies and equipment and the deportment and service of the crew. Many of our stewards have been with us a long number of years and are well known and highly thought of by the regular travelers over our line and numerous letters of commendation are received which prove conclusively they are exerting every effort to provide satisfactory meal service and injecting a bit of personality which helps to make friends for the Old Reliable.

The kitchen is presided over by the chef and is a source of much pride to him. It is not as large as a kitchenette in the modern apartment; however, most any dish served from the large kitchens of hotels and restaurants is prepared in it. This is made possible by the plan of construction which utilizes each inch of space, every detail having been carefully worked out by representatives of the mechanical and dining car departments after having given years of study and experience to the task. The cooking utensils are aluminum, which have replaced copper ones of former years. The kitchens are inspected often and are kept immaculately clean, but it is not necessary to force the men to do this because each crew of cooks takes a personal pride in their kitchen. It takes years of service for the younger cooks to develop into competent chefs, for the preparation of the various foods prepared by these men requires experience and technical knowledge of the culinary art . . .

A steward welcomes a guest entering the dining car in this advertising illustration created in the 1930s for the Great Northern Railroad. The setting is typical of what passengers could expect to find on first-class trains of all major railroads of that era, including the Louisville & Nashville Railroad. Courtesy Great Northern Railway Company, Minnesota Historical Society

Our waiters are imbued with the thought that the keystone to successful meal service is courtesy to the patrons. (Our) older waiters impress upon the younger men that to be successful in their work the passenger must be pleased. In the frequent letters of commendation received from the traveling public the pleased passenger usually comments about the courteous attention of the waiter.

A. E. Flock, assistant superintendent, and two traveling inspectors . . . are continually riding the cars to assist the crews in maintaining the service at the high standard for which the Louisville & Nashville is widely and favorably known.

Frankly we are proud of our department and do not mind telling people so. Frequent letters of praise are received which prove . . . that our efforts are not in vain, our losses justified and that we not only draw old friends closer but make hosts of new ones annually for our Company.

Dining car operations on the Louisville & Nashville Railroad came to an end on April 30, 1971. May 1 of that year saw the cessation of passenger operations on the L&N, and on most other U.S. railroads, and their takeover by Amtrak.

The L&N's Dining Car Department created a number of specialty dishes that reflected the region of the country it served. These items were drawn from local ingredients, or employed the region's favored cooking techniques, or highlighted menu favorites of famous hotels or resorts along the right-of-way. Here is a sampling of such fare.

Fresh Shrimp Gumbo, New Orleans Style

Before You Begin

You'll need:
8-quart stockpot, two 3-quart saucepans

Prep: 30 minutes

Cook: 2 hours

Yield: 24 servings

¾ cup cooking oil

3 onions, chopped fine

2 green bell peppers, diced

3 sprigs parsley, chopped fine

2 bay leaves

¼ lb. raw ham, diced

½ tsp. thyme

¼ cup paprika

2 cups tomatoes, peeled and diced

1 lb. okra, sliced

¾ cup flour

6 qts. strained shrimp stock, heated

2 qts. chicken stock, heated

1 tsp. salt

½ tsp. cayenne pepper

1 qt. small oysters, chopped

2 lbs. lake shrimp, cooked

4 tsp. filé powder

1 cup cooked rice

In the stock pot over medium heat, warm cooking oil and sauté onions, green peppers, parsley, bay leaves, ham, thyme, and paprika until tender, about 5 minutes. Add tomatoes and okra and let cook five more minutes, taking care not to burn. Add flour to make roux and continue simmering for 5 minutes to brown but not burn. Add hot shrimp stock, hot chicken stock, salt, and cayenne pepper. Bring mixture to a boil, reduce heat, and slow boil for 1 hour 30 minutes. Add the cooked shrimp and chopped oysters to gumbo 10 minutes before removing from stove. After removing from stove, add filé. Do not permit to boil after adding this ingredient. To serve, put a heaping teaspoon of boiled rice in serving cup and pour gumbo over.

CHEF'S TIPS: Management instructed chefs: (1) never to boil the gumbo with the rice; (2) never add the filé while the gumbo is on the fire (boiling after the filé is added will make the gumbo stringy and unfit for use); and (3) never reheat directly over a fire (instead, reheat using a double boiler).

Russian Dressing for Salads

Even everyday basics, this salad dressing for example, were prepared fresh on board the train during its run.

Before You Begin

You'll need:
medium bowl

Prep: 15 minutes
(plus 1 hour to chill)

Yield: 1½ cups

1 cup mayonnaise

3 soupspoonfuls French salad dressing
(see NOTE)

2 soupspoonfuls chili sauce

2 soupspoonfuls chopped pimientos

1 soupspoonful chopped green olives

1 tsp. Worcestershire sauce

salt and pepper to taste

NOTE: Today's rough equivalent of a "soupspoonful" is a heaping tablespoon.

Mix all ingredients well and refrigerate one hour to chill.

Southern Corn Muffins

Before You Begin

You'll need: 12-cup muffin pan, 2 mixing bowls

Preheat the oven to 425°F.

Prep: 15 minutes

Cook: 20 minutes

Yield: 12 muffins

This "unusually delicious" specialty of the L&N Dining Car Department was made with "water-ground white corn meal" from Wolf Pen Mill in Prospect, Kentucky, a local product that was widely praised, even in the November 29, 1941, issue of The New Yorker, *for its fresh and fragrant flavor.*

1½ rounded cups stone-ground white cornmeal	1 egg, beaten
1½ tsp. baking powder	1 cup milk
1 tsp. salt	¼ cup bacon drippings, melted (substitute: cooking oil)

Grease muffin pan and set aside. In one mixing bowl, stir dry ingredients together. Separately, thoroughly mix egg, milk, and bacon drippings together. Combine mixtures and stir to just dampen cornmeal. Fill muffin pans ⅔ full. Bake in 425°F oven about 20 minutes.

You are instructed by the Dining Car Superintendent to "serve hot, butter well, and eat."

Kentucky Ham with Red-Eye Gravy

Before You Begin

You'll need: large bowl, large skillet

Prep: 30 minutes

Cook: 15 minutes (includes making gravy)

Yield: 3–6 servings

6 slices aged country ham	2 tsp. pure maple syrup
1 qt. milk	cold water

Remove the rind, do not cut fat off with rind but leave fat on slice of ham. Cut the hard and dark streak around the top edge of slice of ham to prevent curling. Remove all residue from ham by scraping with knife. In a large bowl, combine milk and syrup. Place ham slices in milk/syrup mixture and allow to soak for approximately 20 minutes. After soaking, drain and dry. Cut about half of fat off each slice, placing same in large skillet over medium heat to render. After all grease has been rendered from the fat, remove the fat. Put ham slices in hot skillet, brown quickly on one side, allowing 1 to 2 minutes, turn and brown on the other. Repeat this a second time. (**NOTE:** If cooked too long, ham will become hard and dry.) Remove ham slices and keep warm. Leave grease and residue from ham in skillet to brown. When sufficiently browned, add small amount of cold water, stirring constantly to give a very nice red gravy. If prepared in this manner it will not be necessary to add paprika or anything else. Pour gravy over ham and serve.

Notes from the Dining Car Superintendent to the chef included these tips: (1) if handled in the above manner there is no reason for our country ham to be over-hard, salty, or dry when served; (2) after ham has been soaked for 20 minutes it can be removed from milk and syrup mixture, drained and dried and placed on platter in ice box to be used as ordered; (3) chef should endeavor to soak approximately the number of slices he believes will be needed each morning; and, (4) the milk and syrup mixture should not be used from day to day.

CHEF'S TIP: Substitute cold strong black coffee for the water to produce a darker, more flavorful red gravy.

Spiced Hawaiian Pineapple

Before You Begin
You'll need: strainer, medium saucepan

Prep: 15 minutes

Cook: 45 minutes

Yield: 8 servings

4 cups canned Hawaiian pineapple tidbits
whole cloves
1 cup granulated sugar

¼ cup Hawaiian pineapple juice
¼ cup cider vinegar
grated rind of ½ lemon
1 piece stick cinnamon

Drain and reserve juice from pineapple tidbits. Insert a whole clove into every other piece. In a medium saucepan over medium-high heat, combine sugar, pineapple juice, and vinegar. Add lemon rind and stick cinnamon, and bring just to a boil. Reduce heat and add pineapple. Simmer 20 to 30 minutes, or until syrup is thick and becomes a light caramel color. Remove from heat and cool to accompany ham or other roast meats.

Miss Catherine's Blackberry Jam Cake

Before You Begin
You'll need: sifter, mixer, 2 large mixing bowls, 1 small bowl, three 9-inch round cake pans

Preheat oven to 350°F.

Prep: 30 minutes (allow additional 1–2 hours to cool before icing

Cook: 30 minutes

Yield: 1 three-layer cake

3 cups sifted flour
2 tsp. ground allspice
3 tsp. ground cinnamon
2 Tbsp. cocoa powder
1 cup raisins (see NOTE)
1 cup walnuts, chopped coarse
1 cup blackberry jam

1 cup butter, room temperature (substitute: shortening)
2 cups sugar
4 eggs, well beaten
1 tsp. baking soda
1 cup buttermilk
¼ cup red wine

Grease cake pans and set aside. Sift flour, measure, then in a large bowl, sift with allspice, cinnamon, and cocoa. Fold in raisins, walnuts, and jam. In a large mixing bowl, cream butter and sugar until smooth, add well-beaten eggs, and mix well. In a small bowl, dissolve baking soda in buttermilk. To creamed butter mixture, alternately add flour mixture and buttermilk/soda mixture. Add wine and mix well. Divide batter among three cake pans and place in 350°F oven to bake until a depression in the center bounces back, about 25 to 30 minutes. Cool on a wire rack, then fill and ice with any desired icing. A caramel icing makes this cake really delicious.

NOTE: You can substitute 2 cups jam instead of 1 cup jam and 1 cup raisins.

Amcuisine: Amtrak Intercity Trains

Meet Max Sanoguet, Jr. ("That's right, there's more than one of me," he chuckles), typical of the Amtrak chefs found on board when food service was reformed in 1994. "Madd Max" to his friends, husband and father to his extensive family, poet to his inner self (he willingly shares some of his poems with those who show an interest), and larger-than-life-chef to Crew 1 on Amtrak's *Southwest Chief*. Madd Max indeed.

Aggressive in personalizing the meals coming out of his kitchen, Max is one of that new breed of Amtrak chef who views himself as the master of his own restaurant, and the passengers as his guests. He began his career at New York City's Riker's Island Correctional Facility ("As a cook, not an inmate," he insists). After stints on Cunard Line cruise ships and at Hilton Hotels, he'd been with Amtrak ten years in 1996, and been on the *Southwest Chief* seven years to rise to head up Crew 1 (there are eleven crews assigned to the *Chief*). "I like working down here," he says of the lower-level galley on Superliner equipment. "I come down at 4:30 A.M. and work a couple hours by myself. But don't get me wrong. I like the travel and the opportunity to meet people too."

Evidence of Max's attitude and skill is prevalent throughout his menu. "At breakfast, I'll make omelets to order with whatever I have" (on one trip it was green peppers, fresh mushrooms, and diced onion). Another night, at the suggestion of a guest, he prepared curried chicken as an entrée, first creating a crispy-coated—or baked-fried—half chicken using oil, Cajun seasoning, melted butter, and a dusting of flour; them improvising a curry sauce seasoned mildly with sliced fresh Serrano peppers and a dash of Habanero pepper sauce. "I always check the *Coast Starlight*'s menu," he says, alluding to the fact that the *Starlight* features a wider variety of fresh ingredients (hence the serrano peppers) than is available for other trains. "So to accompany our red snapper, I've made roasted red potatoes with fresh rosemary."

Max Sanoguet is a colorful, down-to-earth, creative fellow who just happens to

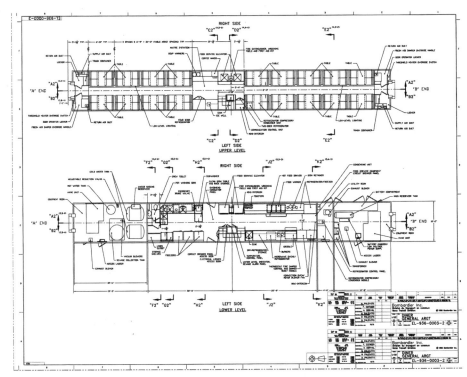

The layout of Amtrak's newest food service car, the Superliner II Dining Car. Courtesy Amtrak

love what he does for a living. So it shouldn't come as a surprise that his conversation is peppered with opinions about his craft, his customers, and his co-workers. He calls them "Max-ims".

- "When you can sunny-side a fried egg on a grill, with you and the eggs moving along at 90 miles an hour, you can cook anywhere."

- "I work for my guests. I work for me. I work for Amtrak. In that order."

- "If you eat something of mine you don't like, and you don't say anything about it to anyone on board, you share the blame for your experience. Tell me and I'll do something about it."

- "I enjoy the opportunity to work with true chemists."

Of this latter observation, it should be pointed out that the highest praise Max can heap on a coworker is to label him or her a "chemist." By that he means the person understands food and can use ingredients to create distinctive, flavorful dishes that please the guest. On one trip, for example, Max is assisted by a First Cook who normally works the *Coast Starlight,* but on this trip is serving off the "extra board," railroad jargon for an unscheduled assignment. "He is a chemist," Max says as the younger man uses blueberry conserve intended for breakfast pancakes to dress up a sauce for the fruit platter served at lunch. Over coffee between meals in the dining car, a train conductor with over ten years' experience in the restaurant industry stops to chat, and promptly shares a recipe of his own for a seafood marinade using the serrano peppers Max has requisitioned from the commissary. "Now he is a real chemist," Max observes when the conductor detrains at Albuquerque.

Were he to follow Amtrak's recipes to the letter, here's what might have been on Max's menu throughout one day on the *Southwest Chief*:

Bagel and Fresh Fruit

Simple elegance and a light start to the day. Best taken as the sun rises on the stark desert landscape drifting by outside the window.

1 orange	1 bagel, sliced, toasted	**Before You Begin**
equivalent amounts of two other varieties of fresh fruits	2 to 3 Tbsp. cream cheese	**Prep:** 10 minutes
	6 oz. fruited yogurt, any flavor	**Yield:** 1 serving

Rinse fruit and prepare as necessary: trim, remove peel, core, seed, slice, or leave whole, according to specific fruit. Fruits that tend to turn brown (apples, pears, bananas) should be dipped in orange juice to prevent browning. To serve, place toasted bagel to one side of plate, arrange fruit on remaining plate surface, and accompany with cream cheese. Spoon yogurt into a pedestal glass and serve alongside.

※ ※ ※

Omelets: One Recipe, Six Varieties

Before You Begin

You'll need:
medium skillet or
griddle (plus a sauté
skillet for various of
the fillings)

Prep: 15 minutes

Cook: Varies, 5–15
minutes

Yield: 1 serving

No better demonstration of one key to success in both the restaurant and dining car business: Amtrak's omelets are simple, consisting of common ingredients, and offer variety. While it would be uncommon to find all six varieties of omelet on a single train, at least two, and often more, may be presented by the menu.

⅔ cup liquid pasteurized eggs   fillings (see below)

Lightly grease griddle or skillet and preheat to medium. Ladle egg mixture onto surface and spread to achieve a circle of approximately 7 to 8 inches (**NOTE:** Pour approximately ⅓ of the mixture on griddle, allow the egg to set slightly, then slowly add remaining ⅔ to form omelet shape.) Allow the egg to set until slightly firm, add filling to center, spreading to within ½ inch from each side. Fold approximately ⅓ of one side over the filling, then fold the opposite ⅓ flap over the first fold. Plate the omelet with the seam underneath. Garnish as appropriate.

Omelet Fillings

CHEESE: Two slices cheddar cheese. Cut one slice diagonally and use for filling. Julienne one slice and drape slices over the top of the folded omelet and allow to soften slightly before plating.

MUSHROOM: Sauté ⅔ cup sliced fresh mushroom pieces in butter until soft. Use ⅓ cup for filling, ⅓ cup for topping (see NOTE).

VEGETABLE: Sauté ⅔ cup diced fresh vegetables (e.g., onions, green bell pepper, celery, zucchini, etc.) in butter until soft. Use ⅓ cup for filling, ⅓ cup for topping (see NOTE).

SPANISH: Sauté ⅔ cup of a mix of diced seeded fresh tomatoes, onions, and green bell pepper, sliced black olives, and capers, seasoned with garlic powder or granules, basil, oregano, salt and pepper, in butter until soft. Use ⅓ cup for filling, ⅓ cup for topping (see NOTE).

CREOLE: Sauté ⅔ cup of a mix of diced seeded fresh tomatoes, onions, green bell pepper, and celery mixed with ¼ cup of Creole sauce or ¼ teaspoon Creole seasoning. Use ⅓ cup for filling. ⅓ cup for topping (see NOTE).

NOTE: After plating, drape ⅓ cup of appropriate filling over top or at open edge of omelet.

※ ※ ※

Amtrak Grilled Cheese Club Sandwich

2 slices bacon

3 slices white bread

butter or margarine, softened

2 slices American cheese

2 slices tomato

1 lettuce leaf

¾ oz. potato chips (for garnish)

1 pickle spear (for garnish)

Before You Begin

You'll need: small skillet, griddle, or large skillet, frill toothpicks

Preheat griddle or large skillet to medium-high

Prep: 20 minutes

Cook: 6 minutes

Yield: 1 serving

Cook bacon slices until crispy and set aside. Meanwhile, spread butter on one side of each slice of bread. Arrange two slices of American cheese between two unbuttered sides of bread. On a griddle or in a skillet preheated to medium-high, place the buttered sandwich and grill until golden-brown, about 3 minutes. Turn and grill the opposite side until golden-brown. Meanwhile, place remaining slice of bread on the griddle, buttered side down, and grill until golden brown. Set aside.

To serve, on top of the grilled cheese portion of the sandwich, arrange tomato slices, cooked bacon broken in half, and lettuce leaf folded to the approximate dimensions of bread slices. Place the remaining slice of grilled bread on top.

Insert a frill toothpick into each quarter of the sandwich and slice the sandwich diagonally into quarters. Arrange sandwich quarters around the outer edge of the dinner plate; garnish with potato chips in the center of the plate and pickle spear to one side.

※ ※ ※

Oven-Fried Chicken

This standard Amtrak menu item has survived any number of menu revisions to become a classic for the railroad. And it is just waiting for a "chemist" to alter the seasonings used.

6 chicken splits

1 cup cooking oil

½ tsp. garlic powder

½ tsp. onion powder

1½ tsp. salt

½ tsp. black pepper

1¼ cups flour

Before You Begin

You'll need: 9" × 13" roasting pan

Preheat the oven to 350°F.

Prep: 10 minutes

Cook: 45 minutes

Yield: 6 servings

Wash chicken, pat dry, and coat evenly with oil. Combine dry ingredients and mix well. Dredge chicken in coating mix, shake and brush excess off, and arrange in roasting pan. Bake in 350°F oven uncovered for 30 minutes, increase oven temperature to 450°F, and finish baking 15 minutes to an internal temperature of 165°F. Serve with mashed potatoes with gravy, a baked potato, or rice pilaf (see page 70), and steamed vegetables of the season.

VARIATION: Substitute cornflake crumbs for one-half of the flour.

Jimmy's Catfish with TJ's Rice

Before You Begin

You'll need:
9 inch × 13 inch roasting pan

Preheat the oven to 350°F.

Prep: 10 minutes

Cook: 20 minutes

Yield: 6 servings

1 Tbsp. basil
1 Tbsp. salt
1½ tsp. white pepper
1½ tsp. garlic powder
1½ tsp. onion powder

6 catfish fillets
6 Tbsp. mustard, prepared
3 cups cracker or bread crumbs
6 oz. butter or margarine, melted
4 oz. white wine

Grease roasting pan and set aside. Combine basil, salt, white pepper, garlic powder, and onion powder. Rub each fillet with dry seasoning mix, spread with 1 tablespoon of mustard, and place in roasting pan. Sprinkle cracker or bread crumbs over and drizzle with melted butter or margarine. Pour wine around fish. Place in 350°F oven and bake until an internal temperature of 140°F is reached, approximately 20 minutes.

TJ's Rice

Before You Begin

You'll need:
medium sauté pan, 9" × 13" roasting pan, small saucepan, aluminum foil, 2-quart saucepan

Preheat the oven to 350°F.

Prep: 20 minutes

Cook: 20 minutes

Yield: 6 servings

4 Tbsp. butter or margarine, divided
4 oz. onion, diced small
1 tsp. curry powder
8 oz. converted rice
½ tsp. garlic powder
½ tsp. onion powder
½ tsp. salt

⅛ tsp. white pepper
2 cups beef broth
1 lb. Italian mixed vegetables, fresh or frozen, at room temperature (carrots, zucchini, yellow squash, broccoli florets, Italian green beans, lima beans)

In a medium sauté pan over medium heat, melt 2 tablespoons butter and sauté onions until soft, about 3 minutes. Season with curry powder. Melt remaining butter or margarine in roasting pan. Add raw rice, sautéed onions, and remaining seasoning, and mix well. In a small saucepan over high heat, bring beef broth to a boil and pour over seasoned rice and onion mixture. Cover with foil and place in 350°F oven for 20 minutes, or until all liquid is absorbed. Meanwhile, dice Italian mixed vegetables small. Then, in a 2-quart saucepan of boiling water, plunge vegetables to heat through, 2 to 5 minutes depending on the type of vegetables used. Drain and stir vegetables in to cooked rice just before service.

Steak "Rory" with Potatoes Josette and a Baked Stuffed Tomato

Steak "Rory"

2½ tsp. salt

½ tsp. black pepper

6 10-oz. sirloin steaks

Before You Begin

You'll need: 4-cup mixing bowl, small mixing dish, griddle or skillet

Preheat the griddle to 400°F.

Prep: 5 minutes

Cook: 15 minutes

Yield: 6 servings

Basting Sauce

10 oz. A.1. steak sauce

5 oz. Worcestershire sauce

2 oz. vegetable oil

1 oz. red wine

Combine all ingredients for Basting Sauce in mixing bowl, mix well, and set aside. Combine salt and black pepper. Season each steak with ½ teaspoon of the salt and pepper mix. On hot griddle, cook steak to within ⅔ of desired doneness. Brush both sides of each steak with 1½ ounce of Basting Sauce, return to griddle, and finish cooking to desired doneness.

CHEF'S TIP: Amtrak Chef Rory Bland, to whom credit for this recipe goes, uses the Basting Sauce as a marinade as well, allowing steaks to rest in the sauce for 2 or 3 hours before cooking them. He will often use a grill or a cast-iron skillet when cooking the steaks at home.

Potatoes Josette

2 29-oz. cans white potatoes, sliced

2 Tbsp. butter or margarine, melted

4 egg yolks, beaten

⅛ tsp. white pepper

¾ cup white cream sauce

12 slices American cheese

Before You Begin

You'll need: strainer, 9" × 13" roasting pan, small mixing bowl

Preheat the oven to 350°F.

Prep: 15 minutes

Cook: 30 minutes

Yield: 12 servings

Rinse the potatoes with water and drain. Liberally brush the bottom and sides of the roasting pan with melted butter. Combine beaten egg yolks, white pepper, and cream sauce. Gently fold the potatoes into the sauce mixture. Place ⅓ of the potatoes and sauce mixture into roasting pan. Top with 4 slices of cheese, being careful not to overlap. Repeat the layering process twice, equally distributing the remaining ingredients. Place in 350°F oven until golden brown, approximately 30 minutes. Let stand 5 minutes, then cut into 3-inch squares to serve.

Baked Stuffed Tomato

Before You Begin

You'll need:
8" × 11" baking dish, medium mixing bowl

Preheat the oven to 375°F.

Prep: 45 minutes

Cook: 10 minutes

Yield: 6 servings

6 large tomatoes
2 cups bread crumbs, Italian flavored
2 Tbsp. onions, finely diced
2 Tbsp. green bell pepper, finely diced
1 Tbsp. Parmesan cheese, grated

1 tsp. basil, dried
1 tsp. oregano, dried
1 Tbsp. olive oil
salt and pepper to taste

Slice off top of tomato just below stem blemish, remove a thin slice from the bottom to allow the tomato to stand upright. Scoop out, chop and save the pulp of the tomato. Lightly salt the interior of the tomato and invert to allow excess juices to drain. Meanwhile, mix bread crumbs, onion, green pepper, and Parmesan cheese, add the reserved tomato pulp and olive oil, and mix thoroughly. Stir in basil, oregano, salt, and pepper (**NOTE:** Stuffing mix should be moist, but not overly wet. If the mixture is too dry, add water slowly until desired moisture content is achieved. The stuffing should have the consistency to be shaped without falling apart). Fill the tomato shells with enough stuffing mixture to be slightly above top edge of shell. Arrange tomatoes in an 8" × 11" baking dish and place in a 375°F oven until internal temperature is at or above 140°F, as measured with a stem thermometer, about 15 minutes. Can be kept in warm oven at 140°F for no longer than 1 hour.

Steamed Vegetables with Brown Rice

Before You Begin

You'll need:
steaming pot for vegetables

Prep: 30 minutes (includes cooking brown rice according to package directions)

Cook: 10 minutes

Yield: 1 serving

¼ cup green bell pepper, julienne cut
¼ cup onion, chopped coarse
¼ cup celery, sliced diagonally
½ cup chopped mixed vegetables
    (zucchini, yellow squash, carrots, etc.)

¼ cup tomato, chopped
⅛ tsp. garlic powder
½ tsp. curry powder
salt and pepper to taste
1½ cups cooked brown rice

In a vegetable steamer over high heat, bring water in steaming (bottom) pan to full boil. Place all vegetables, except tomato, in perforated (top) pan. Insert perforated pan onto pan containing boiling water and cover. Allow steam to cook vegetables until slightly undercooked. (**NOTE:** Cooking times vary from 3 to 6 minutes depending on vegetables being used. Vegetables will reach their peak color when cooked to correct degree of doneness.) Remove vegetables, toss with tomato, spices, salt and pepper to coat completely. To serve, place cooked brown rice on a dinner plate and spread the rice over the plate surface, leaving a well in the center. Spoon the steamed vegetables into the well. Serve hot.

How does an Amtrak chef meet the challenge of preparing up to three hundred meals at one time while working on a tight schedule in a compact kitchen? Finalists in the railroad's "Chef of the Year" competition offer this list of tips. The chef on George M. Pullman's first dining car, the *Delmonico*, would recognize the advice.

1. Plan ahead. Preplan your menus and make sure all ingredients and equipment are in reach.

2. Clean as you go to keep work surfaces clear for food preparation.

3. Use your microwave to thaw frozen foods and to cook some foods, especially vegetables.

4. Make sure your kitchen is well organized. If everything is in its proper place, you will not waste time searching for utensils and ingredients.

5. Do not take short-cuts on nutrition. Use fresh fruits and vegetables and take time to plan balanced meals.

6. Use lemon juice, herbs, and spices rather than salt to season foods.

Versatility is another quality critical to a dining car chef's success. Consider these instructions, taken from the *Amtrak Dining Service Chef's Cookbook,* which use common ingredients found in most kitchens to make various sour cream sauces in just fifteen minutes.

Instructions for making sour cream sauces and when to offer them in the menu, from the Amtrak Dining Service Chef's Cookbook. *Courtesy Amtrak*

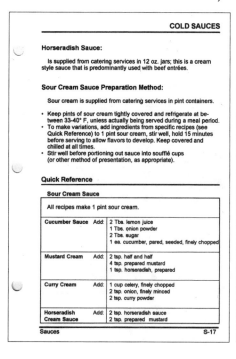

Amcuisine, *Coast Starlight*–Style

The mood onboard the *Coast Starlight* is festive. Here, the dining car is party central. The dining room is downright busy. In high season, as many as four hardworking, enthusiastic waiters and a steward hustle about nonstop to bring a unique array of foods to as many as seventy-two guests at one time (it is more customary elsewhere on Amtrak to find two waiters and a steward serving no more than forty guests at each seating in only half of a Superliner dining room). The resulting tumult—conversations at eighteen tables mixing with the clink of dishes, calls from waiters to the kitchen and to each other, the gleeful chatter of children, the steward beckoning new arrivals—is more reminiscent of a gala than of a dining room.

Below, the galley is quieter but no less hectic. A chef and three food specialists (not the more typical one and one) attentively hover over the range and grill, steam tables, and cutting boards to bring distinction to an already exceptional menu. In the course of their long day, they will conjure seven lunch offerings, a house garden salad with balsamic herb vinaigrette dressing, and six dinner entrées; roast baby red potatoes, steam summer vegetables, and cook black-and-white rice for the side; apply finishes to six desserts; and prepare two children's meals. On the second day

Many argue that Amtrak's most scenic route is followed by the Seattle-Los Angeles Coast Starlight, *shown here running along part of its 140-mile trip on the shore of the Pacific Ocean north of Los Angeles. The northern portion of the trip takes the train past the many volcanic mountains of the Cascades, beginning with Mt. Shasta in northern California and ending with Mt. Ranier in northern Washington. Courtesy Amtrak*

of the day-and-a-half trip they will offer a breakfast with seven selections, plus side dishes, and repeat lunch.

Recipes for the *Coast Starlight,* when it was a stand-alone train operated by the Amtrak West SBU, emphasized ingredients and wines found along the train's route, here including artichokes from Castroville, California, cherries from Washington state, and wines from Sonoma and Napa Valley.

Onion-Mushroom-Spinach Omelet

1 tsp. olive oil
¼ oz. white onions, diced
¼ oz. fresh mushrooms, sliced
¼ oz. fresh spinach leaves
4 oz. liquid eggs

¼ oz. cheddar cheese, shredded
¼ oz. salsa
1 orange slice
1 sprig parsley

Before You Begin

You'll need: small skillet, nonstick omelet pan

Prep: 5 minutes

Cook: 10 minutes

Yield: 1 serving

In a small skillet over medium heat, warm oil and sauté onions, mushrooms, and spinach until soft, about 3 minutes, and set aside. Preheat an omelet pan over medium heat, add egg mixture, swirl to coat surface evenly, and cook until firm. Add onion, mushroom, and spinach. Fold and plate the omelet and top with cheddar cheese. Add salsa on the side. Garnish with an orange slice cut through to the peel of one side and twisted over a sprig of parsley. Serve with ½ cup of home fries.

Coast Starlight Castroville Cheese Tortellini

2 lbs. cheese tortellini
1 cup artichoke hearts in oil
½ cup sun-dried tomatoes in oil
1 clove fresh garlic, chopped fine
1 cup marinara sauce

1 cup pesto
½ cup small black olives, halved lengthwise
Parmesan cheese, grated (for garnish)

Before You Begin

You'll need: 2 small saucepans, large bowl, pan to follow tortellini instructions

Prep: 10 minutes

Cook: 20 minutes

Yield: 4 servings

Cook cheese tortellini according to package directions. In a small saucepan over medium-low heat, combine artichoke hearts, sun-dried tomatoes, garlic and olives, bring to 145°F, and retain. Meanwhile, in a small saucepan over medium heat, combine marinara sauce with pesto, bring to 145°F, and retain. Place pasta in a bowl and toss lightly with marinara/pesto sauce. Arrange pasta on the plate and top with a portion of vegetable mixture, using a slotted spoon to strain off oil. Sprinkle with Parmesan cheese and serve with garlic bread cut into triangles.

Coast Starlight Chicken Breast Pinot Noir and Dried Cherries

Before You Begin

You'll need: large skillet, 8" × 11" roasting pan, 2-quart saucepan

Preheat oven to 350°F.

Prep: 5 minutes

Cook: 30 minutes

Yield: 4 servings

4 8-oz. boneless chicken breast, skin removed
1 Tbsp. cooking oil
½ cup red wine vinegar
¼ cup granulated sugar

1 cup Pinot Noir
1 lb. dried cherries
2 cups demi-glace
salt and pepper to taste
sprig Italian parsley

Wash and clean chicken, and pat dry. Season chicken breast with salt and pepper. In a large skillet over medium-high heat, warm oil, add chicken breasts, and cook until golden brown, 4 to 6 minutes per side. Place in an 8" × 11" roasting pan and bake in a 350°F oven until it reaches an internal temperature of 165°F, about 20 minutes. Meanwhile, in a 2-quart saucepan over medium heat, bring vinegar and sugar to a simmer, reduce heat, and let simmer until mixture reaches the consistency of syrup. Add demi-glace and simmer for 10 more minutes. Add Pinot Noir and cherries, stir to mix, and heat through. To

An Amtrak Chef puts the finishing touches on dessert in a Superliner II dining car kitchen. Like many fine restaurants, several of the railroads and trains included here have their desserts prepared according to proprietary recipes by specialty caterers. One chef here owns a bakery that supplies desserts for a number of fine restaurants across America. Courtesy Amtrak

serve, cut chicken breast in half lengthwise and overlap the halves on a plate. Ladle ½ cup sauce over chicken. Garnish with sprig of Italian parsley, and serve with summer vegetables and roasted red potatoes.

Coast Starlight Seasonal Summer Vegetables

16 oz. frozen mixed vegetables
1 Tbsp. olive oil
¼ tsp. garlic, minced
1 large zucchini, ½-inch slice or dice
1 large yellow squash, ½-inch slice or dice

½ each red and green bell peppers, ½-inch dice or short julienne
¼ tsp. herbs
salt and pepper to taste

Before You Begin

You'll need:
2-quart micro-waveable covered dish, large skillet

Prep: 10 minutes

Cook: 15 minutes

Yield: 8 serving

Cook frozen vegetables in microwave according to directions. Drain and keep warm. Meanwhile, in a large skillet over medium heat, warm olive oil, garlic and herbs. Add fresh vegetables and sauté until tender, 3 to 5 minutes. Season and add frozen vegetables, stir to mix, and remove from heat.

Coast Starlight Roasted Red Baby Potatoes

3 lbs. red baby potatoes, washed, quartered
fresh rosemary leaves

2 Tbsp. olive oil
salt and pepper to taste

Before You Begin

You'll need:
9" × 13" roasting pan

Preheat oven to 350°F.

Prep: 5 minutes

Cook: 50 minutes

Yield: 8 servings

Place potatoes in a roasting pan. Add olive oil, rosemary leaves, salt and pepper. Mix ingredients well to coat potatoes completely. Bake in a 350°F oven for 50 minutes, or until golden brown, stirring every 15 minutes.

A railroad's commissary not only stores the provisions needed to stock its dining cars, it also whips up some of the railroad's unique ingredients in bulk. For example, despite being filled with instructions for making small batches of such delicacies as fresh sliced peaches with cream, oyster croquettes, and orange meringue pie, the *Canadian Pacific Railway Dining Car Service* book of standards, dated July 1, 1920, also includes this massive preparation. It is typical for this type of specialty, intended for use throughout the system.

Canadian Pacific Mince Meat

160 lbs. corned beef	22 lbs. cassia
120 lbs. suet	6 lbs. cloves
800 lbs. currants	5 lbs. ginger
750 lbs. raisins, seeded	5 lbs. nutmeg
10 cases apples	2 gallons molasses
4 bags sugar	5 gallons apple cider
100 lbs. orange peel	5 dozen lemons
180 lbs. lemon peel	4 gallons rum
120 lbs. citron peel	

Boil meat and suet together until tender. Drain and cool, then dice fine. Combine remaining ingredients except rum, and simmer 1½ hours. Add rum and mix well. Jar and seal. Yield: 3,600 pounds.

"It has usually been my observation," Paul Reiss, once Supervising Chef of the Southern Pacific Lines, route of the *Daylights,* the *Lark,* and other great trains, said in 1926, "that travelers starting on a long trip usually eat too much the first day." He and others of his day should know: They dealt regularly with the effects of meals taken on a train.

Why do people overeat on trips? Reiss suggested that "everybody is pleasantly excited over the beginning of the journey," and, "being a slave to the eating habit," eat even though they know they are inviting trouble. He explains: "Did you ever observe the crowd on a dining car the first evening out on a transcontinental train? . . . Heavy orders go into the kitchen. People who are light eaters at home will start with an oyster cocktail, take on an order of broiled pork chops or steak with fried potatoes on the side, drink two cups of coffee and eat a slice of pie—not to mention other things.

"Next morning not so many show up for breakfast. Those who do show up have a tendency to be a little grouchy. They'll gladly tell you how well they didn't sleep last night. 'Never can sleep,' they'll say, 'the first night on a Pullman.' . . . And by mid-afternoon, after another heavy meal for lunch, the listlessness that follows from lack of exercise sets in. A headache comes on, and everything is just right for the catching of a bad cold."

To combat this, Paul Reiss recommended a carefully planned diet for the entire first day of a trip. A thoughtful man who was likewise a keen observer of human behavior and psychology, Reiss recommended what he termed a "model menu" to reduce discomfort when traveling. It has stood the test of time and is worth remembering the next time you ride the rails, or set out in your RV or car.

BREAKFAST

Fresh Fruit in Season
or
Breakfast Prunes with Cream
Plain Omelet with Bacon
One Roll   Two Bran Muffins
Coffee

LUNCH

Consommé, Hot or Cold according to season
Fresh Fish in Season
or
Poultry
Potatoes
Lettuce and Tomato Salad with French Dressing
Corn Bread   Bran Muffins
Coffee

DINNER

Tray of Fresh Relish
Soup (all but creamed)
Fritters with Fruit Sauce
Roasted Meat, Potatoes, Vegetables
Tea Biscuits   Bran Muffins
Coffee

Acela Express

It really was by the dawn's early light, on the northbound platform of Amtrak's BWI Airport Station outside Baltimore, Maryland, from a point far to the left, where the rails converge as they disappear into a curve to the right, the New York–bound 8:23 A.M. *Acela Express* out of Washington, D.C., swept soundlessly into view. The shovel-nosed machine, Amtrak's newest train, designed to operate at up to 150 miles per hour, resembles a puppy, head down, sniffing the floor as it hurries through new territory.

A ticket for a First Class accommodation entitles passengers to the foods designed expressly for that service level on that train. *Acela*'s food is one of the train's unsung successes. The First Class menu, carefully thought out and precisely executed, features unusual, imaginative, and inviting selections that change frequently. If success is in the numbers, consider that more than three thousand First Class meals alone are served every day, making *Acela* a pretty big restaurant. (**NOTE:** In Business Class, the lounge car offers food from the standard Amtrak menu, which includes several specialty sandwiches, salads, wraps, and the like.)

On board the First Class car, the seating area is spacious, its aisle covered with an inviting blue-gray carpet, with side panels of a soft, flecked, gray that rise to meet a solid gray canopy. Oversized chairs invite relaxation or comfortable work. Single seats have tables that fold up and out of the seat back ahead. Elsewhere, facing pairs of seats make up sections for four and have a permanent table between them.

Acela Express
*hurries along on
its run between
Washington,
D.C., and Boston.*
Courtesy Amtrak

The ride is smooth, with the few bumpy stretches due to track conditions. The occasional noisy whirring din and squeak can be attributed to the train itself, which, like the thoroughbred it is, is acting balky at being held back from its desire to run at speed.

Meals are offered on departure, with breakfast served until mid-morning, lunch replacing it until midafternoon, and dinner following. Washington and Boston departures serve breakfast and lunch most heavily. Trains out of New York in either direction can offer breakfast, but the primary meals are lunch or dinner.

At breakfast, Amtrak's plan is to offer a fruit bowl, an egg dish, or an non-egg dish, plus either a croissant or bagel. Lunch consists of a hot or cold sandwich, or a salad topped, if the passenger wishes, with hot or cold meat (fish, chicken, or duck), and a hot or cold pasta, all with a dinner roll. Dinner is a larger serving of the lunch pasta, or a beef and a poultry or fish entrée.

Gate Gourmet is the company responsible for foods served on *Acela Express*. Tim Costello, Culinary Institute of America graduate and the Gate Gourmet Amtrak Account Executive Chef responsible for Amtrak's menus, has been working on *Acela* food service since the train was launched. His comments describe a model for the well-run kitchen for busy people on the move and who love food.

"Amtrak has several goals for *Acela,*" says Chef Tim. "One is, the company wants to offer seasonal menus, with lighter fare and more cold dishes in the spring and summer, and heartier foods and more hot items in fall and winter. Another is, management does not want to clutter the menu with more items, but wants to offer more choices. So we use ingredients that can be combined in interesting ways. Green salads can be served plain, or accompanied by seasoned meats that can be served hot or cold. Pasta dishes can be served hot or cold, and the lunch portion increased and the side dishes varied for dinner. The sandwiches are good served either hot or cold. Finally, Amtrak strives to make the whole dining experience more passenger-friendly." To that end, a two-week menu cycle assures variety for this train with heavy repeat riders.

Commissaries in Boston, New York, and Washington, D.C., are critical to pulling all this off. "Breakfast is loaded at all three," says Chef Tim. "Lunch and dinner are loaded in New York." The meals in each city are prepared in Gate Gourmet's airport flight kitchens. The food is then trucked to Amtrak's commissaries, where it is loaded into carts that will go on the trains. From there it is taken to trackside and put on board. At each step—in the kitchen, on the truck, in the commissary, and on carts headed for the train—the "chill factor," or desired temperature, is maintained. The New York operation is the trickiest. Costello explains: "You have to allow for traffic, and the train's schedule. Even on uneventful days, you have only about ten minutes to get the empty carts off the train and the full carts on. To do that, everything has to be in place when the train arrives."

Back on board, the First Class galley is eight feet long and occupies both sides of the aisle at one end of the car. Overhead, three metal cubes on each side hold glasses, paper products, and the like, and are secured in place with latches. They slide in and out for speedy replacement. Atop one side's counter is the oven, where food is warmed to its service temperature, a toaster, and a microwave. Beneath, the food is stored in refrigerated lockers, and two racks hold the service trays set up with cold items. The other side's counter is the beverage setup area, with beverages, including alcohol that is protected by a lock, stored beneath.

The crew boards at the station and inventories each item. The meals requiring it are put in the oven, and the car made ready for passengers. For First Class passengers, the only chore is to make a menu selection. Once that's done, they can relax and watch the Northeast Corridor flash by outside the window.

Chef Tim Costello's recipes for *Acela Express* First Class Service are classic railroad. True to the high-speed train's mission, each recipe can be prepared ahead of time, refrigerated, then finished without fuss later, when you are ready to serve.

At breakfast, classic French Toast with Blue Cranberry Compote served with chicken-apple sausage and garnished with fresh berries in season.

French Toast with Blue Cranberry Compote

Before You Begin

You'll need: medium bowl, large skillet or griddle, absorbent towels

Prep: 10 minutes

Cook: 5–10 minutes

Yield: 4 servings, 3 slices each

1 cup pasteurized egg
2 cups whole milk
3 Tbsp. heavy cream
1 tsp. pure cinnamon, ground
1 oz. sugar
dash of salt

1 French baguette loaf (2- to 2 ½-inch diameter)
vegetable spray
8 links chicken-apple sausage (Williams-Sonoma, see page 264)

In a medium mixing bowl, stir eggs to mix. Add milk, heavy cream, cinnamon, sugar, and salt, and mix slowly until well incorporated. Refrigerate until ready to use. Slice baguette on the bias at ½ inch intervals. In a large skillet or on a griddle heated to hot, spray lightly with oil. Dip bread slices into egg batter, turning to coat both sides. Pan-fry baguette in skillet on both sides until well browned, about 2 minutes per side. Transfer to toweling to drain. Meanwhile, cook sausage according to package instructions.

Blue Cranberry Compote

Before You Begin

You'll need: large saucepan

Prep: 5 minutes

Cook: 20 minutes

Yield: 6 cups

½ lb. blueberries, fresh or frozen
1 ½ lbs. cranberries, fresh
1 ½ lbs. granulated sugar
2 oz. raisins, dark

pinch salt
¼ tsp. plus dash ground cinnamon
¼ tsp. plus dash cayenne pepper
⅓ oz. fresh lemon juice

If using frozen blueberries, defrost under refrigeration. In a large saucepan over medium heat, combine all ingredients and cook until sugar dissolves. Increase heat and cook over high heat for 3 to 5 minutes or until cranberries have popped.

To serve, arrange three slices of French toast on individual plates, ladle Blue Cranberry Compote over French toast, and position two links of sausage on the side. Refrigerate remainder of compote.

For lunch:

Duck Confit Sandwich Wrap

For each serving:

1 Tbsp. Hoisin Oyster sauce

4 oz. Oriental stir-fry vegetables

2½ oz. pan-seared duck breast, ¼" × 2" julienne

1 12" sun-dried tomato lavash wrap

Cut lavash to 10-inch round and lay on flat surface. Coat one side evenly with Hoisin Oyster sauce. Place vegetable mixture and duck evenly down center of the bread. Fold lavash over vegetable/duck mixture, then tightly roll into a cylinder. Wedge-cut on bias exposing sandwich contents.

Hoisin Oyster Sauce

¼ cup hoisin sauce

½ cup oyster sauce

Combine and mix well. Cover and refrigerate until ready to use.

Before You Begin

You'll need: small bowl

Prep: 5 minutes

Yield: ¾ cup

Oriental Stir-Fried Vegetables

2 Tbsp. sesame oil

¾ oz. garlic, minced

¼ oz. gingerroot, minced

10 oz. bok choy, ¼" × 2" julienne

3 oz. green onion, ¼" × 2" julienne

1 oz. shitake mushroom, ¼" × 2" julienne

1 oz. red bell pepper, ¼" × 2" julienne

1 oz. shredded carrot

1 oz. yellow bell pepper, ¼" × 2" julienne

3 oz. hoisin sauce

3 oz. oyster sauce

Before You Begin

You'll need: large skillet

Prep: 20 minutes

Cook: 10 minutes

Yield: 6 servings

In a large skillet over medium heat, warm oil and sauté garlic and ginger for 1 minute. Add vegetables and continue to cook until tender but not overcooked, about 5 minutes. Add hoisin and oyster sauce, mix well, and heat through. Remove from heat.

Pan-Seared Duck Breast

Before You Begin

You'll need: 1-qt freezer bag, medium skillet, sheet pan

Preheat oven to 350°F.

Prep: 1 hour

Cook: 20 minutes

Yield: 6 servings

1½ cups teriyaki marinade   3 5-oz. duck breast, skin on

Pour marinade in 1-quart freezer bag, immerse duck, seal, and refrigerate for at least 1 hour. In a medium skillet preheated to medium-high, place duck skin-side down and sear for 3 minutes. Turn breasts and continue cooking for additional 3 minutes. Place breasts on sheet pan and finish in 350°F oven until internal temperature reaches 145°F.

CHEF'S TIP: The Pan-Seared Duck Breast can be chilled and served over salad greens.

For dinner:

Grilled Halibut with Chili-Lime Sauce

Grilled Halibut

Before You Begin

You'll need: sheet pan

Preheat the oven to 350°F.

Prep: 5 minutes

Cook: 20 minutes

Yield: 4 servings

4 5-oz. halibut fillets
vegetable oil
salt and white pepper to taste

4 oz. Chili-Lime Grilling Sauce (American Spoon Foods, see page 263)

Rub fillets with oil, season with salt and white pepper. Mark halibut on a broiler, making a crosshatch pattern, about 1 minute per side. Remove from broiler and place on a sheet pan. Bake at 350°F until internal temperature reaches 150°F, about 15 minutes.

Lentil Ragout

1 lb. dried red lentils
5 cups water
1 bay leaf
2 tsp. unsalted butter
1 medium yellow onion, fine dice
2 tsp. curry powder

2 oz. garlic, minced
1 tsp. cumin seed
2 tsp. fresh lemon juice
½ oz. sea salt
½ tsp. coarse ground black pepper

Before You Begin

You'll need: 3-quart saucepan, medium skillet

Prep: 10 minutes

Cook: 30 minutes

Yield: 8 servings

Cover lentils with water in a 3-quart saucepan. Over medium-high heat, bring just to a boil, add bay leaf, reduce heat, and simmer until water is absorbed, about 20 minutes. Do not overcook. Remove bay leaf. Meanwhile, in medium skillet over medium heat, melt butter and sauté onions until tender, about 3 minutes. Add curry powder, garlic, and cumin. Cook briefly, then stir in lentils to heat through. Season with lemon juice, salt, and pepper. Remove from heat.

Lyonnaise Carrots

1 lb. carrots, peeled, halved, cut ⅛"
    thick diagonally
5 Tbsp. unsalted butter
10 oz. Spanish onion, cut ⅛" × 2"
    julienne

¾ tsp. salt
¼ tsp. ground white pepper

Before You Begin

You'll need: large skillet

Prep: 10 minutes

Cook: 10 minutes

Yield: 8 servings

In a large skillet over medium heat, melt butter and sauté carrots for 4 to 5 minutes. Add onions, continue to sauté until onions are tender, about 3 more minutes. Season with salt and white pepper.

To serve, on individual plates, position Lentil Ragout to the right, position carrots in the center, touching the lentils, and center the halibut fillet above the carrots. Position asparagus (see page 248 or 258 to prepare) to the left with the tips pointing up. Pour 1 ounce chili-lime sauce over the halibut fillet.

CHEF'S TIP: You can prepare this meal a day or two in advance. For each serving, in an ovenproof individual casserole, prepare as instructed above, wrap in foil, and refrigerate. When ready to serve, heat in oven to 350°F, remove foil from casserole(s), and reheat dish 20 minutes, or until internal temperature is 145°F.

VIA Rail Canada

www.viarailcanada.com

VIA Rail Canada's Toronto-Vancouver Canadian, *a three-day trip of uncommon splendor, is shown here running in the Canadian Rockies. VIA Rail Canada Inc.*

On VIA Rail Canada's trains, exclusive first class service can be found on board a combination of trains that take you "from sea to shining sea." On the *Ocean,* between Halifax and Montreal, *Easterly Class* is described as a "cozy 'bed & breakfast' experience," complete with private quarters, a shower in each car, continental breakfast in the private *Park Car,* and meals in the dining car. From Montreal to Toronto trains offer *VIA 1* service, which includes a hot breakfast or a four-course hot or cold lunch or dinner, and an inviting assortment of aperitifs, wine, and liqueurs, all served at your seat. This puts you in position for a trip on one of the undisputed greatest trains in the world, the famed *Canadian* between Toronto and Vancouver. VIA's premier train, this transcontinental beauty is made up of restored stainless steel cars from the 1950s and offers a *Silver & Blue Class* service, which also

includes dining cars, sleeping cars, domed lounge cars, and exclusive use of a *Park Car,* the round-ended observation car that contains several sleeping compartments, its own dome, a lounge, and an observation salon.

A *Silver & Blue* Service meal in a dining car on this train is what people recalling the mythical "golden age" of rail travel describe. It is proof of the observation sung in that era, that "nothing could be finer" than a repast on a long-distance train moving at speed and with a purpose.

Imagine departing a single roomette, one of four at one end of each sleeping car, and following the hall forward as it wraps out around and along six double compartments, then returns to the car's center. At this second turn, the entry to a large dressing room and shower stall for the car's passengers, and opposite it, and again facing each other ahead, are three berths. (The only discernable variation from Pullman berths of more than 150 years ago is that Velcro has replaced hooks at certain locations on the curtains.)

Go on through two additional identical sleeping cars to encounter the dining car. The room is remarkable in that it is both grand and embracing. Highlights include a cream-colored ceiling, bold rose-colored wall covering, a pair of four-top booths at each end of the main dining room, separated by etched glass partitions; various stylish stainless lighting fixtures, strategically placed mirrors that appear to enlarge the dining room, and unifying grey-green accents and carpeting.

Waiting there, tables covered with white linen and, at an angle, a smaller rose-colored tablecloth. The tables are flanked by black wooden chairs with rose seat and back cushions or grey-green upholstered booth benches. Noritake china and service pieces, heavy stainless-steel flatware of a simple design, and a small vase with pink and white carnations adorn the table at breakfast and lunch. At dinner the topping tablecloth is of dark blue piped with gold, and the chairs are covered with dark blue shams. The effect is one of serenity and anticipation.

The Service Coordinator greets all who enter the dining room, seats them, presents menus, and takes drink orders. The atmosphere is one of reserved pleasantry. Three servers work from an area measuring 8 feet by 12 feet to pour drinks, assemble salads, and put together the breadbasket. They also set up desserts, assist in food preparation, including slicing or dicing vegetables, and do dishes.

The menu sparkles with variety, At breakfast, assorted juice, a choice of yogurt, cereal, or fruit cocktail, five main courses, one of which changes daily, and a beverage. At lunch, soup or juice, a choice from among four main courses, one of which changes daily, and dessert and beverages. Dinner is a gastronomic blowout. The menu is different from top to bottom every day, with a choice of soups, salad, one of four main courses—red meat, seafood, chicken, and vegetarian offerings, and two desserts. Consider, for example, the typical seafood selections on a westbound trip. Day One: Northern Ontario Lake Trout, pan-fried, coated with a corn crumb mixture, topped with caramelized Bermuda onion. Day Two: From the icy waters of Manitoba, pickerel lightly seasoned, pan-fried, and served with a white wine tar-

The dining car on VIA Rail Canada's Canadian *has been prepared for passengers who will meet here for lunch. For dinner, the topping tablecloth is of dark blue piped with gold, and the chairs are covered with dark blue shams. VIA Rail Canada Inc.*

ragon sauce. Day Three: Wild Pacific Chinook Salmon, marinated in a blend of herbs, ginger, and garlic, baked "to perfection."

All of this comes from one or two chefs (depending on the number of passengers) working in a space measuring 8 feet by 18 feet. Their tools consist of one grill, one hot plate, two ovens, and a steam table. From here they serve as many as ninety-six guests, in two seatings, three meals each day.

The *Canadian* is headquartered in Winnipeg, with one on-board crew working to Toronto and return, and another working to and from Vancouver. The dining cars are initially provisioned in Winnipeg, and resupplied as needed in Toronto and Vancouver. A separate dome-lounge offers coach passengers an equally diverse, but unchanging menu for each meal.

This is a serene first-class travel experience with a focus on fine and varied dining enjoyed in a calm setting at intervals that pleasantly break up the trip. Canada's stunning natural beauty is taken in through picture windows, along with lively conversations with local and world travelers. All as the train hurries at mainline speed to reach a destination. The "Golden Days" relived.

To begin your day, consider having the *Canadian* Omelet, a specialty of the train that harkens back to the days when each railroad typically had one or more signature dishes to encourage patronage, not to mention the loyalty of shippers.

Canadian Omelet

1 cup liquid eggs
2 oz. roasted ham, diced
1 oz. Monterey Jack cheese, shredded

1 oz. green onion, fine diced
1 oz. tomatoes, diced
1 Tbsp. sour cream

Before You Begin

You'll need: medium skillet or griddle

Prep: 10 minutes

Cook: 5 minutes

Yield: 1 serving

Prepare as you would a standard ham and cheese omelet (see page 208) to order. Top with diced tomato and onion. Add sour cream to a squeeze bottle and garnish omelet in a lattice decoration. Serve with hash brown potatoes and garnish with fresh fruit and one leaf of flowering kale.

At lunch, watch the prairie pass outside and remind yourself of a time when foragers provided fresh game for the trains.

Bison Burger with Caramelized Onion

1 tsp. butter
3 thin slices Bermuda onion
1 5-oz. bison burger
1 onion sandwich bun

1 tsp. Chef's Spread
1 leaf iceberg lettuce
2 large slices tomato
salt and pepper to taste

Before You Begin

You'll need: 1 small skillet and griddle, or two small skillets

Prep: 5 minutes

Cook: 30 minutes

Yield: 1 serving

In a small skillet over low heat, melt butter and sauté onion until golden brown, about 30 minutes, season and set aside. On a medium-hot griddle or skillet over medium-high heat, cook burger, turning once, until medium-well done (about 12 minutes). Assemble burger bun with Chef's Spread, lettuce and tomato. Top with caramelized red onions and season. To serve, arrange burger on bun open-faced on a dinner plate. Serve with either Potato Salad (see page 27) or Caesar Salad (see page 135 or 182). Garnish with kale and fresh fruit.

Chef's Spread

1 cup mayonnaise
¼ cup ketchup
3 Tbsp. grainy Dijon mustard

2 tsp. horseradish
1 tsp. Tabasco sauce
1 tsp. Worcestershire sauce

Before You Begin

You'll need: small mixing bowl

Prep: 5 minutes

Yield: 1½ cups

Combine all ingredients and mix well. Cover and refrigerate.

And at dinner, imagine running out of Jasper through the rugged terrain of the route to Vancouver as you await this selection from the evening's menu:

Silver & Blue Field Greens with Ginger Lime Dressing

Field Greens

Before You Begin

You'll need: serving plate

Prep: 15 minutes

Yield: 1 serving

1 cup lettuce field greens

1 oz. corn shoots

1 oz. pea shoots

2 leaves endive

Ginger Lime Dressing

1 tomato wedge

1 thin slice cucumber

Wash lettuce field greens in cold water and drain well. On a salad plate, mound field greens in the center, keeping the rim of the plate clean. Top with corn shoots, pea shoots, and endive. Drizzle dressing over. Garnish with tomato wedge and cucumber slice.

Ginger Lime Dressing

Before You Begin

You'll need: small bowl, whisk

Prep: 15 minutes

Yield: 2 cups

1 cup olive oil

3 oz. lime juice

½ oz. gingerroot, grated

½ oz. roasted garlic

zest of 2 limes

1 oz. orange juice

1 oz. fresh cilantro, chopped fine

2 oz. creamed honey

sea salt to taste

black pepper to taste

In a small bowl, whisk together olive oil and lime juice. Add remaining ingredients and mix well. Cover, refrigerate, and mix before using. Drizzle ½ ounce dressing on salads just prior to service.

CHEF'S TIP: Store made-up liquids, including such things as this dressing, sour cream, and the Chef's Spread above, in squeeze bottles. Set out as appropriate to reach room temperature, and shake before using when and as called for.

Baked Wild Pacific Chinook Salmon

¼ lb. butter

2 cloves garlic, minced

1 tsp. gingerroot, minced

1 oz. dill weed, chopped

1 oz. parsley, chopped

4 6-oz. salmon fillets

4 green onions, finely diced

12 slices lemon

Before You Begin

You'll need: small saucepan, griddle or large skillet, roasting pan, foil

Preheat oven to 350°F

Prep: 10 minutes

Cook: 20 minutes

Yield: 4 servings

In a small saucepan over medium heat, melt butter. Add garlic, ginger, dill, and parsley, and sauté to heat through, about 1 minute. Brush seasoned butter onto salmon and sear both sides on hot griddle, about 1 minute per side. Carefully transfer to a foil-lined roasting pan and top each fillet with green onions and 3 lemon slices. Bake in a 350°F oven for 15 minutes. Garnish with fresh dill sprig, lemon wedge and chopped chives.

Honey-Almond Roasted Potatoes

2 lbs. organic potatoes

sea salt to taste

black pepper to taste

¼ tsp. rosemary

¼ tsp. thyme

1 tsp. butter

½ cup sliced almonds

2 Tbsp. creamed honey

Before You Begin

You'll need: small bowl, 9" × 12" baking dish, small skillet

Preheat oven to 350°F.

Prep: 15 minutes

Cook: 55 minutes

Yield: 8 servings

Wash potatoes, pat dry with a paper towel, then cut in to approximately 1-inch pieces. In a small bowl, mix seasonings, sprinkle over potatoes, and toss to coat. Bake in a 350°F oven for 40 minutes. Meanwhile, in a small skillet over medium heat, melt butter and sauté almonds, tossing occasionally, until lightly brown, about 5 minutes. Add honey, mix, pour over roasting potatoes, and gently toss or stir to coat. Continue cooking for 15 minutes.

Champagne Risotto

2 Tbsp. butter

2 shallots, diced fine

1½ cups Arborio rice

1¼ cups champagne

3 cups vegetable stock

⅔ cups heavy cream

¼ cup Asiago cheese

sea salt to taste

black pepper to taste

¼ cup parsley, chopped

Before You Begin

You'll need: 2-quart saucepan

Prep: 10 minutes

Cook: 30 minutes

Yield: 24 servings

In a 2-quart saucepan over medium heat, melt butter and sauté shallots until soft, about 3 minutes. Add risotto and mix until grains are well coated with butter. Add champagne and bring to a boil. Reduce heat and simmer until liquid is absorbed, about 10 minutes. Add vegetable stock ½ cup at a time, making sure the last has been absorbed before adding the next. When rice is tender, add cream and cheese. Season with salt and pepper. Add parsley just prior to service.

French Bean Medley

Before You Begin

You'll need:
4-quart saucepan, strainer, large skillet

Prep: 5 minutes

Cook: 10 minutes

Yield: 4 servings

1 lb. green beans, French cut
2 Tbsp. butter
⅛ tsp. sea salt

⅛ tsp. black pepper
nutmeg to taste

In a 4-quart saucepan, boil lightly salted water to cover beans. Add beans to blanch 1 minute. Drain well and plunge into cold water to arrest cooking. Meanwhile, in a large skillet over medium heat, melt butter. Add drained green beans, salt, pepper, and nutmeg, and sauté, stirring occasionally, until heated through, about 5 minutes. Remove from heat, cover, and hold for service.

CHEF'S TIP: Add just enough nutmeg to enhance the flavor, not so much it is overpowering.

Maple Buttered Carrots

Before You Begin

You'll need: 3-quart saucepan, small saucepan, large skillet

Cook: 15 minutes

Yield: 4 servings

1 lb. baby carrots
3 Tbsp. butter, divided
1 Tbsp. maple syrup

sea salt to taste
black pepper to taste
chopped parsley

In a 3-quart saucepan over high heat, bring sufficient water to cover carrots to a boil. Cook carrots until tender, about 3 minutes. Drain and cool. Meanwhile, in a small saucepan over medium heat, melt 2 tablespoons butter. Stir in maple syrup. In a large skillet over medium heat, melt 1 tablespoon butter, add carrots, and sauté until heated through. Drizzle maple butter over top. Stir to coat, cover, remove from heat, and hold hot for service. Season to taste and garnish with chopped parsley.

In the galley of one of the dining cars in VIA's Vancouver–Toronto *Canadian,* Chef Ron Woods is too busy. He is to have a cook to assist him when more than seventy-five passengers are on his section. A section is typically made up of from three to six sleeping cars, a dining car, and a dome-lounge forward of the dining car. In high season as many as four sections can make up one train.

On this run, however, somewhere the decision was made that with only eighty-one passengers in his section, he will have to do without help. His creativity under these circumstances is especially apparent at lunch on day two.

A self-confessed perfectionist, Woods had already been in the kitchen for over six hours and had just feed his section's crew at 9:30 A.M. Looking ahead to the chef's luncheon on the day's menu, Chef Ron, short a cook, conceptualizes a substitute that he can prepare ahead and finish for service at lunch. The result is an open-faced roast beef sandwich, and his recipe is captured below.

Chef Ron, a Metis (one whose parents are a mix of white settlers and First Nations people), studied the culinary arts at Northern Alberta Institute of Technology, and previously worked on cruise ships and at lodges, restaurants, and hotels. "I'm twenty-two years in the kitchen," he says. "I worked at the lodge in Jasper and would watch the train go through. I wanted to find out what it was like to cook in there, with your kitchen moving at seventy-five miles an hour." His passion is for healthy cuisine. "I'm known among VIA's chefs as 'the herb man,' " he says. "I use herbs liberally."

Here, then, Chef Ron Woods's impromptu Roast Beef Sandwich.

Roast Beef Sandwich

Before You Begin

You'll need: small bowl, large skillet

Preheat oven to 350°F.

Prep: 20 minutes (plus 1 hour for seasonings to blend)

Cook: 5 minutes

Yield: 4–6 servings

2 Tbsp. dried or fresh mixed herbs, chopped (use some combination of parsley, chevil, cilantro, rosemary, sage, dill, chives, tarragon, etc.)

4 Tbsp. butter, room temperature

salt to taste

fresh ground black pepper to taste

juice of ½ lemon

2 Tbsp. butter

½ large Bermuda onion, sliced, halved, rings separated

1 14-inch loaf focaccia bread

1 lb. thin-sliced roast beef, chopped coarse

1 cup shredded, mixed, Monterey Jack and colby cheese

dried, chopped rosemary, sage, or basil to taste

In a small bowl, combine mixed herbs, room temperature butter, salt, pepper, and lemon juice well and set aside 1 hour or more for flavors to blend. Meanwhile, in a large skillet over medium heat, melt 2 tablespoons butter. Sauté chopped Bermuda onion until soft, about 3 minutes, and set aside. Carefully slice bottom crust off focaccia loaf horizontally and spread herbed butter evenly on the exposed side of the top of the loaf. Place on a griddle or large skillet over medium heat with the buttered side down, and brown for 2 or 3 minutes, taking care not to burn. Sprinkle chopped roast beef, sautéed onion, and shredded cheese over buttered side of the focaccia loaf. Sprinkle favorite dried herb(s) lightly over all and place in a 350°F oven to heat through and melt cheese, about 5 minutes. Cut sandwich into 8 wedges and serve with Mixed Greens Salad (see page 80) and/or Potato Salad (see page 27).

Great Southern Railway

www.trainways.com.au

Billed as one of the world's longest and greatest train journeys, a run across Australia on the Great Southern Railway's *Indian Pacific* covers 2,829 miles between Sydney and Perth in sixty-five hours. Departing twice each week in each direction, with through passengers spending two days and three nights on the train, this "transcontinental hotel on wheels" connects the two oceans that are its namesake. Its many highlights include scenic views of the Blue Mountains, the treeless plains of The Nullarbor, and an outpost named Cook (population: 2); a fascinating array of wildlife, among them the Australian wedge tailed eagle that is the symbol of this great train; and the longest stretch of straight railroad track in the world, the 310-mile right-of-way across the Nullarbor.

Finishing touches are being applied to the dining room of the restaurant car "Adelaide" in anticipation of guests on Australia's transcontinental Indian Pacific. *Courtesy Great Southern Railway*

With the private takeover of the *Indian Pacific,* as well as of *The Ghan* between Adelaide and Alice Springs, and *The Overland* between Melbourne and Adelaide, in 1997, the Great Southern Railway now runs these famous trains once operated by Australian National Passenger Rail. In deluxe accommodations on the *Indian Pacific* and *The Ghan,* Gold Kangaroo Service offers comfortable seating in private cabins by day that converts to sleeping berths at night. Meals feature local specialities and are served at table in tastefully decorative, discrete "restaurant cars," each decorated with a different historic theme. Deluxe cabins include a lounge area, bar, and private video player. For the ultimate in private travel, *The Chairman's Car,* a private car that can be coupled up to the train, offers a spacious lounge with CD and video entertainment systems, a private dining room, and cabins to sleep up to eight guests.

Fine food and wine, in a train moving on a schedule to a destination, with changing panoramic views of a vast and beautiful continent passing outside the window: The Great Southern Railway's *Indian Pacific* is a classic rail travel experience.

Pumpkin and Coconut Soup with Crabmeat

1 Tbsp. shrimp paste

2½ lbs. pumpkin, peeled, cut into
    1¾-inch cubes

¼ cup canola oil

7 oz. onion, diced fine

1 tsp. sambal olek (substitute: chili
    paste)

6¼ cups coconut milk

3 cups chicken stock

salt and pepper to taste

½ lb. crabmeat, cooked, picked clean

Before You Begin

You'll need: baking sheet, roasting pan, 3-quart saucepan, blender, deep-fryer (optional)

Preheat oven 225°F, later to 500°F

Prep: 30 minutes

Cook: 30 minutes

Yield: 10 servings

Spread the shrimp paste on a baking sheet and dry roast in a 225°F oven until crumbly, about 30 minutes. Set aside. Coat pumpkin in oil, arrange in a roasting pan, and place in 500°F oven until golden, about 20 minutes. Pour oil from tray into a 3-quart saucepan over medium heat and sauté onion until soft, about 3 minutes. Add shrimp paste and sambal olek and cook, stirring occasionally, for 5 more minutes. Add pumpkin, coconut milk, and chicken stock and simmer until pumpkin is soft, about 10 minutes. Pour pumpkin mixture into a blender and puree until smooth. Adjust with salt and pepper to taste. Ladle soup into serving bowls and sprinkle crabmeat over. Garnish with deep-fried pumpkin shreds and coriander sprigs. (**NOTE:** To make deep-fried pumpkin shreds, peel pumpkin using a vegetable peeler, and carefully and quickly deep-fry peels in 300°F oil until crisp.)

Lamb with Native Spice Rub and Bush Tomato Sauce

Before You Begin

You'll need: mortar and pestle or spice grinder, large skillet, baking sheet, aluminum foil

Preheat oven to 375°F.

Prep: 10 minutes

Cook: 30 minutes (plus 5 minutes to rest)

Yield: 10 servings

2 tsp. native pepper berries
2 tsp. sea salt
¾ tsp. parsley flakes

10 8-oz. lamb rumps
¼ cup olive oil

Crush pepper berries in mortar and pestle or spice grinder. Combine pepper berries with sea salt and parsley. Coat lamb rumps with olive oil and rub on spice mixture. In a large skillet over high heat, sear lamb rumps on all sides, allowing about 30 seconds per side. Transfer lamb to a baking sheet and roast at 375°F until medium rare (internal temperature: 150°F), about 30 minutes. Cover baking sheet with foil and rest in a warm place for 5 minutes. Cut lamb rumps into ¼-inch slices and serve with Bush Tomato Sauce.

Bush Tomato Sauce

Before You Begin

You'll need: heavy 4-quart saucepan, blender

Prep: 15 minutes

Cook: 45 minutes

Yield: 3 quarts

¼ cup olive oil
10½ oz. onion, diced fine
2 large cloves garlic, crushed
1½ tsp. salt
2 carrots, peeled, diced fine
6¼ cups canned diced tomato

8-oz. can tomato paste
4 cups chicken stock
1¾ Tbsp. bush tomato, ground
½ cup light brown sugar
½ tsp. fresh coarsely ground pepper

In a heavy 4-quart saucepan over medium heat, heat oil and sauté onion, garlic, salt, and carrots for 15 minutes. Add canned tomato, tomato paste, chicken stock, bush tomato, and brown sugar. Bring to a boil and simmer gently for 20 minutes. Stir in pepper. Pour tomato mixture into a blender and puree until smooth, about 5 minutes.

CHEF'S TIP: Excess sauce can be used for burgers, roast meats, hot dogs, and the like, or frozen for later use.

Chocolate Whiskey Pudding

1 lb. unsalted butter, roughly chopped

10½ oz. Callebaut dark couverture
   (substitute: see NOTES)

1 lb. 5 oz. caster sugar, plus to dust
   molds (see NOTES)

2 cups + 2 Tbsp. hot water

2 Tbsp. + 2 tsp. Trablit coffee essence
   (substitute: see NOTES)

⅔ cup Scotch or Irish whiskey

12 oz. all-purpose flour

3½ oz. self-rising flour

3 oz. Callebaut Dutch cocoa powder
   (substitute: see NOTES)

5 eggs, beaten to lemon color

Before You Begin

You'll need: 24
4-oz. pudding
molds, double
boiler, large bowl,
large roasting dish

Preheat oven to
300°F.

Prep: 30 minutes

Cook: 45 minutes

Yield: 24 servings

NOTES: (1) If Callebaut is not available, substitute Lindt, Ghirardelli, or other high-quality (60 percent or 70 percent cocoa solid content) chocolates and cocoa powder. (2) If you don't have caster sugar, grind granulated sugar for a couple of minutes in a food processor to substitute. (3) Trablit products come in institutional portions. Substitute using any strong coffee or with thick liquid made of high-quality instant coffee granules.

Lightly grease pudding molds with butter or vegetable oil spray, dust with caster sugar, and set aside. In the top pan of a double-boiler, combine butter, chocolate, sugar, water, coffee essence, and whiskey. Gently heat over simmering water until chocolate has melted and sugar is dissolved. Remove from heat and cool to room temperature. Meanwhile, sift both flours with cocoa powder, add to chocolate mixture, and whisk to combine. Add eggs and stir to combine. Spoon mixture into prepared molds. Place molds in large roasting dish and pour water in dish to come halfway up the side of the molds to make a water bath. Bake at 300°F until tops crack and spring back when touched, about 45 minutes. Cool on a wire rack. To serve, display Bittersweet Chocolate Sauce on individual serving plates, top with a pudding, and dust with confectioners' sugar. (**NOTE:** This recipe and the one below may be halved to produce 12 servings.)

Bittersweet Chocolate Sauce

1 lb. unsalted butter

2½ cups Callebaut dark couverture

1 cup water

8 oz. caster sugar

⅔ cup Scotch or Irish whiskey

1 cup heavy cream

Before You Begin

You'll need:
2-quart saucepan,
whisk

Prep: 10 minutes
(plus 1 hour chill)

Cook: 30 minutes

Yield: 2 quarts

In a 2-quart saucepan over low heat, combine butter, chocolate, water, and sugar. Heat very slowly until chocolate is melted and sugar has dissolved to form a smooth mixture. Remove from heat, whisk in whiskey and cream, and refrigerate to chill, about 1 hour.

From the Business Car

The operation of a railroad is an immense undertaking. Unlike other businesses, which have fixed operations run out of permanent headquarters, the railroad executive oversees both a headquarters and a far-flung network of physical plant that may be only ten feet wide but run to a length of 30,000 miles or more. Even the industry's subdivisions stretch several thousands of miles from their respective division headquarters. Concerns over safety for workers, passengers, and the general public, over local, state, and national jurisdictions and regulations, and over customers, competitors, investors, and politicians, all may require attention right outside the office door or half a continent away. On the same day. To assist in managing such an operation, in visiting and inspecting the vast setting in which

BNSF Business Car Train. The Burlington Northern and Santa Fe Railway Company

railroading takes place, and in enabling managers at all levels of the company to be where they are needed at the same time they complete their work, railroads of all sizes employ a fleet of business cars to ferry executives and guests to and fro.

When it is time to dispatch a business car on an appointed round, a crew is assigned to do the work that allows the railroad executive to concentrate on business. Such a crew customarily consists of a mechanic, a steward, and of course, a chef. Here, then are three examples of meal service typically offered to executives or a guest of the railroad—a large shipper, perhaps, or a politician, regulator, or other official whose business affects the health and well-being of the railroad—and enjoyed in the business car.

A BNSF Business Dinner: A Class I Corporate Dining Room

www.bnsf.com

Among the more than 5,000 locomotives and 190,000 freight cars the Burlington Northern Santa Fe Railway has on its roster, there are also twenty-two business cars. This favorite meal among guests of the Class I carrier's fleet begins with a tossed salad of fresh greens accompanied by a Balsamic Vinaigrette Dressing. The showpiece, though, is the Roasted Tenderloin of Beef with Pomme au Gratin and Buttered Asparagus Spears. For dessert, Amaretto Mousse. (**NOTE:** See page 119 for one BNSF chef's prize-winning adaptation of the Roasted Tenderloin of Beef, suitable for the grill.)

Roasted Tenderloin of Beef

4 lb. beef tenderloin (see NOTE)	4 cloves garlic, minced
1 Tbsp. black pepper, ground	1 Tbsp. Lawry's seasoned salt

Season tenderloin heavily with pepper, garlic, and seasoned salt. In a large skillet or on flat-top griddle over high heat, or under the broiler, sear tenderloin on all sides. Remove to a roasting pan and place in 350°F oven until meat is medium rare (internal temperature of 140°F), approximately 60 minutes. Let stand 5 minutes before slicing. To serve, slice tenderloin using three medallions per serving and place the medallions over bordelaise sauce and garnish with sprig of fresh rosemary.

NOTE: Use choice-grade whole tenderloin weighing 5 pounds or less, depending on number of servings, with silverskin removed.

Before You Begin

You'll need: large skillet, roasting pan, meat thermometer

Preheat oven to 350°F

Prep: 10 minutes

Cook: 60 minutes

Yield: 8 servings

Pomme au Gratin

Before You Begin

You'll need: large heavy saucepan with cover, colander, three 6-inch round cake pans, plastic wrap, sheet pan

Preheat oven to 350°F.

Prep: 15 minutes

Cook: 30 minutes, plus 10 minutes to reheat

Yield: 6 servings

8 baking potatoes, peeled, sliced very thin
½ lb. butter
¼ cup minced shallots
¼ cup minced garlic
salt and pepper to taste
¾ grated Parmesan cheese, divided
2 cups heavy cream

Butter three 6-inch round cake pans and set aside. Peel and thinly slice potatoes and place in cold water to hold. In a large heavy saucepan over low heat, place butter, shallots, and garlic, cover, and sweat 3 to 4 minutes. Meanwhile, drain potatoes, then add to saucepan and increase heat to medium. Folding constantly, sauté potatoes several minutes until they become transparent, about 3 minutes. Add salt, pepper, ½ cup Parmesan cheese, and cream. Simmer until cream reduces just enough to coat potatoes. Divide and arrange potato mixture in cake pans. Divide and sprinkle ¼ cup Parmesan cheese over tops, and bake at 350°F until top is browned, about 20 minutes. Cool enough to handle, then remove potatoes from cake pans, wrap in plastic wrap, and refrigerate. (**NOTE:** These potatoes cut cleaner when cool, and are easily reheated). To serve, preheat the oven to 375°F. Remove plastic wrap from potatoes, cut in to wedges as you would a pie, and place on a sheet pan. Warm for 10 minutes and serve.

Buttered Asparagus Spears

Before You Begin

You'll need: 9" × 13" roasting pan, plastic wrap

Prep: 5 minutes

Cook: 10 minutes

Yield: 8 servings

There may be no more splendid example of the versatile and resourceful flexibility of a dining car chef than this method for preparing the vegetable.

2 lbs. asparagus spears, trimmed
4 Tbsp. butter
juice of 1 lemon
salt to taste

Spread trimmed asparagus spears in a roasting pan. Bring sufficient water to cover to a boil. Meanwhile, sliver butter over asparagus and sprinkle with the juice of one lemon and salt to taste. Pour boiling water over asparagus, seal roasting pan with plastic wrap, and set aside. Drain to serve.

Amaretto Mousse

The business car staff declares this dessert to be a favorite and the most-requested of their recipes.

4 Tbsp. sweet butter

5 eggs

¾ cup sugar

1½ tsp. unflavored gelatin

¾ cup macaroon cookies, crushed, divided

1½ Tbsp. amaretto liqueur, plus as needed

1½ cups heavy cream, chilled

¼ cup slivered or sliced almonds, toasted

Before You Begin

You'll need: baking sheet, double boiler, bowl, 8 soufflé cups

Preheat oven to 350°F.

Prep: 20 minutes (plus approximately 1 hour to chill before serving)

Cook: 15 minutes

Yield: 8 servings

Spread almonds in a single layer on a baking sheet and place in a 350°F oven to dry and lightly brown, about 5 minutes. Set aside. Meanwhile, in top pan of a double boiler, over boiling water, melt butter. In a separate bowl beat eggs with sugar, then add unflavored gelatin. Add to butter and cook, stirring, until it thickens, about 8 minutes. Remove from heat and add ½ cup of crushed cookies and amaretto liqueur. Blend well until the mixture cools and begins to set. Whip heavy cream to form soft peaks and gently fold into amaretto mixture. Pour sufficient amaretto liqueur to cover into the bottom of each soufflé cup. Put mousse mixture into soufflé cups. Add toasted sliced almonds and the rest of the cookie mixture to the top of the mousse. Chill before serving.

Christmas Dinner on the Union Pacific

A major railroad's executives of sufficient rank to merit the use of a business car when traveling would turn to the dining car department for a two-man staff when the car was "out on the line." Each executive would select a favorite chef and steward, ones whose dispositions and specialties would make for a pleasant trip. The Union Pacific Railroad, operating one of the largest fleets of dining cars in the 1920s, had no shortage of skilled chefs for such occasions. For an idea of what, say, the president of the railroad might have enjoyed on a Christmas Day trip to a year-end meeting in the east, consider these recipes for holiday favorites from the then-best chefs and stewards in Union Pacific's roster. They were solicited by the editors of *Union Pacific,* an employee magazine, and ran in a column entitled "The Real Home Terminal" in the holiday issues between 1925 and 1927.

For starters, a creation of UP chef-caterer Otto Hoffstaetter:

Grapefruit and Crème de Menthe Cocktail

Before You Begin

You'll need: covered dish

Prep: 15 minutes (plus 1 hour to chill)

Yield: 8 servings

4 large fresh grapefruit

¼ cup granulated sugar

½ cup crème de menthe

Halve grapefruit and remove the fruit sections, taking care to leave behind all traces of the section walls. Place sections in covered dish, sprinkle sugar over, and chill at least 1 hour. To serve, mix sections well, place in individual dishes, and sprinkle 1 tablespoon crème de menthe over each portion.

Food authority James Beard urged that turkey be reserved for a special place at Thanksgiving. The Christmas meal, he argued, should feature some other meat as the main course. Here, from Chef Edward Jones of the UP subsidiary Los Angeles & Salt Lake Railroad, is a main course that satisfied Beard's suggestion:

Roast Ham St. Angel

Before You Begin

You'll need: large pot, large saucepan, covered roasting pan, bowl

Preheat oven to 325°F.

Prep: 20 minutes (plus 1½ to 1¾ hours to cook ham)

Cook: 45 minutes

Yield: 8 servings

6 to 7 lbs. raw smoked ham

8 large sweet potatoes

1 cup light brown sugar

1 Tbsp. flour

½ tsp. ground black pepper

4 to 5 whole cloves

Ask the butcher for a center-cut piece of ham from which the bones have been removed, and have the ham rolled and tied securely, similar to a roast of beef. (**NOTE:** You may need to order this in advance.) Place the ham in a deep pot with water to cover. Bring to a boil, reduce heat, and slow simmer, allowing 15 minutes for each pound of ham. Meanwhile, in a large saucepan, place sweet potatoes in water to cover, bring to a boil, and cook until tender but not soft, about 15 to 20 minutes. Drain, cool, peel, and quarter the potatoes. When ham is cooked remove it from the water and pat dry, retaining the water in which it was cooked. Place ham in a covered roasting pan with the fat side of the meat up. In a bowl, mix brown sugar, flour, and pepper together well. Spread mixture thickly over the ham. Press cloves along ham's upper side. Arrange cooked sweet potatoes around the ham in the roasting pan. Place in a 325°F oven and bake 45 minutes. (**NOTE:** Use a meat thermometer, which should read 140°F when finished.) Baste frequently using a portion of the liquid in which the ham was boiled. To serve, slice ham and place on a platter with sweet potatoes arranged neatly around.

On the side, a recipe from Union Pacific steward Verne A. Snyder:

Scalloped Corn

Before You Begin

You'll need: mixing bowl, 2-quart baking dish

Preheat oven to 325°F.

Prep: 15 minutes

Cook: 30 minutes

Yield: 8 servings

4 cups uncooked corn kernels

3 eggs, well beaten

1½ cups milk

1½ tsp. salt

1½ tsp. granulated sugar

⅛ tsp. ground white pepper

3 Tbsp. butter, melted

In a mixing bowl, stir the corn, well-beaten eggs, milk, salt, sugar, and white pepper together to mix well. Pour mixture into a 2-quart baking dish and drizzle melted butter over. Bake in a 325°F oven until browned, about 30 minutes. Serve hot in the dish in which it was baked.

And for dessert, from Chef-Caterer Charles Mitchell:

Date and Nut Pudding

Before You Begin

You'll need: 3-quart pudding mold or baking dish, small saucepan, large mixing bowl, small bowl

Preheat oven to 350°F.

Prep: 30 minutes

Cook: 30 minutes

Yield: 8 servings

3 cups milk

4 cups soft bread crumbs

1½ cups pitted dates, chopped

flour

2 egg yolks, well beaten

1½ cups granulated sugar

2 Tbsp. butter, melted

1 tsp. vanilla extract

½ cup pecan pieces

2 egg whites, beaten stiff

1 tsp. baking powder

1 pint whipping cream

Butter a pudding mold or baking dish well and set aside. In a small saucepan, scald milk. In a large mixing bowl, pour scalding hot milk over bread crumbs, mix thoroughly and let stand 5 minutes. Meanwhile, toss pitted and chopped dates with flour to coat well. Beat egg yolks until of light lemon color. Then add beaten egg yolks, sugar, melted butter, vanilla, floured dates, and pecans to soaked bread crumbs. Mix together well. Beat egg whites until stiff, sprinkling baking soda over as they begin to stiffen. Fold beaten egg whites into bread mixture. Pour into buttered mold or baking dish, set mold/dish in an ovenproof pan or larger dish with hot water, and place all in 350°F oven to bake 30 minutes or until knife inserted in center comes out clean. Let cool and serve with whipped cream.

Montana Rail Link

www.montanarail.com

Montana Rail Link, Inc., an FRA Class II regional railroad with more than nine hundred miles of track, serves one hundred stations in Montana, Idaho, and Washington. The line employs one thousand men and women who operate a fleet of more than 2,100 freight cars, 120 locomotives, and 4 business cars. A continuous schedule of business meetings, employee and shipper appreciation events, and community involvement keeps the business cars and other corporate facilities busy. Food, of course, plays a central role.

So it is not unusual to find Montana Rail Link Executive Chef Norma Geng busy serving eight hundred guests steak dinners at a golf outing, or overseeing an employee picnic at "the ranch." Cooking for a crowd was part of growing up for her. "I was one of the oldest of eight children," says the Montana native. "One of my jobs was to cook. My mother and grandmother were wonderful cooks and teachers, and I seemed to take to it naturally."

She has cooked for Montana Rail Link for over fifteen years.

An advocate "good, old-fashioned cooking," Ms. Geng's experience has encouraged her to "try this and that" over the years. She offers this dinner, which collects some of her most popular items, to the company's executives and their guests, and now to you.

Montana Rail Link business car dining room. Montana Rail Link, Inc.

Deep-Fried Ravioli with Tomato Dipping Sauce

Tomato Dipping Sauce

1 15-oz. can tomato sauce
1 cup finely chopped fresh tomatoes
½ cup finely chopped sun-dried
    tomatoes, packed in olive oil and
    herbs

1 tsp. dried Italian seasoning
2 tsp. green onion, chopped

Before You Begin

You'll need:
medium bowl, large
pot, deep-fryer or
large skillet

Prep: 20 minutes
(plus overnight to
chill dipping sauce)

Cook: 30 minutes

Yield: 6 servings

In a medium bowl, combine tomato sauce, fresh tomatoes, sun-dried tomatoes, and seasoning. Cover and refrigerate overnight. To serve, garnish with
green onion, set bowl on a platter, and surround with fried ravioli.

Fried Ravioli

1 25-oz. package frozen small square
    cheese-filled ravioli

4 cups olive oil

In a large pot of boiling water, cook frozen ravioli according to package directions and drain well. Meanwhile, in a deep-fryer, warm olive oil to 375°F or, in
a large skillet over medium-high heat, warm ½ inch of oil. Place cooked ravioli
in the fry basket and immerse in oil to cook until golden brown, shaking basket occasionally, about five minutes. If using a skillet, place sufficient cooked
ravioli to form a single layer in the hot oil and fry both sides until golden
brown, about 2 minutes per side. Repeat until all ravioli are fried. Remove
fried ravioli to plate lined with paper towels and keep warm.

Cocktail Snack Kabobs with Dip

Before You Begin

You'll need: large cocktail picks, small bowl, whisk

Prep: 30 minutes

Yield: according to need

pimiento-stuffed pitted ripe olives

cauliflower florets

assorted pickled vegetables (mushrooms, hot peppers)

cheese cubes (Swiss, Monterey Jack, and cheddar)

baked ham, cubed

turkey, cubed

51- to 60-count (medium) shrimp, cooked

cucumber, ¼-inch slices

red, green, and/or yellow bell pepper, 1-inch dice

red or sweet onion, 1-inch dice, layers separated

cherry tomatoes

melons, 1-inch cubes

pineapple, 1-inch cubes

Offer a variety of combinations of ingredients above on different picks, or arrange ingredients on platters and accompany with picks so guests can make their own.

Dip

1 cup olive oil

⅓ cup balsamic vinegar

3–4 drops Tabasco sauce

½ tsp. granulated sugar

1½ Tbsp. minced cilantro

In a small bowl, combine all ingredients well and sugar is dissolved. Cover and chill at least 1 hour in refrigerator. Whisk to blend before serving.

Parmesan Potato Soup

Before You Begin

You'll need: 2-quart saucepan, small saucepan

Preheat oven to 350°F.

Prep: 30 minutes (plus 2 hours to bake and chill potatoes)

Cook: 1 hour

Yield: 8 servings

2–3 baking potatoes, about 2 lbs.

2¼ cups rich chicken stock (see NOTE)

⅓ cup + 2 Tbsp. onion, chopped

¼ cup celery, chopped

¼ tsp. basil

¼ tsp. seasoning salt

¼ tsp. thyme

¼ tsp. onion salt

¼ tsp. garlic powder

¼ tsp. pepper

¼ cup. butter

3 Tbsp. flour

¼ lb. bacon, cooked and chopped

½ cup grated fresh Parmesan cheese

3–4 cups half & half (substitute: whole milk)

parsley, chopped

NOTE: To make rich stock, begin with 3 cups stock, bring to a boil, reduce heat and simmer to reduce by ¼ to 2¼ cups. This can be done ahead.

Bake potatoes in 350°F oven until done firm, about 1 hour. Refrigerate to chill, then peel and cut into ½-inch cubes. Meanwhile, in a 2-quart saucepan, bring rich chicken stock to a boil, add onions, celery, and all seasonings, then reduce heat and simmer until onions and celery are tender, 15 minutes. Add baked potato cubes and cook for an additional 30 minutes. Meanwhile, in a small saucepan over medium heat, melt butter. Add flour, stirring constantly, to make a blond roux, about 3 minutes. Add roux to the soup a little at a time while cooking, continuing to simmer. Stir until soup thickens, then reduce heat to low, add bacon, Parmesan cheese, and half & half to desire texture and richness. (**NOTE:** Do not boil.) Garnish with chopped parsley.

Easy Oriental Salad

1 large head lettuce, torn into small pieces

4 stalks celery, sliced thin

3 or 4 whole green onions, chopped coarse

1 large can bean sprouts, drained

1 lb. pineapple tidbits, drained

1 large bunch green grapes, cut in half

1 large bunch red grapes, cut in half

1 can Mandarin oranges, drained

1 cup broken cashew nuts

Before You Begin

You'll need: large salad bowl, small bowl

Prep: 20 minutes

Yield: 8 servings

In a large, decorative bowl, arrange lettuce. Top with celery, onions, and bean sprouts. Scatter fruit over top and sprinkle with nuts.

Dressing

½ cup soy sauce

1 cup mayonnaise

In a small bowl, blend soy sauce and mayonnaise well (longer is better), and chill before serving. Serve dressing on side of salad portions.

Baron of Beef

Before You Begin

You'll need: large bowl, whisk, roasting pan with rack, meat thermometer

Preheat oven to 500°F.

Prep: 10 minutes (plus overnight to marinate)

Cook: 1 hour 40 minutes to 3 hours

Yield: 8–12 servings

1 5–8-lb. baron of beef
2–4 garlic cloves, chopped
4 tsp. coarsely ground pepper

¾ cup Worcestershire sauce
1½ cups soy sauce
1⅓ cups beef broth

In a bowl sufficient to hold cut of beef, combine garlic, pepper, Worcestershire sauce, and soy sauce, and whisk well. Rub mixture onto beef. Cover and refrigerate overnight. To cook, preheat oven to 500°F. Drain marinade and discard. Place beef on a rack in a roasting pan and pour beef broth around. Place in oven to roast 45 minutes, turn reduce heat down to 325°F and cook until of an internal temperature of 160°F, about 20 total minutes per pound for "rare," 22 minutes per pound for "medium." Remove and let stand 5 minutes, then slice and serve accompanied by juice from roasting pan. You may also garnish with sliced button mushrooms that have been sautéed in butter.

Roasted Asparagus

Before You Begin

You'll need: 2 sheet pans

Preheat oven to 350°F

Prep: 10 minutes

Cook: 15 minutes

Yield: 4 servings

½ cup slivered almonds, toasted
1½ tsp. butter

1½ tsp. olive oil
1 lb. asparagus, trimmed

Scatter slivered almonds on a sheet pan and place in a 350°F oven to toast to light brown, about 5 minutes, and set aside. In a large skillet over low heat, melt butter. Remove from heat and blend with olive oil. Roll asparagus spears in butter and oil mixture, and place on sheet pans. Roast in a 350°F oven until slightly tender, about 10 to 15 minutes. Garnish with toasted slivered almonds.

Swedish Mashed Potatoes

10 to 12 medium red potatoes, peeled
⅓ cup sour cream
½ cup butter, divided

½ head green or red cabbage, shredded
1 cup shredded cheddar cheese

In a large saucepan, place potatoes in water to cover. Bring to a boil and cook potatoes until tender, about 20 minutes, and drain. In a large bowl, mash potatoes with sour cream and 1/3 cup butter until fluffy. Meanwhile, in a medium skillet, melt remaining butter and sauté cabbage until soft. Mix cabbage into potatoes. Stir shredded cheddar cheese into potatoes. Put potato mixture to a 3-quart casserole and place in a 350°F oven until golden brown, about 30 minutes.

Before You Begin

You'll need: large saucepan, large bowl, medium skillet, potato masher or electric mixer, 3-quart casserole

Preheat oven to 350°F.

Prep: 30 minutes

Cook: 30 minutes

Yield: 8 servings

Apple Raspberry Pie

5 cups peeled, thinly sliced tart apples
1 cup raspberries (see NOTE)
1 cup granulated sugar, or to taste
1 Tbsp. butter, cold
1 tsp. ground cinnamon

1 Tbsp. tapioca
1 egg white
1 tsp. water
vanilla ice cream

NOTE: Fresh raspberries will do, but frozen are preferred because of the juices present when thawed.

Prepare pastry for a two-crust pie (see page 82), and line 9-inch deep-dish pie plate with bottom crust. Combine sugar and cinnamon. (**NOTE:** The amount of sugar depends on how tart the apples are.) Arrange a layer of apples in pastry-lined pie plate and sprinkle with sugar and cinnamon. Follow with a layer of raspberries and sprinkle with sugar and cinnamon. Repeat to use all apples and raspberries. Dot top layer with small pieces of cold butter and sprinkle with tapioca. Cover with top crust, seal edge, and cut four 1-inch slits to vent. In a small bowl, whisk egg white with water. Brush egg wash on top crust and sprinkle with 1 tablespoon sugar. Place on lowest rack in a 450°F oven. Bake 10 minutes, reduce oven to 350°F and bake for 30 to 35 minutes longer until bubbly and crust is of light golden brown. Let stand 5 minutes and serve warm with vanilla ice cream.

Before You Begin

You'll need: 9-inch deep-dish pie plate, large mixing bowl, small bowl

Preheat oven to 450°F.

Prep: 15 minutes

Cook: 45 minutes

Yield: 6–8 servings

Chef Christian deLutis Reinvents Classic Railroad Cuisine

The Harbor Court Hotel

www.harborcourt.com

At Baltimore's Harbor Court Hotel, Chef Christian deLutis of Brighton's Restaurant has adapted, interpreted, or simply presented, a number of dishes taken from railroad dining cars of the Golden Age. The result is an interesting view of how menu items of that era might be presented today.

Brighton's specializes in seasonal American cuisine. Chef Christian is committed to preserving what he calls "classic American countryside cooking," with an emphasis on ingredients and techniques that spring from the American experience. A focus on the foods found here, and the culinary possibilities they offer, led him to explore dining car menus of yore.

What Chef Christian does with classic railroad recipes sheds light on how our food styles have changed. Here, then, are three menu items you might have found on a train in the 1930s, accompanied by Chef Christian's contemporary offering.

Arabian Peach Salad from the Western Pacific Railroad

Before You Begin

You'll need: 3 small plates to roll and save date bars in coatings, grater.

Prep: 30 minutes

Yield: 4 servings

2 cups black dates, chopped

French dressing

⅓ cup pistachio nuts, chopped fine

⅓ cup Swiss cheese, grated fine

1 fresh peach

4 romaine leaves

8 pimiento strips

4 watercress rosettes

Mold chopped black dates into bars ½-inch square by 1½-inch long. Dip or gently roll bars in French dressing to coat, then roll in finely chopped pistachio nuts and grated Swiss cheese. To serve, peel and cut peach in half, remove the pit, and cut in ¼-inch slices. Place one leaf of romaine on an individual serving plate. Using 3 peach slices and two date bars, alternate peach slices and date bars across the romaine. Pour a small portion of French dressing over the salad and garnish with a cross of pimiento and a rosette of watercress.

From this, Chef Christian creates:

Arabian Peach Salad with Pistachio Scallops

Before You Begin

You'll need: blender, small roasting pan, ovenproof sauté pan

Preheat oven to 350°F.

Prep: 10 minutes

Cook: 11 minutes

Yield: 4 servings

1 bunch watercress

5 ice cubes

juice of ½ lemon

1 hard-boiled egg

½ cup heavy cream

salt and pepper to taste

2 fresh underripe peaches

oil for cooking

8 sea scallops

2 dates, chopped coarse

1 cup crushed pistachio, divided

Place watercress, ice cubes, lemon juice, hard-boiled egg, and cream in blender, season with salt and pepper, and puree. Refrigerate to chill. Quarter peaches and discard pit. Toss peach sections with oil to coat lightly, season with salt and pepper, place in a roasting pan, and roast at 350°F until tender, about 10 minutes. (**NOTE:** If peaches are ripe, roast about 5 minutes.) Let rest in pan to stay warm. Season scallops with salt and pepper and roll in crushed pistachio until evenly coated. Place 2 tablespoons of oil in an ovenproof sauté pan, add scallops, and cook in a 350°F oven for 11 minutes. To serve, space two scallops 3 inches apart, top each with 1 peach wedge, and top peach slices with mound of chopped dates. Drizzle with chilled watercress sauce, and dust plate with crushed pistachios.

Pork Sausage and Sweet Potatoes from the Chicago, Milwaukee, St. Paul & Pacific Railroad

Before You Begin

You'll need: large saucepan, potato masher or ricer, small bowl, small saucepan, 1-quart casserole

Preheat oven to 350°F.

Prep: 30 minutes

Cook: 45 minutes

Yield: 4 servings

4 sweet potatoes

2 Tbsp. butter, plus to butter casserole

½ tsp. salt

2 eggs, well beaten

¼ cup light cream, heated

1 lb. ground pork sausage

Butter a 1-quart casserole and set aside. Wash sweet potatoes thoroughly and place in large saucepan with water to cover. Bring to a boil and cook until potatoes are tender, about 25 minutes. Drain, peel, and mash potatoes. Add butter, salt, eggs, and cream. Beat or whip to make light and fluffy. Place potatoes in buttered casserole. Shape sausage into 4 patties and press each into potatoes. Place in oven and bake until sausage is nicely browned and done, about 30 to 45 minutes.

Christian DeLutis's main course is:

Sweet Potato with Tapioca and Sausage

Before You Begin

You'll need: cooking sheet, large saucepan, bowls

Preheat oven to 350°F.

Prep: 10 minutes (plus time to bake sweet potatoes)

Cook: 30 minutes

Yield: 4 servings

4¼-lb. links duck sausage (see NOTE)

8 1-inch slices fresh baguette

2 Tbsp. oil

1 shallot, chopped

2 garlic cloves, chopped

1 cup wild mushrooms, chopped

¾ cup dried cherries

1 cup instant tapioca

1 cup milk

2 cups water

2 sweet potatoes, baked, skin removed, coarsely mashed

½ bunch sage, chopped

fresh thyme for garnish

NOTE: Use duck sausage seasoned with herbs or herbs and fruit, not spicy sausage.

Cut 2 sausages in half, then in half lengthwise, and place on a cooking sheet. Roast at 350°F until done, about 10 minutes. Remove duck from roasting pan and set aside to keep warm. Increase oven to 400°F, place baguette slices in renderings in cooking sheet and return to oven to brown, approximately 4 minutes per side. Meanwhile, dice remaining 2 sausages to any size. In a large saucepan over medium heat, warm oil and add shallots, garlic, and diced sausage. Cook, stirring occasionally, until fat is rendered, about 3 minutes. Add mushrooms and dried cherries and continue to sauté until browned, about 3 minutes. Add tapioca and stir gently to toast 15 seconds only. Stir in milk, water and sweet potatoes. Simmer, stir, and add more water as needed until tapioca is cooked through and mixture has a creamy consistency. Stir in sage and heat through. To serve, stack 2 browned baguette slices in individual serving bowl, ladle potato/sausage mixture over, and prop 2 roasted sausage pieces alongside. Garnish with fresh thyme.

Melon Mint Cocktail as Served on the Pennsylvania Railroad

Before You Begin

You'll need: small saucepan, strainer, melon baller, small bowl

Prep: 20 minutes (allow 1 hour for syrup to chill)

Cook: 10 minutes

Yield: 4 servings

½ cup sugar
1½ cup water
1 Tbsp. mint leaves, chopped
juice of 1 lemon, strained

juice of 1 orange, strained
1 large melon or 2 half-melons of the season

In a saucepan, stir sugar and water together, bring to a boil, and reduce heat to slow boil for 5 minutes. Meanwhile, place chopped mint in bowl. Pour boiling syrup over mint, stir to mix, and set aside to cool. Strain syrup and stir in lemon juice and orange juice. Place in refrigerator and chill through for 1 hour. Meanwhile, halve the melon(s), remove seeds, cut into balls, and chill. To serve, place 10 melon balls in a dish, pour syrup over all, and garnish with fresh mint leaves.

Melon Mint Cocktail as Served by Chef Christian

Before You Begin

You'll need: medium bowl, small saucepan, electric beater and mixing bowl

Prep: 20 minutes

Cook: 10 minutes

Yield: 4 servings

1 cup chopped honeydew, in small bite-size pieces
1 cup chopped cantaloupe, in small bite-size pieces
1 cup chopped watermelon, in small bite-size pieces
1 cup sugar

1 to 2 ozs. brandy, divided
1 cup water
1 Tbsp. peppermint extract
1 cup heavy cream, whipped
2 Tbsp. confectioners' sugar
1 Tbsp. curry powder

Chop and combine melon and set aside to chill. In a small saucepan, combine sugar, 1 ounce brandy, and water. Bring to a boil, reduce heat, and simmer until sugar is dissolved and a thin syrup forms, about 5 minutes. Stir in peppermint extract and brandy to taste, let cool at room temperature, and set aside. Meanwhile, whip cream until thick and light, and peaks form when beaters are lifted. Add confectioners' sugar and curry powder. Blend until creamy and bright yellow. To serve, fill individual martini glasses with chopped fruit. Drizzle mint/sugar syrup over fruit. Add a splash of brandy. Spoon a dollop of curry cream on each glass and garnish with a wedge of melon used and peppermint leaf at the base of the glass.

Quad/Graphics Quad/Cuisine

www.qg.com

On a recent afternoon in New Orleans's Union Station, the buzz that announces the arrival of a passenger train swept through those awaiting the arrival of Amtrak's *City of New Orleans*. Those taking up a position on the platform to watch were in for a surprise: The Superliners backing in were preceded by a dashing four-car set of restored 1950s-era flute-sided streamliners, the markers carried by a domed, round-end observation car whose round end was in fact a platform.

This four-car consist has a name: the *Silver Rail Fleet*. It is the business train of Quad/Graphics, a large printing company headquartered in Sussex, Wisconsin. Founded in 1971 by the late Harry R. Quadracci, it is the largest privately held printer in the world, with output that includes *Time, Newsweek*, and *People* magazines, L. L. Bean and Lands' End catalogs, commercial pieces, newspaper inserts, trading cards and game pieces, fine art posters, and more.

"Senior," as Harry Quadracci was known, built the company on the belief in thinking small and nurturing close personal relationships. And what better way to build such relationships than to treat clients to a delicious meal aboard a scenic train ride? Representatives of Quad/Graphics can conduct a presentation at the corporate offices in Sussex, then board the train to talk further over lunch on the roughly hour-long run to the Lomira plant. On the return trip, specialists on board address any questions a customer may raise. In addition, the train is displayed at

The "Silver Lodge," the "Silver Shore," and the dome/observation car "Silver Chalet," part of the Quad/Graphics Silver Rail Fleet, *follow Amtrak's* Lake Shore Limited *out of Hammond, Indiana, en route to Chicago. John H. Kuehl*

professional association meetings, carries clients to special events like the Super Bowl, and is made available to client firms for use in their own marketing efforts. The cozy, attractive train also serves employees well. The company organizes business meetings aboard the train, complete with dinner and drinks served.

Executive Chef Bob Clairmont is one of several chefs who manage food service on the *Silver Rail Fleet*. His culinary background includes work at hotels, restaurants, and a catering service. But what prepared him for work on a train was a stint working on a cruise boat. "That taught me how to keep a kitchen," he says. With Quad/Graphics now more than eleven years, he oversees off-premises events, the corporate dining room, and the growing number of runs the train makes each year. Come join him for a four-course dinner.

Salmon Persilade on Mesclun Greens with Fresh Basil Beurre Blanc

Before You Begin

You'll need:
8 skewers (or 16 toothpicks), 2 small bowls, sheet pan, 1-quart saucepan

Preheat oven to 375°F.

Prep: 30 minutes

Cook: 10 minutes

Yield: 8 servings

3 lbs. Copper River king salmon fillet, skinned

2 tsp. fresh garlic chopped fine

2 Tbsp. white wine

¼ cup Dijon mustard

½ cup extra-virgin olive oil

1 cup fresh bread crumbs, crust removed

1 Tbsp. fresh minced parsley

1 Tbsp. lemon zest

salt and white pepper to taste

4 cups mesclun greens or spring greens mix

Remove pin bones from salmon and cut into 1½-ounce strips. Place 2 pieces of salmon against each other yin-and-yang fashion, secure with 2 toothpicks or a skewer, and set aside. In a small bowl, combine garlic, wine, and mustard, then whisk in olive oil a little at a time and thoroughly infuse. In another small bowl, combine bread crumbs, parsley, lemon zest, salt, and white pepper, and set aside. To finish, brush each portion of salmon generously with mustard mix, top with bread crumbs, and place on a sheet pan. Place in a 375°F oven to bake until just done, 8 to 10 minutes. To serve, put ½ cup mesclun greens on individual plates, top with 2 portions of salmon, and drizzle with Fresh Basil Beurre Blanc.

Fresh Basil Beurre Blanc

¼ cup white wine

2 Tbsp. fresh lemon juice

½ cup heavy cream

½ lb. sweet butter

⅓ cup chopped fresh basil

In a heavy 1-quart saucepan over medium-low heat, slowly reduce wine and lemon juice to 1 tablespoon, stir in cream and simmer to reduce to ¼ cup. Reduce heat to low, stir in butter 1 tablespoon at a time. (**NOTE:** Do not boil.) Add basil just before serving.

Pasta Della Quadracci

8 oz. uncooked linguini

¼ cup olive oil, or enough to coat
  cooked pasta

2 Tbsp. extra-virgin olive oil

1½ Tbsp. fresh garlic

1 lb. fresh shitake mushrooms, stems
  removed, sliced ¼ inch thick

1 cup red bell pepper, ¼-inch dice

1 cup Kalamata olives, pitted, sliced

2 Tbsp. chopped fresh oregano

1 cup grated Parmesan cheese

Before You Begin

You'll need: pasta pot, colander, sauté skillet

Prep: 10 minutes (plus time to cook linguini)

Cook: 5 minutes

Yield: 8 servings

Cook linguini according to package directions, drain well, and toss with olive oil to coat. Meanwhile, in a sauté skillet on medium-high heat, heat extra-virgin olive oil and add garlic to cook until garlic starts to turn golden, about 2 minutes. Add mushrooms, peppers, and olives, and sauté until tender, about 3 minutes. Add oregano and stir to mix and heat through. To serve, place hot pasta on individual plates and top with sautéed vegetables and Parmesan cheese.

Roasted Veal Loin with Morel Mushroom Glace

1 3–4-lb. veal loin (see CHEF'S TIP)

2 Tbsp. olive oil

cracked pepper to taste

2 tsp. chopped fresh rosemary

1 medium onion, diced coarse

1 carrot, diced coarse

1 stock celery, diced coarse

Before You Begin

You'll need: large skillet, roasting pan, meat thermometer, small bowl, 1-quart heavy-bottomed saucepan

Preheat oven to 325°F.

Prep: 10 minutes (does not include making veal stock)

Cook: 1 hour

Yield: 8 servings

Rub the veal loin with olive oil, cracked pepper, and chopped fresh rosemary. Arrange diced onion, carrot, and celery to form a "raft" on which to set the loin in the roasting pan. In a large skillet over high heat, sear veal on all sides, about 2 minutes per side, and remove to the roasting pan. Place in a 325°F oven to roast until internal temperature is 120°F, about 40 minutes.

CHEF'S TIP: I buy veal short loins and have the meat company bone them out and cryovac the loins and tenderloins separately, then use the bones to make the veal glace.

Morel Mushroom Glace

3 oz. dried morels
½ cup brandy
1 Tbsp. olive oil

⅓ cup chopped fresh shallots
2 cups glace de viande (see NOTE)

NOTE: Substitute "Glace de Viande Gold" from Kitchens of More Than Gourmet (see page 264), or similar from Knorr Swiss.

In a small bowl, soak dried morels in brandy to moisten, about 20 minutes. In a 1-quart heavy-bottom saucepan over medium heat, warm oil, add shallots and caramelize, about 3 to 4 minutes. Add morels in brandy and simmer until liquid is almost gone. Add veal glace, stir, and bring to a boil. Remove from heat.

Bundled Asparagus

Before You Begin

You'll need: small bowl, large pot, colander, large bowl

Prep: 20 minutes

Cook: 7 minutes

Yield: 8 servings

1 6-inch or longer zucchini, plump preferred
2 lbs. fresh asparagus spears
½ red pepper, cut lengthwise into 8¼-inch strips

½ yellow pepper, cut lengthwise into 8¼-inch strips

Slice zucchini across in ½-inch pieces, remove centers, and place in small bowl with cold water to hold. In a large pot bring water sufficient to cover asparagus to a boil, add asparagus, and blanch for 5 minutes. Drain and plunge into a large bowl of ice water to arrest cooking. To assemble, depending on the size of the asparagus, use 3 to 5 spears per serving. Combine spears and one piece of each pepper and secure by sliding a zucchini ring over. (**NOTE:** Alternatively, tie with a ¼-inch strip of leek.)

To serve, slice veal into ¼-inch slices. Put Morel Glace on individual plates, taking care to reserve some mushrooms for garnish. Arrange 3 slices of veal in sauce, offset with a bundle of asparagus, and top with a few mushrooms. Can be accompanied by Pasta Della Quadracci or potatoes (see the Recipe Index by Course, page 265, for suggestions).

Chocolate Decadence with Raspberry Coulis

1½ lbs. Callebaut bittersweet chocolate
   (see NOTE)
7 oz. sweet butter, room temperature
6 eggs, well beaten

2 Tbsp. sugar
fresh raspberries (for garnish)
gaufrette cookies (for garnish)

Before You Begin

You'll need:
1 medium and 1
large stainless-steel
mixing bowl and
saucepan to hold
each over simmering
water, candy
thermometer, 10-
inch cake pan,
electric beater,
blender, small bowl

Preheat oven to
375°F.

Prep: 30 minutes
(plus 4 or more
hours to freeze cake)

Cook: 10 minutes

Yield: 8 servings

NOTE: Substitute Lindt, Ghirardelli, or other high-quality chocolates (60 percent or 70 percent cocoa-solid content).

Butter and flour a 10-inch cake pan and set aside. In a medium stainless-steel mixing bowl over a simmering water bath, melt together and mix bittersweet chocolate and butter, and set aside. In a large mixing bowl over a simmering water bath, combine eggs and sugar, and whisk until sugar dissolves. Bring mixture to 70°F. Whip with an electric beater on high for 15 minutes, or until full volume is reached. (NOTE: Look at the side of the mixing bowl to see when the volume starts to fall.) Fold in the butter and chocolate and pour into the prepared 10-inch cake pan. Place in a 375°F oven to bake for 8 to 10 minutes. (NOTE: The center of the cake will be loose.) Freeze the cake, allowing 4 or more hours. To remove the cake from the pan, heat the pan slightly in a shallow tray of hot water, then invert. Serve with Raspberry Coulis and garnish with fresh raspberries and gaufrette cookie.

Raspberry Coulis

1¼ cups fresh raspberries
2 Tbsp. granulated sugar

½ tsp. fresh lemon juice

In a blender, puree raspberries with sugar and lemon juice, and pour through a fine sieve into a bowl, pressing to extract all liquid. Refrigerate at least 1 hour before serving.

It could be argued that the railroad dining car single-handedly elevated French toast to its iconic place at the American breakfast table. In the Golden Age of rail travel from the 1920s to the 1950s, French toast was third in popularity among all menu dishes, behind beef steak (remember, most passengers in that bygone era were men), and that legendary patriotic staple, apple pie. Among the three, French toast allowed the greatest opportunity for creative innovation.

So it is fitting that in selecting his signature dish, Amtrak Corporate Executive Chef Lamar Gilbert, Sr., who is in charge of, among other things, meals served on Amtrak's business car, the *10001*, without hesitation presented his French toast. He calls it Santa Fe French Toast, in tribute to what was once the most famous of railroad French toast recipes. But, as good chefs always do, Chef Lamar made a recipe that is his own. His interpretation of Atchison, Topeka & Santa Fe French Toast follows:

Santa Fe French Toast

Before You Begin

You'll need: large bowl, whisk, large skillet

Prep: 5 minutes (plus overnight to blend ingredients)

Cook: 6 minutes per serving

Yield: 8 servings

6 eggs, beaten

1 qt. whole milk

½ tsp. nutmeg

3 Tbsp. vanilla extract

1 Tbsp. ground cinnamon

1 cup heavy cream

vegetable oil

16 pieces fresh white bread, cut in ½-inch slices

confectioners' sugar

In a large bowl, use a whisk to combine the first six ingredients well, then refrigerate the mixture overnight. In a large skillet over medium heat, warm sufficient oil to coat bottom of skillet. Using two slices of bread for each serving, dip bread into egg mixture to coat, then place in hot oil to fry until golden brown, 2 to 3 minutes. Turn and repeat to finish. Replenish oil in skillet and repeat for each serving. Serve dusted with confectioners' sugar accompanied by bacon, sausage, ham, or all three.

CHEF'S TIP: The heavy cream keeps the egg mixture from saturating the fresh bread. But take care not to allow bread to soak up too much mixture as bread will tear if too wet.

Appendix 1

Sources for Further Information

Rail travel and dining is a dynamic activity. The information in this book is accurate as of its date of publication. Below are some additional sources for up-to-date information on each category of train. Or consult a professional travel agent.

Private Luxury Trains

See a travel agent to research and book travel on domestic and international private trains. Two companies that specialize in such trips are:

> Trains Unlimited Tours, found on the Web at www.trainsunlimitedtours.com or by calling 800-359-4870, 800-266-8751, 775-852-4448 or 530-836-1745 (in Canada: 800-752-1836), offers access to a variety of public and customized trips for tourists and rail fans.

> Abercrombie & Kent, on the Web at www.abercombiekent.com, or accessible by telephone at 800-554-7094, books the *Royal Scotsman, Northern Belle, Venice Simplon-Orient-Express, Eastern & Oriental Express,* and *Great South Pacific Express,* among others.

Private Cars

For more information about the private rail car travel, or to learn about the cars available for charter, contact the American Association of Private Railroad Car Owners (AAPRCO) on the Web at www.aaprco.com, or by telephone at 202-547-5696.

Dinner Trains

Always contact a dinner train prior to planning a visit. Most require advance reservations. Some expect an entrée selection at the time a reservation is made. Virtually all trains can, with notice, accommodate special dietary or lifestyle menu preferences. Most are available for group charter at times other than those scheduled throughout the year. For current information on dinner trains, see:

www.dinnertrainsofamerica.com: An interactive site operated by a voluntary association of a growing number of dinner trains in North America.

www.americandinnertrains.com: A comprehensive, if occasionally out-of-date, list of dinner trains arranged by state. It is worth checking prior to planning any trip.

Railfan & Railroad: Each year, the June issue of this monthly magazine includes a center-section pullout briefly describing each rail dining experience in North America. Here you'll also find the author's monthly "On the Menu" column about dinner trains and other aspects of rail dining. For more information on the magazine, go to www.railfan.com; for more about the author, visit the Web site www.jamesdporterfield.com.

Empire State Railway Museum's Tourist Trains, an annual guide to tourist railroads and museums available from Kalmbach Publishing Co., 21027 Crossroads Circle, P.O. Box 1612, Waukesha, Wisconsin 53187-1612. (Look for the "attendant holding a tray aloft" symbol, which denotes a dinner train.)

The Railroads

Amtrak: A number of long-haul trains with first-class accommodations, including dining cars, connect America's major cities. *Acela Express* service operates frequently each day between Washington, D.C., and Boston, via New York City. Contact Amtrak on the Web at www.amtrak.com or by telephone at 800-USA-RAIL (872-7245).

VIA Rail Canada: VIA operates an extensive array of trains throughout Canada that include first-class accommodations and meal service. Contact VIA on the Web at www.viarail.ca or by telephone at 888-VIA-RAIL (842-7245).

Appendix 2

Sources for Specialty Food Items

Below are some recommended sources for regional or specialty ingredients called for in the recipes here.

ALASKA WILD BERRY PRODUCTS
5225 Juneau Street
Anchorage, AK 99518
Phone: 800-280-2927
Web: www.alaskawildberryproducts.com
Notes: While the Alaska Wild Berry Syrup used on the *Midnight Sun Express* (see page 32) is a custom blend made just for the train, recommended substitutes are raspberry sauce, blueberry sauce, and salmonberry sauce.

AMERICAN SPOON FOODS
P.O. Box 566
Petosky, MI 49770-0566
Phone: 888-735-6700
Web:www.spoon.com
Notes: The source of the chili-lime sauce used on dishes served on Amtrak's *Acela Express* First Class Service (see page 224).

CHRISTMAS POINT WILD RICE COMPANY
975 Edgewood Drive
Baxter, MN 56425
Phone: 218-828-0603
Web: www.christmaspoint.com
Notes: A source for authentic, hand-picked, wild rice growing in the lakes and streams of the Minnesota North-woods.

EASTERN STATES BISON COOPERATIVE
RR9, Box 9100
Lake Ariel, PA 18436
Phone: 570-689-2427
Web: www.easternbison.com
Notes: A source of the various buffalo products called for. Or consult your local specialty grocer.

FINCHVILLE FARMS

P.O. Box 56
Finchville, KY 40022
Phone: 800-678-1521 or
502-834-7952
Web: www.finchvillefarms.com
Notes: Authentic Kentucky aged country ham, called for by the Louisville & Nashville Railroad to make its Kentucky Ham with Red-Eye Gravy (see page 203).

MINOR'S

P.O. Box 21743
Cleveland, OH 44121
Phone: 800-TASTEBUD (827-8328) or
216-381-9925
Web: www.soupbase.com
Notes: A complete line of soup bases, sauce preps, gravies, and flavor concentrates.

KITCHENS OF MORE THAN GOURMET

929 Home Avenue
Akron, OH 44310
Phone: 800-860-9385 or 330-762-6652
Web: www.morethangourmet.com
Notes: Classic French sauces and stocks made with no chemicals, MSG, or preservatives. A number of chefs here recommend these to their passengers.

NORA MILL GRANARY

7107 South Main Street
Helen, GA 30545
Phone: 800-927-2375
Fax: 800-927-1280
Web: www.noramill.com
E-mail: NoraMill@aol.com
Notes: Stone-ground corn products such as those used by the Louisville & Nashville Railroad to make its Corn Muffins (see page 203).

WILLIAMS-SONOMA

P.O. Box 7456
San Francisco, CA 94120–7456
Phone: 800-541-2233
Fax: 702-363-2541
Web: www.williams-sonoma.com
Notes: Specialty sausages such as are called for in the breakfast recipe on *Acela Express* (see page 222).

Appendix 3
Recipe Index by Course

SOUPS AND STEWS

SALADS AND SALAD DRESSINGS

Greens, Mixed Salad with House Vinaigrette (*J. Pinckney Henderson*), 80

Huckleberry Vinaigrette Dressing (*Mt. Hood Dinner Train*), 149

Japanese Pickled Cucumber Salad (*Napa Valley Wine Train*), 162

Mandarin Orange Salad (*Northern Sky*), 84

Melon Mint Cocktail (Pennsylvania Railroad), 253

Pancetta Vinaigrette (*The Survivor*), 105

Paul's Special Salad Dressing (*Montana Daylight*), 118

Pasta Salad (Montana Rockies Rail Tours), 23

Pears, Poached, with Stilton Blue Cheese, Cranberry Compote, and, Toasted Poppy Seed Dressing (*Royal Canadian Pacific*), 43

Potato Salad (*The Royal Scotsman*), 27

Potato Salad, Family Roundup (*Marlboro Unlimited*), 35

Raspberry Vinaigrette (*Virginia City*), 115

Raspberry Vinaigrette Mixed Salad (*Scenic Rail Dining*), 176

Red Leaf and Mesclun Salad à la Café (*Café Lafayette Dinner Train*), 129

Romaine, Grapefruit and Toasted Almond Salad (*Spirit of Washington Dinner Train*), 190

Russian Dressing (Louisville & Nashville Railroad), 202

Salmon Persilade on Mesclun Greens with Fresh Basil Beurre Blanc (Quad/Graphics), 256

Slaw, Pepper (*Marlboro Unlimited*), 36

Soft Lettuce Salad with Champagne and Roasted Beet Vinaigrette (*My Old Kentucky Dinner Train*), 157

Spinach Salad (*Tamalpais*), 108

Tomato Salad, Summer, with Fresh Mozzarella, Sweet Red Peppers, Roasted Shallot and Basil Vinaigrette (RailCruise America), 170

Waldorf Salad (*Chapel Hill*), 72

BEEF, BISON, AND VEAL

Alberta Beef Tenderloin with Portobello Duxelle with Blueberry-Ice Wine, Demi-Glace (*Royal Canadian Pacific*), 48

Baron of Beef (Montana Rail Link), 248

Beef, Hash Cakes, Browned on Buttered Toast Points (Rufus Estes/Pullman Company), 76

Beef, Roasted Tenderloin of (BNSF), 239

Beef, Roasted Tenderloin of, Kansas City Barbecue-Style (BNSF), 119

Beef Tenderloin Fillet on Wild Mushroom Ragout with Demi-Glace (*Northern Sky*), 86

Beef Tenderloin, Sliced, with Red Wine Mushroom Sauce (*Scottish Thistle*), 100

Beef Wellington with Sauce Béarnaise or Merlot Sauce (*Shasta Sunset Dinner Train*), 183

Bison, Beartooth, with Roasted Tomato and Pepper Medley Chipotle Salsa (*J. Pinckney Henderson*), 80

Prime Rib (*Tamalpais*), 110

Steak, "Rory" (Barbecue) (Amtrak), 211

Veal Loin, Roasted, with Morel Mushroom Glace (Quad/Graphics), 257

GAME

Alaskan Reindeer Chili (*Midnight Sun Express*), 29

POULTRY

Chicken Breast Pinot Noir and Dried Cherries (*Coast Starlight*), 216

Chicken Breast Stuffed with Wild Mushrooms and Smoked Gouda (*Spirit of Washington Dinner Train*), 191

Chicken in Burgundy Creole Sauce (Amtrak), 198

Chicken, Deviled, with Mustard Sauce (Rufus Estes/Pullman Company), 76

Chicken, Oven-Fried (Amtrak), 209

Chicken Roulade with Maple-Chipotle BBQ Sauce (*American Orient Express*), 14

Chicken, Smoked Sonoma Range, on Crispy Wonton with Mustard Cream, Sauce and Maui Onion-Apple-Mustard-Red Pepper-Sweet Corn Chow Chow (*Napa Valley Wine Train*), 163

Cornish Hens, Roasted with Cajun Cornbread Stuffing (*Great Smokey Mountain Railroad*), 140

Duck Breast, Pan-Seared (*Acela Express*), 224

Index

Note: The general recipe index begins on page 277.

Subject Index

Woods, Ron, 233–234
Woolworth, F. W., 104
writers, 89–92

Recipe Index

mesclun greens. *See also* salad(s)
    red leaf and, à la Café with caramelized
        almonds, 129
    salmon persilade on, with basil beurre
        blanc, 256
mince meat, 218
mixed greens salad, with vinaigrette sauce, 80
morel mushroom glace, veal, roasted loin
    with, 257–258
mousse
    Amaretto, 241
    blueberry, chocolate-laced pastry tulip
        with white chocolate, raspberry sauce
        and, 173–174
    scallop, spinach Anaglotti with salmon
        medallions and Champagne saffron
        cream beurre blanc, 45–46
mozzarella
    basil vinaigrette, tomato salad with sweet
        red peppers and roasted shallots,
        170–171
    buffalo mozzarella, ensalata caprese, 31
muffins
    corn, Southern, 203
    Milwaukee Road deluxe, 122
Mulligan stew, 154
mushroom(s)
    beef tenderloin, Alberta, with portobello
        duxelle and blueberry ice wine demi-
        glace, 47
    morel mushroom glace, veal, roasted loin
        with, 257–258
    omelet, 208
    portobello, and sweet potato hash, 136
    portobello, beef tenderloin, Alberta, with
        portobello duxelle and blueberry ice
        wine demi-glace, 47
    portobello napoleon, 139
    sauce, red wine, beef tenderloin with,
        100–101
    shitake, pasta della quadracci, 257
    soup, Hungarian style, 176
    turnovers, 128
    wild mushroom, chicken breast stuffed
        with, and smoked Gouda, 191
    wild mushroom ragout, beef tenderloin
        fillet on, with demi-glace, 86–87
    wild mushroom sauce, pork medallions
        with, spiced, 66–67
mustard cream sauce, chicken, smoked
    Sonoma range, on crispy wonton with,
    and Maui onion-apple-mustard-red
    pepper-sweet corn chow chow, 163–164
mustard sauce, deviled chicken with, 76
mustard spread, lamb, roast rack of,
    Provençale, 177–178

olives, stuffed with blue cheese and shrimp,
    57
omelets, 229
    all-purpose, 208
    onion-mushroom-spinach, 215
onion, caramelized, bison burger with,
    229–230
onion-mushroom-spinach omelet, 215
orange ginger soy glaze, halibut, black and
    white sesame-encrusted with, 171–172
orange soup, with chantilly and chocolate
    zests, 49–50
Oriental salad, 247
orzo, golden, 117. *See also* pasta
oven-fried chicken, 209–210
oyster bisque, 144

pancakes, peach hotcakes, 62–63
pancetta vinaigrette sauce, baby greens salad
    with warm goat cheese and dried
    cherries, 105–106
pan-fried potatoes, 73
parfait, mountain berry, 185–186
Parmesan potato soup, 246–247
parsley potatoes, 111
pasta
    linguini, della quadracci, 257
    orzo, golden, 117
    ravioli, deep-fried, with tomato dipping
        sauce, 245
    spinach Anaglotti, with scallop mousse,
        salmon medallions with Champagne
        saffron cream beurre blanc, 45–46
    tortellini, Castroville cheese, 215
pasta della quadracci, 257
pasta salad, 23–24
pastry crust, chocolate pecan tart, 82–83. *See
    also* phyllo dough, apple blossoms
pâté, chicken liver, 127–128
peaches
    bread pudding, with bourbon sauce, 112
    hotcakes, 62–63
    pecan sundae, 59
    pie, 168
    salad, Arabian, 250–251
pears
    caramelized, dark Belgian chocolate cups
        filled with pumpkin mousse and
        drizzled with ("Golden Kisses"), 137
    chocolate-stuffed, 147
    poached with almond meringue and
        chocolate mousse, 152–153
    poached with Stilton blue cheese,
        cranberry compote, and poppy seed
        dressing, 43–44